Personality in Work Organizations

FOUNDATIONS FOR ORGANIZATIONAL SCIENCE
A Sage Publications Series

Series Editor
David Whetten, *Brigham Young University*

Editors
Peter J. Frost, *University of British Columbia*
Anne S. Huff, *University of Colorado* and *Cranfield University* (UK)
Benjamin Schneider, *University of Maryland*
M. Susan Taylor, *University of Maryland*
Andrew Van de Ven, *University of Minnesota*

The FOUNDATIONS FOR ORGANIZATIONAL SCIENCE series supports the development of students, faculty, and prospective organizational science professionals through the publication of texts authored by leading organizational scientists. Each volume provides a highly personal, hands-on introduction to a core topic or theory and challenges the reader to explore promising avenues for future theory development and empirical application.

Books in This Series

PUBLISHING IN THE ORGANIZATIONAL SCIENCES, 2nd Edition
Edited by L. L. Cummings and Peter J. Frost
SENSEMAKING IN ORGANIZATIONS
Karl E. Weick
INSTITUTIONS AND ORGANIZATIONS
W. Richard Scott
RHYTHMS OF ACADEMIC LIFE
Peter J. Frost and M. Susan Taylor
RESEARCHERS HOOKED ON TEACHING:
Noted Scholars Discuss the Synergies of Teaching and Research
Rae André and Peter J. Frost
THE PSYCHOLOGY OF DECISION MAKING: People in Organizations
Lee Roy Beach
ORGANIZATIONAL JUSTICE AND HUMAN RESOURCE MANAGEMENT
Robert Folger and Russell Cropanzano
RECRUITING EMPLOYEES: Individual and Organizational Perspectives
Alison E. Barber
ATTITUDES IN AND AROUND ORGANIZATIONS
Arthur P. Brief
IDENTITY IN ORGANIZATIONS: Building Theory Through Conversations
Edited by David Whetten and Paul Godfrey
PERSONNEL SELECTION: A Theoretical Approach
Neal Schmitt and David Chan
BUILDING STRATEGY FROM THE MIDDLE: Reconceptualizing Strategy Process
Steven W. Floyd and Bill Wooldridge
MISSING ORGANIZATIONAL LINKAGES: Tools for Cross-Level Research
Paul S. Goodman
THE CONTINGENCY THEORY OF ORGANIZATIONS
Lex Donaldson
ORGANIZATIONAL STRESS: A Review and Critique of Theory, Research, and Applications
Cary L. Cooper, Philip J. Dewe, and Michael P. O'Driscoll
INSTITUTIONS AND ORGANIZATIONS, Second Edition
W. Richard Scott
ORGANIZATIONAL CULTURE: Mapping the Terrain
Joanne Martin
PERSONALITY IN WORK ORGANIZATIONS
Lawrence R. James and Michelle D. Mazerolle
CAREERS IN AND OUT OF ORGANIZATIONS
Douglas T. Hall

Lawrence R. James
University of Tennessee at Knoxville

Michelle D. Mazerolle
Philips Consumer Electronics North America

Personality in Work Organizations

Foundations for
Organizational
Science
A Sage Publications Series

Sage Publications
International Educational and Professional Publisher
Thousand Oaks ■ London ■ New Delhi

For information:

 Sage Publications, Inc.
2455 Teller Road
Thousand Oaks, California 91320
E-mail: order@sagepub.com

Sage Publications Ltd.
6 Bonhill Street
London EC2A 4PU
United Kingdom

Sage Publications India Pvt. Ltd.
M-32 Market
Greater Kailash I
New Delhi 110 048 India

Library of Congress Cataloging-in-Publication Data

James, Lawrence R.
    Personality in work orgazizations / Lawrence R. James and Michelle D. Mazerolle.
        p. cm. — (Foundations for organizational science)
    Includes bibliographical references and index.
        ISBN 0-7619-0295-3 (cloth) — ISBN 0-7619-0296-1 (pbk.)
        1. Psychology, Industrial.   2. Personality.   I. Mazerolle, Michelle D.
    II. Title.   III. Series.
        HF5548.8.J256   2002
        158.7—dc21   2001005871

01   02   03   04   05   10   9   8   7   6   5   4   3   2   1

Acquiring Editor:	Marquita Flemming
Editorial Assistant:	Candice Crosetti and Maryanne Vail
Production Editor:	Claudia A. Hoffman
Copy Editor:	Judy Selhorst
Typesetter/Designer:	Janelle LeMaster
Indexer:	Molly Hall
Cover Designer:	Jane Quaney

Contents

Introduction to the Series

The title of this series, **Foundations for Organizational Science** (FOS), denotes a distinctive focus. FOS books are educational aids for mastering the core theories, essential tools, and emerging perspectives that constitute the field of organizational science (broadly conceived to include organizational behavior, organizational theory, human resource management, and business strategy). Our ambitious goal is to assemble the "essential library" for members of our professional community.

The vision for the series emerged from conversations with several colleagues, including Peter Frost, Anne Huff, Rick Mowday, Ben Schneider, Susan Taylor, and Andy Van de Ven. A number of common interests emerged from these sympathetic encounters, including: enhancing the quality of doctoral education by providing broader access to the master teachers in our field, "bottling" the experience and insights of some of the founding scholars in our field before they retire, and providing professional development opportunities for colleagues seeking to broaden their understanding of the rapidly expanding subfields within organizational science.

Our unique learning objectives are reflected in an unusual set of instructions to FOS authors. They are encouraged to: (1) "write the way they teach"—framing their book as an extension of their teaching notes, rather than as the expansion of a handbook chapter; (2) pass on their "craft knowledge" to the next generation of scholars—making them wiser, not just smarter; (3) share with their "virtual students and colleagues" the insider tips and best-bets for research that are normally reserved for one-on-one mentoring sessions; and (4) make the complexity of their subject matter comprehensible to non-experts so that readers can share their puzzlement, fascination, and intrigue.

We are proud of the group of highly qualified authors who have embraced the unique educational perspective of our "Foundations" series. We encourage your suggestions for how these books can better satisfy your learning needs—as a newcomer to the field preparing for prelims or developing a dissertation proposal, or as an established scholar seeking to broaden your knowledge and proficiency.

—DAVID A. WHETTEN
SERIES EDITOR

Preface

This is a book about the past, present, and future of personality in work organizations. It introduces principal concepts of current personality theory. The "two disciplines" of personality, namely the trait approach and the social cognitive approach, receive equal emphasis. Moreover, we make a concerted effort to integrate these two approaches and to communicate the sense of coherence that exists among them. Strategies for measuring personality in organizational settings receive considerable attention. Included here are new approaches for assessing implicit or unconscious motives, such as motives to aggress or to avoid failing. We devote the final chapter in the book to those who wish to conduct research in personality. We make suggestions about how promising new themes in personality could be integrated into organizational research. We wish to thank Ben Schneider and Sage Publications for the encouragement to write this book and for their perseverance. Sage also provided superb editing. This book took a long time to write because a number of new concepts (e.g., channeling models, conditional reasoning, differential framing) were just on the cusp of being validated and introduced to psychology, and we wanted to include them in the book. We also wish to thank those who provided support and informal reviews, including Michael McIntyre, Terry Mitchell, Charles Glisson, Larry Williams, Jack Feldman, and the University of Tennessee Conditional Reasoning Research Group. June Trbovitch, our administrative assistant for I-O psychology, shepherded the final manuscript to the publisher. Writing this book was not an ordeal; in fact, it was stimulating, challenging, interesting, and, at times, even exciting. We thank our families for supporting us during a period that they most likely frame in slightly less cheerful terms.

—*LAWRENCE R. JAMES*
—*MICHELLE D. MAZEROLLE*

 **1**   The Role of Personality
in Organizations

P*ersonality* refers to dynamic mental structures and coordinated
mental processes that determine individuals' emotional and behavioral adjustments to their environments (see Allport, 1937; Millon,
1990). The term *dynamic* suggests that personality continues to evolve
throughout an individual's lifetime. Evolution for a given individual is
predictable, however, for there is also considerable coherence in personality over time. For example, "mental structures" include needs, memo-
ries, and self-images. These attributes may adjust and modify to
correspond to changes in activity level, development, education, occupation, marital status, health, and socioeconomic status. But we also
witness consistency over time. The achievement-oriented person will
continue to seek success, the conscientious person will continue to be
reliable, and the aggressive person will continue to be combative over
time and across situations. The same may be said for "mental processes"
such as perception and reasoning. Over time, a person's attributions for
why he or she acts in particular ways may sharpen and reflect greater
understanding. However, unrecognized rationalizations in these attributions may remain with the individual throughout the life span.

Interest in personality among organizational theorists and researchers has waxed and waned over the past 50 years. The latest cycle began in the 1960s, a troublesome time for personality research, especially for attempts to measure personality. Guion and Gottier (1965) engendered considerable consternation about personality testing with their conclusion that there is little predictive validity in personality test scores. Similar devastating views were expressed in Guion's (1965) widely acclaimed testing book. Another well-thought-of text in psychometrics proclaimed that the major source of variance in self-report measurements of personality is social disability (Nunnally, 1967). Critiques from such respected sources placed personality assessment in both industrial-organizational psychology and organizational behavior in poor regard.

The ensuing period of 20 or so years in these domains is aptly captured by Goldberg's (1993) statement, "Once upon a time, we had no personalities" (p. 26). Goldberg goes on to say, "Fortunately, times change." The resurgence of interest in personality in organizational research is evident in such recent contributions as the 1996 special issue of *Applied Psychology: An International Review* on "work and personality." Additional indications of this resurgence of interest include Furnham's book *Personality at Work: The Role of Individual Differences in the Workplace* (1992), Lillibridge and Williams's chapter "Another Look at Personality and Managerial Potential: Application of the Five-Factor Model" (1992), and House, Shane, and Herold's article "Rumors of the Death of Dispositional Research Are Vastly Exaggerated" (1996). Nicholson (1996) notes that the study of personality in work settings has developed along three themes: (a) the search for universal truths in personality description and prediction, (b) the search for personality development through learning and change, and (c) the search for interactional models to bridge the gap between these objectives. Nicholson suggests further that there is a need for a new "strong" interactionism, one that "recognizes the relative immutability and power of deep personality structures, as well as the importance of situational constraint" (p. 190). We agree; the interaction between personality and work environments receives considerable attention in the chapters that follow.

Several factors were responsible for the renewed interest in personality in the 1990s. Chief among these was the ever more pressing need for employers to select people with high probabilities of adjusting and succeeding in work situations. Technological advances over the past several decades have had enormous impacts on the nature of work in organizations. As work becomes more complex and demanding, the ratio of work produced by a good engineer (or computer programmer, or nurse, or manager) becomes even greater compared with that produced by a poor engineer (computer programmer, nurse, manager). Organizations have turned to personality experts to assist them in the early identification of employees who are likely to be achievement motivated, conscientious, prosocial, and stable.

A second cause of the enhanced interest in personality in organizations is cultural and reflects a general political and philosophical shift in American opinion. Thirty years ago, behavior was framed as being strongly influenced by uncontrollable situational forces (e.g., the richness or deprivation of the environment into which a person was born). Over the intervening years, behavior has come to be framed as a product both of the environment and of the individual's dispositional capacity and fortitude to take the initiative and responsibility to adapt to environmental influences. This shift toward attention to dispositional factors is exemplified in organizational behavior in the aforementioned article by House et al. (1996). These authors emphasize the need to reinvigorate examinations of how dispositions influence behavior in work settings (see also Nelson & Sutton, 1990; Staw, Bell, & Clausen, 1986). Critics of dispositional influences argue that personality does not account for a great amount of the variance in the behavior of individuals in organizations (see Davis-Blake & Pfeffer, 1989). Such arguments are out of phase with the culture and with the prevailing focus of the social sciences, as well as with recent evidence.

A third cause of enlivened interest in personality has been furnished by advances in our understanding of the cognitive and emotional bases of human behavior. From a scientific standpoint, these advances are particularly exciting because they provide a foundation for truly creative advances in the understanding and measurement of personality. It is possible to make this statement because, in the past 20 or so years, substantial breakthroughs have been made in our understanding of the cognitive structures and processes employed by humans to give meaning to, and determine their functioning in, social contexts. This domain of research is generally referred to as *social cognition*.

The study of social cognition involves examination of the inferences, judgments, explanations, and theories people have about the causes and effects of their own behavior and the behavior of others in social environments. A representative sampling of specific research domains in social cognition includes attributions for the causes of behavior (including emotions), framing or interpretation of social events, heuristics in decision making, implicit personality theories, biases in person perception, and cognitive mechanisms for self-protection and self-enhancement (for reviews, see Fiske & Taylor, 1984, 1991). Organizational researchers have harnessed advances in social cognition research to help increase their understanding of supervisors' ratings of employees (see Feldman, 1981; Green & Mitchell, 1979), subordinates' perceptions of what makes a good leader (Lord, Foti, & DeVader, 1984; Lord, Foti, & Phillips, 1982; Rush, Thomas, & Lord, 1977), and tendencies on the part of executives to escalate their commitment to losing causes (Staw, 1976; Staw & Ross, 1987).

Other factors also stimulated revitalization of interest in personality, a prime example being the establishment of the first generally accepted taxonomy of personality known as the *five-factor model*. We address these factors in the course of the chapters that follow. For now, we would like to underscore the potential for using social cognition to synergize creative advances in our understanding and measurement of personality in work settings. We use the illustration that follows to demonstrate how social cognition provides us with a means to understand how and why the same environmental events are framed differently by diverse individuals.

John's Description of His Supervisor

John, a computer programmer for Microfirm, believes that he is being exploited and oppressed by David, his supervisor. John's description of the situation is as follows:

David's sense of self-esteem and competence as a supervisor is determined by how successfully he competes with me and my coworkers. If he cannot show that he is technically and intellectually superior to us, then he feels inferior and questions whether he should be a leader. To demonstrate his superiority, he continually tries to show how my work could be done better. For example, he rewrites all of my programs. To be specific, he critiques a program, then he implies that errors in the program were due to my incompetence and carelessness, and finally he rewrites the entire program, including parts that he did not criticize. All of this is designed to make him look good and to make me feel inadequate. I always experience a great deal of anxiety as I am completing a program because I know that nothing I do will be accepted by David.

Things can get worse because David is not satisfied with just being technically superior. He wants to show that he is in control at all times. To illustrate, he makes us fill out requests to obtain even the most minor materials, such as pencils. We have to write memos describing every interaction we have with someone outside our department, including telephone calls. We have to sign out, leaving an address and telephone number if we are going to be away from our desks for even 15 minutes. And we have to ask for things that are due us, like vacation time, in a humble and deferential manner. If we are not sufficiently submissive, or if we complain, then we are punished. For example, we are asked to work irregular hours and to give up weekends to work overtime.

Trying to please David by deferring to his authority or by acceding to his egotistical criticisms often invites additional abuses. He takes advantage of docile workers by overloading them with work. He is not interested in our problems, such as when I or a member of my immediate family have a serious illness. He never asks me or my coworkers for our opinions. If we take the initiative and make suggestions, David ignores our ideas or rejects them without fully listening to them. David never informs us of what he is planning, and he never explains his decisions. He just tells us what to do and expects us to obey.

I believe that I and my coworkers are victims of oppression. We are treated unfairly and inequitably by a tyrannical supervisor with an inferiority complex. I believe that in the interest of righting the many wrongs that have been done to us, we are justified in seeking retribution. We have a right to defend ourselves against supervisory abuses.

Unfortunately, going to management will not help. David has his boss fooled into believing that he is a great supervisor. I suppose that this is a result of our being harassed into being rather productive. It is also due to the fact that David is a sycophant to management. He doesn't rock the boat by standing up for the rights of his subordinates. He is more than happy to please his bosses by going along with whatever decisions they make about our work assignments, benefits, and pay raises.

My coworkers are not of much assistance either in striking out against the tyranny of our supervisor David. They are afraid of David, which shows that they are weak and impotent. Indeed, their weakness and compliance invites more oppression by David because it shows that they are willing to submit. I have been the only one to stand up to David. This has been difficult because the sole way to deal with a tyrant is to confront him. I have had to fight fire with fire. David must learn that he cannot tyrannize his employees without fear of retaliation. In time, my coworkers will see the results of my striking back at David, and I will gain their respect. Hopefully, they will find the fortitude to follow my lead and stand up to David as well.

In regard to specifics, I make an effort to undermine David's credibility. I frequently point out David's attempts to coerce and to intimidate me to my coworkers. I attempt to build opposition to his ideas and plans by showing how they benefit him much more than us. I encourage female employees to complain about his oppression as a form of harassment. And I have found ways to resist David, both actively and passively. For example, I started a personal work slowdown. Just the minimum needed to keep my job gets done, and I take as long as possible to do it. I do not give David accurate feedback on how programs and computers are working, which might tarnish some of his credibility with management. I take maximum sick leave, come to work late, read newspapers during meetings, and publicly argue with David about technical matters whenever possible. It's not much, but it's a start.

The View of John's Coworkers

Now let's conduct a reality check, and ask John's coworkers to describe the work environment. If John's description of the situation is accurate, then others should express similar sentiments about David's oppression of employees. This, however, is not the case. John's coworkers report:

David can be a little demanding at times, but this is largely due to the fact that he really wants our team to achieve and be recognized as one of the best computer groups in the company. Basically, David is a good leader. He is technically proficient as a programmer himself and will attempt to assist others when they run into problems. He is also astute enough to understand that many of the programmers in the team have special areas of concentration that exceed his expertise. He provides an umbrella under which these people can work creatively, seeking resources when requested, listening to ideas when asked, providing nurturance and comfort when people are frustrated, and making sure that his people are not overloaded with too much work or unrealistic deadlines.

Even more revealing is the coworkers' description of John. They state:

John is a mediocre programmer. Indeed, the only reason that John is still employed is that David rewrites his defective programs. David gives John credit for the programs and tries to help John build his expertise by suggesting books to read and courses to take at a local college, including one in motivation. John "frames" rewrites of his programs as attempts by David to emasculate and belittle him. According to John, his programs are just fine. He tells us that David's rewrites and David's insinuations that he is inadequately educated and unmotivated are character attacks intended to demonstrate who is the master. According to John, David has an inferiority complex about his leadership skills and thus must control his subordinates. John tries to interpret our interactions with David as signs of oppression as well. We try, unsuccessfully, to explain to John that David is really only trying to help rather than to make us submit to his will.

It appears to us that John thinks he is in competition with David for who will be the "alpha male" of the group. Inasmuch as John lost whatever competition there was to David for the promotion to supervisor (a correct decision, in the team's opinion), John now seems to want to engage in a more personal and visceral form of conflict. For example, he is grossly insubordinate to David (e.g., talks back, is late for meetings and then does not pay attention). He denounces David incessantly behind David's back. He tries to get female members of the team to file harassment charges for nonexistent slights. And his work has gotten even worse. Where before John was imprecise, he is now slow and imprecise. He lets maintenance problems escalate into major damage. He takes maximum sick leave even though he boasts of never being ill. Yet he tells David that either he or someone in his family is seriously sick. David, like the rest of us, has become a bit skeptical of these excuses.

John is unsuccessful in his attempts to convince us that his belligerence toward David is justified. We see none of the oppression and unfairness that John sees. Rather, we think that there is something wrong with John. He appears never to have gotten over the one time that David pleaded with him ("coerced" him, according to John) to work late on a Friday night and then put in a full day on Saturday. It was a very important project that we all worked on for the same extra hours as John. Yet, unlike the rest of us, to this day John still complains that we were bullied and intimidated into neglecting our families and giving up our rights to weekends off. John's perceptions of David's actions also take an unwarranted negative spin in regard to company policies. For example, John blames David for rules over which David has no control, such as keeping memos of conversations with customers and leaving an address/telephone number if away from our desks for more than 15 minutes.

John's aggressiveness toward David is embarrassing to us and to David. David is still trying to salvage John, but his patience is thinning. We have started to worry about just how far John is willing to go in confronting David. We are also concerned about John's reactions to us because we have not supported either his behaviors or his rationalizations. We fear John, and we wish that he would just go away.

Use of Personality and Social Cognition to Explain Individual Differences in Framing and Analysis

How is it possible for John's framing and analysis of his work situation to be so different from the framing and analysis of his coworkers? Why is it that John sees David as a tyrant but his coworkers see an achievement-oriented and empathic leader who offers unheralded assistance to John? Why is it that John describes a supervisory style that involves intentional attempts to demean and dominate subordinates but his coworkers describe a supervisor who creates a nurturing environment characterized by challenging but fair workloads and equitable rewards? And why is it that John sees himself as a victim of oppression who is performing justifiable acts of retribution whereas his coworkers see him as a belligerent and insubordinate employee who might be dangerous?

Answers to these questions are furnished by the fact that John and his coworkers have different personalities. The differences in personalities help shape, define, and sustain social cognitions such as how the supervisor, David, is perceived as well as how John is perceived by himself and by his coworkers. Differences in personalities also help shape and influence the analytic processes that John and his coworkers use to determine whether John's hostility toward David is justified. We present below an overview of the mental structures and processes involved in these framing and analytic aspects of social cognition. In the chapters that follow, we explain many of the issues raised here in greater depth.

We begin by noting that John has an aggressive personality. Aggressiveness evolves from a desire or motive to overcome opposition forcefully, to fight, to revenge an injury, to attack another with intent to injure or kill, and to oppose forcefully or punish another (Murray, 1938). Contemporary work on aggression combines this motive with trait-based behavior to describe the "aggressive individual." An aggressive individual (a) chooses to use some form of aggression to deal with evocative, especially frustrating, situations; (b) dislikes if not hates the target of aggression; (c) desires to inflict harm on this target; (d) has diminished self-regulatory capacities, which suggests underdeveloped internal prohibitions or standards against aggressing (although sufficient self-regulation may be present to make the aggression indirect and/or passive); and (e) sees limited response options, which denotes that aggression is seen as the most efficacious response to frustration and anger (see Bandura, 1973; Baron & Richardson, 1994; Berkowitz, 1993; Gay, 1993; Huesmann, 1988; Laursen & Collins, 1994; O'Leary-Kelly, Griffin, & Glew, 1996).

Expression of the motive to aggress may take many forms (Buss, 1961; Folger & Baron, 1996). We see myriad aggressive behaviors in John's case, including direct behaviors (insubordination), indirect behaviors (sowing discontent among coworkers), and passive behaviors (slowdowns, lack of feedback). All of these behaviors share the common denominator that they are intended to harm another individual—namely, David—or the organization (Folger & Baron, 1996).

Justification Mechanisms for Aggression

People like to believe that their behavior is sensible and rational, as opposed to foolish and irrational. A specific instance of this axiom is that people with strong motives to aggress tend to frame and analyze the world in ways that justify—that is, that enhance the rational appeal of —the expression of aggression (see James, 1998). This justification process is often evident in the reasons that aggressive people give for their actions. For example, aggressive people like John often see themselves as victims of inequitable treatment by powerful entities, such as supervisors or organizations. They then use their perception of their being exploited and abused as justification for their acting aggressively. These individuals do not think of actions such as insubordination and withholding effort as unfounded aggression. Rather, as we have seen with John's framing of his behavior, they regard these as justifiable acts by oppressed persons who are seeking retribution, retaliation, or vindication, or who may even be acting in self-defense (see Anderson, 1994; Averill, 1993; Baron & Richardson, 1994; Baumeister, Smart, & Boden, 1996; Berkowitz, 1993; Brehmer, 1976; Buss, 1961; Crick & Dodge, 1994; Felson & Tedeschi, 1993; Gay, 1993; Huesmann, 1988; James,

1998; Millon, 1990; O'Leary-Kelly et al., 1996; Tedeschi & Nesler, 1993; Toch, 1993).

Basically, aggressive people attempt to enhance the rational appeal of acting aggressively (James, 1998). They often do so unknowingly by engaging in framing proclivities and implicit or unconscious reasoning biases that give their aggression a sense of reasonableness and sensibility. Of particular interest here are the adjectives aggressive individuals use to frame the events surrounding aggression, the theories of causality they invoke to explain aggression, the attributions they make about the intent or character of the targets of aggression, and the probabilities they associate with possible outcomes of aggressive actions.

The literatures in aggression and social cognition (see references above) suggest that aggressive individuals in organizational contexts tend to engage unconsciously in the following framing proclivities:

- They perceive others through a prism of dominance, such as either "wolves" or "sheep."
- They see employees who follow the rules as sycophants who are afraid to stand up for their rights.
- They frame organizational rules and regulations as control mechanisms designed to engender submissiveness.

Aggressive individuals also tend to have implicit or unconscious propensities to favor certain types of assumptions or theories when reasoning, such as the following:

- Coworkers will undermine each other's credibility.
- People in authority will try to make subordinates feel inadequate.
- Lack of aggression indicates weakness.
- Rule infractions are legitimate ways to right the many wrongs that have been done to employees.
- Employee compliance with rules and regulations invites oppression by organizations.
- Insubordination toward authority figures is an act of bravery that other employees secretly respect.
- Organizations will tyrannize employees until they begin to fear employee retaliation.
- Attempts to foment discontent and rebelliousness among employees are justifiable forms of retribution, if not self-defense.

We can see the products of many of these framing proclivities and implicit assumptions in John's description of his work situation. A denominator common to his framing and implicit assumptions is that the ensuing social cognitions are biased toward tacitly enhancing the rational appeal of his aggression toward David. Yet aggressive individuals like John believe in the rationality and sensibility of their framing and implicit hypothesizing. They are unaware that their reasoning is biased toward justifying aggression. For example, like other aggressive people, John fails to recognize the limitations of framing people, contexts, and events through a lens or prism that focuses interpretation on dominance and adversarial intent. John also fails to discern his predilection to favor explanatory theories and causal attributions that cast aggression as a reasonable and sensible course of action. In addition, John fails to detect his propensity to associate primarily positive outcomes with his acts of aggression.

A seminal set of latent or unconscious biases appear to define, shape, and guide the myriad specific instances of framing and analyzing that aggressive individuals use to justify aggressive behaviors. James (1998) has proposed the term *justification mechanisms* to refer to these primary biases. Justification mechanisms are defined as nonconscious biases whose purpose is to define, shape, and otherwise influence reasoning (i.e., framing and analysis) so as to enhance the rational appeal of behaving aggressively.

James (1998) has proposed six key justification mechanisms, or JMs, for aggression. The mechanisms, in slightly revised form, are presented in Table 1.1. We illustrate the operation of several of these JMs briefly below.

The adjectives that aggressive individuals like John use to frame aggressive behaviors are often euphemisms designed to put a positive spin on what in fact are hostile acts. The Retribution Bias, for example, includes a proclivity to rationalize aggressive behaviors by framing them as attempts to protect or to restore one's honor and self-respect. The implicit assumptions of causality that aggressive people use to give rational explanations for their behavior are another key source of attempts to justify aggression. Attributions they make about the intent or character of their targets illustrate this case. The Hostile Attribution Bias involves an unrecognized tendency of aggressive individuals to ascribe intentional malevolence to their targets' behavior. This inference assists aggressive persons in rationalizing their aggression toward their

Table 1.1   Justification Mechanisms Underlying Expression of Aggression

1. *Hostile Attribution Bias:*   A tendency to see malevolent intent in the actions of others. Even benign or friendly acts may be seen as having hidden, hostile agendas designed intentionally to inflict harm. An especially virulent form of this bias occurs when benign or positive acts are attributed to selfish concerns and negative incentives (e.g., an aggressive subordinate interprets a helpful suggestion by a supervisor as an intentional attempt to demean the subordinate's work).

2. *Derogation of Target Bias:*   A tendency to attempt to make the target more deserving of aggression. For example, a number of negative characteristics may be ascribed to the target (e.g., corrupt, dishonest, evil, immoral, underhanded, unethical, untrustworthy) or the positive traits of the target may be ignored, undervalued, or depreciated.

3. *Retribution Bias:*   A tendency to confer logical priority to reparation or retaliation over reconciliation. Reflected in implicit beliefs that aggression is warranted in order to restore respect or exact restitution for a perceived wrong. Bias is also indicated by whether a person would rather retaliate than forgive, be vindicated as opposed to cooperate, and obtain revenge rather than maintain a relationship. This bias underlies classic rationalizations for aggression based on wounded pride, challenged self-esteem, and disrespect.

4. *Victimization by Powerful Others Bias:*   A tendency to frame self as a victim and to see self as being exploited and taken advantage of by the powerful (e.g., government agencies). Sets the stage for arguing that aggression is acting out against injustice, correcting inequities, redressing wrongs, or striking out against oppression.

5. *Potency Bias:*   A tendency to frame and reason using the contrast of strength versus weakness. For example, people with a strong Potency Bias tend to frame others on a continuum ranging from strong, assertive, powerful, daring, fearless, or brave to weak, impotent, submissive, timid, sheepish, compliant, conforming, or cowardly. This bias is used to justify aggression via arguments such as (a) aggression (e.g., confrontations with teachers, fights with coworkers) results in one's being perceived as brave or as a leader by others, and (b) weakness/submissiveness invites aggression because it shows that one is willing to submit.

6. *Social Discounting Bias:*   A tendency to call on socially unorthodox and frequently antisocial beliefs in interpreting and analyzing social events and relationships. People with this bias are disdainful of traditional ideals and conventional beliefs; they may be insensitive, unempathic, and unfettered by social customs. They are often directly cynical or critical, with few subliminal channels for routing antisocial framing and analysis.

---

targets as justifiable acts of self-defense. The Derogation of Target Bias consists of an implicit tendency on the part of the aggressive individual to characterize a target as deserving of aggression because he/she/it is evil, immoral, untrustworthy, or exploitative.

Aggressive individuals are selectively attentive to, indeed may seek out, what they regard as acts of inequity, exploitation, injustice, and oppression by their supervisors and/or their organizations. Selective attentiveness and confirmatory searches both engender and reinforce these individuals' implicit tendencies to assume that they are being victimized by powerful others. This reasoning is shaped by the Victimization Bias and contributes to attempts to justify acts of aggression toward supervisors and/or organizations as warranted corrections of inequities or legitimate strikes against oppression.

As noted above, John, like other aggressive individuals, is generally unaware of the effects of JMs on his reasoning. A particularly compelling exemplar of this point is the Potency Bias. Aggressive individuals, including John, tend to filter interactions with others through a prism that frames these interactions as contests to establish dominance versus submissiveness. Such framing is the cornerstone for the aggressive person's assumption that acting aggressively is a demonstration of strength, bravery, or fearlessness, and that not acting aggressively is equivalent to showing weakness, fearfulness, cowardliness, or impotence. An aggressive person may thus reason that (a) aggression is an act of strength or bravery that gains respect from others, and (b) to show weakness is to invite powerful others to take advantage of you.

In sum, aggressive individuals such as John see themselves as victims of exploitative leaders/organizations or hostile coworkers and view aggressive behaviors as justifiable acts of bravery, retaliation, or self-defense. They are unaware of the roles JMs have had in defining, shaping, and guiding their framing and analysis. At least some expressions of aggression in the workplace, including their own, thus appear to them to be reasonable.

Socially Adaptive Individuals

Aggression connotes a behavioral disposition to be antagonistic, belligerent, bellicose, combative, contentious, hostile, malicious, malevolent, offensive, obstreperous, pugnacious, truculent, unfriendly, and unkind. Fortunately, based on estimates presented by James and McIntyre (2000), only 8% to 12% (approximately) of workers appear to engage in these types of behaviors. Most workers, including John's coworkers, have no desire to engage in dominance contests with their supervisors, to fight with their coworkers, or to cause harm to their employers by engaging in theft, malingering, fraud, habitual absenteeism, or intentionally disruptive turnover. Rather, they can be relied upon to be considerate and friendly toward their coworkers, to accept the legitimate authority of their supervisors without rancor or contentiousness, to abide by the rules and regulations of their organizations, and to attempt to be useful, cooperative, and congenial. The contrast to antagonism, combativeness, and hostility is a disposition to behave in amicable, civil, congenial, considerate, cooperative, cordial, courteous, good-natured, gracious, friendly, helpful, hospitable, polite, socialized, trusting, and respectful manners (see Wright & Mischel, 1987; see also, on the Agreeableness factor in the five-factor model of personality, Digman, 1990; Goldberg, 1990; John, 1990).

From a motivational perspective, counteracting desires to fight, to overcome perceived opposition forcefully, and to attack coworkers or the organization with intent to cause harm are the desires to seek friendships, to cooperate with others, to have trust in the goodwill of others, and to live in a harmonious, peaceful environment. These are "socially adaptive" motives that approximately 72% of working individuals manifest in the normal course of functioning in most organizations (approximately 16% to 20% of individuals exist in a gray area between aggressive and socially adaptive). Basically, being civil, friendly, polite, congenial, cooperative, and courteous is to act in the typical, acceptable, normative, socially orthodox, expected (role-prescribed) ways that characterize most people in most work environments.

James (1998) uses the term *prosocial* to characterize the socially adaptive motives (and behaviors) of friendliness, cooperation, harmony, and trust. He uses the term in the sense that it is employed in personality to refer to dynamics that move "people closer together" (Buss & Finn, 1987, p. 435) and that act as contrasts to aggression (Wright & Mischel, 1987). However, in social and organizational psychology, *prosocial* has taken on the connotation of discretionary, extrarole forms of altruistic, organizational citizenship, and helping behaviors (see George & Brief, 1992; Lam, Hui, & Law, 1999; McNeely & Meglino, 1994; Organ, 1988; Podsakoff, Ahearne, & MacKenzie, 1997; Williams & Anderson, 1991).

Whereas extrarole behaviors are included in our domain of interest, our bandwidth for motives and behaviors is much broader. We are concerned with the typical, normative, and adaptive motives and behaviors that distinguish the 72% of people who are amicable, friendly, peaceful, and cooperative from the 8% to 12% of people who are hostile, combative, antagonistic, and obstreperous. Thus, to avoid confusion between this general focus and the extrarole connotation of *prosocial*, we use the term *socially adaptive* to specify the motives for friendship, cooperativeness, harmony, and trust, as well as the behaviors that these motives direct and sustain.

Socially adaptive motives have impacts on reasoning. Specifically, whereas aggressive individuals have a propensity to ground reasoning in JMs for aggression, socially adaptive individuals tend to engage in framing and implicit hypothesizing that promote the reasonableness of being friendly, peaceful, trusting, and cooperative. Following are some illustrations of the contrasting framing and implicit theorizing that socially adaptive individuals tend to use in place of the reasoning based on JMs that distinguishes aggressive individuals:

- Opposing the Hostile Attribution Bias is a tendency to see amicable intent in the actions of others. In particular, socially adaptive individuals frame friendly or helpful acts as being based in good-natured agendas designed intentionally to promote cooperation, trust, and friendship.

- Contrasting with the Derogation of Target Bias is a proclivity to experience compassion for the targets of aggression. Also involved are attempts to build dialectics that include both positive and negative characteristics of targets, followed by analyses of whether the targets are deserving of some form of discipline or punishment.

- Reasoning based on the Retribution Bias is replaced by an orientation to promote friendship, harmony, collaboration, and trust over assuaging wounded pride, defending self-esteem, or seeking retribution for perceived disrespect. Social adaptiveness is reflected in reasoning that indicates implicit tendencies to favor forgiving, cooperating, and maintaining relationships as more reasonable options than retaliating, seeking vindication, or obtaining revenge.

- Contrasting with a Victimization by Powerful Others Bias is a proclivity to frame organizations as legitimate sources of authority and to assume that employees can accept subordinate roles without being exploited, demeaned, or made victims of injustices and inequities.

- Socially adaptive people tend not to perceive others through a prism of potency (i.e., the Potency Bias) that evaluates others as dominant or submissive in relation to themselves. Rather, they tend to perceive others through a prism that frames them on a continuum ranging from likely to be a friend, companion, confidante, partner, or colleague to likely to be part of only a neutral, unemotional, or uninvolved relationship.

- The socially unorthodox reasoning that characterizes the Social Discounting Bias is replaced with tendencies to call on socially orthodox and accepted cultural beliefs to interpret and to analyze social events and relationships. Socially adaptive individuals tend to reason that a society benefits from respect for traditional ideals and conventional beliefs as well as from acceptance of social customs (see Hogan & Hogan, 1989).

John's socially adaptive coworkers evidence much of the reasoning described above. It is also noteworthy that, unlike John's reasoning, the reasoning of his socially adaptive coworkers has no sense of justification. This is because there is no need to justify being friendly, cooperative, trusting, or agreeable. More generally, socially adaptive people have no sense of obligation to justify their acting in normative, socially acceptable ways. According to the norms of our society, being agreeable, friendly, polite, peaceful, cooperative, and trusting is the sensible and reasonable thing to do in normal circumstances. It does not require justification in the way that deviating from these norms (by being aggressive) does.

We do not wish to imply that socially adaptive people are immune to social information-processing biases. For example, by framing others through a prism of friendship, socially adaptive individuals may miss cues that they are about to be exploited. However, this is not the type of biased reasoning that is of interest for our contrast with the reasoning of aggressive individuals.

We should also report that we make no assumption that all socially adaptive people are equal in social adaptability. Indeed, we expect individual differences in the strength of social adaptiveness. However, for the purposes of the present discussion, we regard all people referred to as socially adaptive as having satisfied a minimum threshold for social adaptability. (The mirror image of this argument applies to aggressive individuals.)

Conditional Reasoning

When aggressive individuals and socially adaptive individuals frame the same events differently and unknowingly rely on different implicit assumptions to build rational cases for contrasting behaviors, reasoning is said to be conditional on the personalities of the reasoners (James, 1998; James & McIntyre, 2000). By *conditional reasoning*, we mean that reasoning is dependent on personality; that is, reasoning is dependent (i.e., conditional) on the motives, framing proclivities, and implicit hypotheses of the reasoners. Conditional reasoning is used in a manner such as the following: Whether framing and analyses will identify aggression or social adaptiveness as being a sensible behavioral adjustment to an environment is conditional (i.e., dependent) on whether the person doing the reasoning is aggressive or socially adaptive. Aggressive people like John tend to reason in ways that justify the expression of aggression. Socially adaptive people like John's coworkers tend to reason in ways that foster the expression of friendship, harmony, cooperation, and trust.

Conditional reasoning occurs because the interpretations and analyses of events used to furnish logical support to a given type of behavior are unconsciously shaped, defined, and guided by the motives, framing proclivities, and implicit assumptions of individual reasoners. Thus, for example, an individual's reasoning that culminates in his or her viewing hostility as a justifiable behavior is conditional on the individual's personality when this reasoning was shaped by the motivation to act aggressively in the first place and by the use of JMs such as the Hostile Attribution Bias to enhance the logical plausibility of engaging in aggressive behavior.

Whereas conditional reasoning is grounded in a dependency between the reasoning of an individual and that person's personality, the full scope of conditional reasoning is captured only through consideration of individual differences in reasoning, particularly differences in reasoning about the same events. Conditional reasoning conveys the notion that differences in motives, framing proclivities, and implicit theories shape, define, and guide reasoning so as to furnish a predictable pattern of individual differences in the judgments of what are and are not reasonable behaviors in the same environment. Differences in what are considered to be reasonable adjustments in the same environment are thus dependent or conditional on differences in the personalities of the persons doing the reasoning.

Conditional reasoning is an area of social cognition that is concerned with patterns of individual differences in reasoning about behavior that are unknowingly engendered by differences in underlying personalities. A key feature of conditional reasoning is that even though aggressive individuals and socially adaptive individuals come to disparate judgments about what constitutes a reasonable behavior, both sets of individuals believe that their reasoning is sensible and rational as opposed to foolish and irrational. A novel contribution of conditional reasoning to the study of personality has been the initial charting of the types of reasoning biases—referred to above as justification mechanisms—that aggressive individuals employ to enhance the rational appeal of hostile behavior. As we show in later chapters, enhanced understanding of JMs in reasoning opens the door to more sophisticated treatments of social cognition in personality as well as to new measurement systems for personality.

General Comment: Personality in Organizations

As the preceding illustration suggests, personality is perhaps most clearly demonstrated in work settings when individuals react differently to the same or similar environmental stimuli (e.g., leadership, pay and benefits, job demands, characteristics of team members, systems norms and culture) and the differences in reactions can be traced to differences in cognitive structures (e.g., beliefs, theories, values, emotional propensities) and cognitive processes (e.g., framing and analysis). In this volume, we focus on differences in cognitive structures and processes among individuals in the same work environment and how these differences produce systematic variations in what people believe to be reasonable behavioral adaptations to this environment. We have chosen to emphasize individual differences within work environments because this is the area in which organizational theorists and practitioners are most likely to engage personality. Of course, work environments vary, and thus a meaningful treatment of personality requires that we discuss individual differences within each of multiple types of work environments. This is the concern of person-by-situation interaction models, which we discuss in Chapter 2.

Organization of This Book

There are four remaining chapters in this book. In Chapter 2, we introduce many of the principal concepts of current personality theory. We place our emphasis on fundamentals and make a concerted effort to communicate the sense of coherence that exists among the components of personality, such as needs, social cognitions, emotions, and behaviors. To help communicate this sense of coherence, we use the same personality variables for illustrations throughout Chapter 2. To our knowledge, this is the first time this approach has been attempted.

Our objective in Chapter 3 is to identify the key variables in each of the primary components of personality. We begin by introducing a broad taxonomy of characteristic behavioral adjustments in which key traits are clustered or organized around five broad dimensions of behavior. We then turn our attention to identifying broad categories of the cognitive structures and cognitive processes that govern behavioral adjustments.

Chapter 4 presents strategies for measuring personality in organizational settings. We begin the chapter with a brief overview of the standards or criteria that are used to determine whether an instrument designed to measure personality is useful. We introduce and define the concepts of *validity* and *reliability,* and then employ these standards to select and/or evaluate examples of the measurement instruments currently in use in organizations to measure personality. Our review of personality measurement instruments is highly selective and is based on three categories of measures: (a) self-report measures, (b) projective techniques, and (c) conditional reasoning. In our concluding comments offered at the end of Chapter 4, we focus on the need to expand our frontiers of measurement if personality research is to realize its potential in organizational settings.

Chapter 5 is designed for those who wish to conduct research in personality. As we shall show, the guiding lights for recent creative developments in personality research have been interactional psychology and social cognition. In Chapter 5 we make an attempt to identify promising new themes that will guide research in personality in the near future. We offer some suggestions about how each theme could be integrated into organizational research. Enterprising researchers will of course see additional opportunities to integrate these themes into their research programs. An especially exciting aspect of at least two of the themes is that they have already demonstrated their potential to enhance the empirical validities of personality measures.

 **2** Fundamental
Concepts of Personality

In this chapter we introduce many of the principal concepts of current personality theory. We place our emphasis on fundamentals that are germane to organizational theorists and researchers. In addition, we make a concerted effort to communicate the sense of patterning and coordination that exists among the components of personality, such as needs, social cognitions, emotions, and behaviors. To communicate this patterning, we need to maintain continuity in the personality variables we use for illustrations throughout this chapter. We have chosen achievement motivation and fear of failure to serve as exemplars.

We should note that using the *same* personality variables to illustrate the different components of personality is a novel approach, which is to say that no one has done this before (to our knowledge). The traditional path is to illustrate each principal concept with a different personality variable or two. A number of different personality variables are introduced using this approach. Consequently, our employing the same two exemplars so that we may integrate principal concepts may seem restrictive to readers who have some breadth of exposure to multiple personality variables. Whatever sense of restrictiveness you may experience here, however, will be dispelled in the next chapter, where we provide an overview of domains of personality variables. A quick perusal of Chapter 3 will provide reassurance that it is unlikely to be criticized for narrowness of scope. Thus we ask you to wait until Chapter 3 to become acquainted with the full range of personality variables.

Our objective in this chapter is to correct what we believe is a shortcoming in most treatments of personality—that is, the insular, self-contained treatment of each fundamental concept of personality. Presenting an isolated treatment of each concept lends itself to the use of a new personality variable to illustrate each concept, but this approach does little to show how the fundamental concepts are related. We wish not only to introduce basic concepts, but to demonstrate how these concepts are connected—indeed, how they form the integrated networks of mental structuring and processing that make up personality. To satisfy this objective, we need to use the same variables as exemplars as we move across concepts. There is no particular reason these variables should be achievement motivation and fear of failure; most personality variables would suffice. We have chosen these variables as models simply because we were actively engaged in research on them at the time we were writing this book. We begin the treatment of fundamental concepts by introducing the notion of "traits."

Traits: The Behavioral Indicators of Personality

Alex Haley, the author of *Roots*, endured 7 years of having his manuscripts rejected before he received his first acceptance. During this 7-year period, he (a) submitted manuscripts on a regular basis, (b) viewed rejections as learning experiences that would help him to hone his skills as an author, and (c) persisted in his belief that he would, through dedication and tenacity, prevail as a published author. Haley's persistence over 7 years of rejections, and his ultimate publishing of highly regarded articles and books, is an illustration of what is commonly referred to as "achievement motivation." People high in achievement motivation have strong desires to make something of themselves, to accomplish something important in their lives, and to "do better" simply for the pleasure of succeeding at something important and demanding (see McClelland, 1985b). They are willing to commit themselves to intense effort in their approach to achievement-relevant goals and tasks, often for long periods of time. They associate enthusiasm, intensity, and commitment with the pursuit of achievement and connect a sense of accomplishment, self-respect, and pride with attainment of both incentives along the way and the ultimate objective.

Many individuals are attracted to the idea of becoming famous authors. However, some of these people focus on the risk of spending years preparing a manuscript and then having it rejected. Unlike Alex Haley, who continued to concentrate on the rewards of publishing, these individuals fixate on the disappointment, humiliation, embarrassment, and shame that may follow if they attempt to publish and fail. People who habitually focus on failure and its consequences are prone to experience "fear of failure."

Fear of failure is defined as an anticipatory feeling of uneasiness, apprehension, dread, and anxiety about attempting a difficult task, failing, and appearing incompetent (Atkinson, 1957, 1978). Fear of failing—or, more precisely, the desire to reduce anxiety over failing—dampens enthusiasm for achievement and stimulates affected individuals to avoid achievement-oriented tasks completely or to withdraw from such tasks if success is not immediately forthcoming. It is also the case that anxiety over possible failure may become a self-fulfilling prophecy if such individuals do not avoid demanding tasks. Heightened apprehension over substandard performance can increase anxiety to such a level that it interferes with performance on difficult tasks.

Whether or not to attempt to publish is one example of a human dilemma in which individuals must periodically decide whether to approach or to avoid high-press-for-achievement objectives (goals, tasks). For adolescents and young adults, these decisions may involve such things as whether to attempt to obtain a high grade point average in school or whether to devote long hours to developing proficiency as a musician, an athlete, or an actor. Later in life, these decisions could include whether to seek a job in a high-pressure occupation, whether to dedicate the majority of one's waking hours to being a success, whether to seek promotion to a more responsible but less secure position, whether to make a career change, whether to start a business, and whether to engage in an innovative task, such as attempting to publish an article or novel.

Key features of these decisions are that (a) they are evocative—that is, they are important to the individual—and (b) they are decisions that the individual is free to make. Empowerment to make personally evocative decisions is the condition under which personality is most likely to influence decisions and behavior (see Pervin, 1990; Stagner, 1977).

Most individuals experience some aspects of both attraction (e.g., the attractiveness of becoming wealthy by owning a successful business) and apprehension (e.g., misgivings about investing savings in a business venture that may fail) when faced with decisions regarding whether to approach or to avoid a high-press-for-achievement activity. Whether to approach or to avoid becomes a form of "approach-avoidance conflict" (Atkinson, 1978). How such conflicts tend to be resolved provides the foundation for traits, as we explain below.

The Trait of Achievement Motivation

Over some people's life spans, we see a *recurring pattern* in which these individuals consistently resolve their approach-avoidance conflicts in favor of approaching achievement-oriented objectives. An achievement-oriented goal is one that (a) is personally challenging or demanding relative to the individual's skill and ability, (b) requires intense and persistent effort on the part of the individual to attain, and (c) is perceived by the individual as an important and worthwhile accomplishment. Some examples of achievement-oriented goals for college students include selecting a personally demanding major, striving for promotion in the jobs that follow college, seeking and accepting progressively greater responsibilities, and engaging in innovative activities such as research or writing. Over a career, an individual is likely to attempt to accomplish progressively more difficult objectives. These attempts often reflect continuing enhancement of competencies through experience, training, practice, and, of course, engaging in progressively more difficult tasks.

A recurring pattern of seeking successively more challenging goals and tasks is also likely to include the individual's willingness to devote intense effort to whatever demanding objective he or she has selected at the time. Intensity is reflected by such things as competitiveness, long hours devoted to honing the skills required for success, and what may be a level of involvement in goal accomplishment that engenders neglect of other aspects of the individual's life. Accompanying intensity is tenacity, exemplified by a willingness to persevere for long periods to accomplish demanding objectives. Alex Haley's persistence over 7 years to become a published author, the perseverance required to complete a graduate program such as medical school, and willingness to endure years of hard work and low income to start a business are illustrative.

In sum, we have described a consistent tendency to resolve approach-avoidance conflicts in favor of approaching high-press-for-achievement tasks. Accompanying this recurring pattern of selecting challenging objectives is a willingness to devote intense and persistent effort to accomplishing the objectives. These consistent behavioral tendencies, or behavioral dispositions, define the *trait* of "achievement motivation" (see Buss & Craik, 1983; Epstein, 1979; Kenrick & Funder, 1988; Wright & Mischel, 1987).

Characteristics of Traits

The term *trait* refers to a disposition or tendency to behave in a relatively consistent manner over time and across diverse situations. When an individual demonstrates a consistent predilection to select demanding tasks and to pursue their accomplishment with intensity and tenacity, he or she is said to possess the trait of achievement motivation. We might also think of achievement motivation as ranging on a continuum from high to low. High achievement motivation involves consistent exhibition of achievement striving in evocative situations, moderate achievement motivation is marked by indeterminacy in how approach-avoidance conflicts are resolved and less-than-profound intensity/tenacity, and low achievement motivation is reflected in avoidance decisions and decided lack of enthusiasm in the pursuit of high-press-for-achievement objectives. (Low achievement motivation is often indicative of fear of failure [Atkinson, 1978], a trait discussed below.)

Being deemed a trait is not an especially difficult or exclusive attainment—there are thousands of traits. We address a typology of traits in Chapter 3. The salient aspects of a trait that are of concern here are (a) a number of related behaviors can be grouped into one general category, (b) this category can be operationally defined in terms of these behaviors, and (c) the behaviors representing the trait are consistently manifested over time and situations. People who consistently exhibit achievement striving when they must make truly evocative decisions about their education, their training and development, their future career paths, and their productivity have been described as possessing, or being high in, the trait of achievement motivation. The consistency of

behavior furnishes us with a means not only to characterize these individuals but also to predict how they will behave in the future. We must
remember, however, that we are describing *what* people do and not *why*
they are doing it. We shall return to this point shortly, after we have examined the trait of fear of failure.

The Trait of Fear of Failure

Fear of failure is a trait defined by a bonding of emotional and behavioral responses. At its most basic level, fear of failure may be described as
a consistent tendency to respond to achievement-oriented tasks with
apprehension and anxiety about failing and being deemed incompetent. The direct consequence of this apprehension, anxiety, or "fear of
failing" for the individual is that it "oppose[s] and dampen[s] the tendency to undertake achievement-oriented activities" (Atkinson, 1978,
p. 15). A salient aspect of such dampening is that it leads the individual
to resolve approach-avoidance conflicts in favor of avoiding achievement-oriented tasks. A reasonably intelligent person who is high in fear
of failure is likely to have a history that includes choice of a college with
only modestly rigorous standards, choice of an academic major that is
largely devoid of intense competition and "cut courses," and choice of a
career that is high in security and stability.

However, to characterize fear of failure, or those who possess this
trait, as merely avoidant would be to miss many of the trait's important
subtleties. Inasmuch as these subtleties occur frequently, but implicitly,
in organizational settings and can have profound impacts on organizational functioning, we shall take a moment to illustrate behavioral indicators of fear of failure at work. Following Atkinson (see 1978), we refer
to these behavioral indicators as *inhibitory behaviors*. The term *inhibitory* denotes that these behaviors are designed ultimately to reduce anxiety over failing (that is, to reduce fear of failure) by dampening (that is,
inhibiting) the undertaking of achievement-oriented activities.

Inhibitory Behaviors

A moderately subtle form of inhibitory behavior is a "compensatory"
action, which involves the substitution of an easier goal or task for a
more demanding, achievement-oriented goal or task. For example, a
soon-to-be college graduate in computer science may be apprehensive

about the competition and uncertainty of success that accompanies acceptance of a job offer from a high-profile software company. Indeed, fear of failing dampens the job candidate's enthusiasm for the position to such an extent that he spends sleepless nights worrying about failing. Loss of sleep and other indicators of fear-engendered stress (e.g., irritability) create a situation in which job security and stability are more important to this individual than the challenge and opportunity offered by the software company. The candidate thus rejects the job offer, preferring instead to seek employment in a safe, secure work environment.

The subtlety of inhibitory behaviors increases when high-press-for-achievement situations are unavoidable, such as when achievement demands occur only periodically in an otherwise unchallenging job. Behaviors that function to allow the individual to avoid having to engage in achievement-oriented activities may involve "overly conservative" actions. Examples of such actions include discounting the adoption of new ideas (because new ideas could fail), avoiding any form of risk (because risk implies the possibility of failure), and, when given the opportunity, selecting the least demanding tasks rather than more exacting but potentially rewarding tasks. The last of these is also a form of compensatory behavior, and individuals often justify such behavior by imbuing the less difficult tasks with positive, socially desirable qualities (e.g., low risk).

Other subtle forms of inhibitory behaviors include "counterproductive" or "self-defeating" behaviors. For example, students high in fear of failure may engage in a "defensive lack of effort." As the name implies, a defensive lack of effort consists of a purposeful lack of attempt to achieve. Examples of this inhibitory behavior in students include not attending class, not completing homework assignments, and not studying for tests. In their review of self-defeating behaviors, Baumeister and Scher (1988) suggest that this form of inhibitory behavior serves implicitly to shift attributions for low test scores away from deficits in intellectual skills (very threatening) toward lack of interest or exertion (less threatening).

Additional counterproductive behaviors involve "precautionary processes," such as the strategy of attempting only those tasks for which an excuse of nonaccountability is available (e.g., lack of sufficient resources to complete the task) should failure occur. Procrastination is a form of precautionary process, often justified by arguments that it is more reasonable to "remain flexible" and to "withhold judgment" than to act precipitously and commit to what may be a futile action. A key form of precautionary process in business settings is "unnecessary diffusion of responsibility." This occurs when, in an attempt to avoid complete responsibility for important decisions, or to delay decision making, an executive disperses the responsibility to others, such as committees and teams. Unnecessary diffusion of responsibility is often presented as a form of empowerment, delegation, or participation. In truth, however, it is a defensive strategy that some executives use to avoid or to delay making decisions that they should make.

A final set of illustrative inhibitory behaviors are also counterproductive and involve "dispositionally induced lowered performance" on demanding tasks. Lack of persistence is the major problem here. People who fear failing tend to discourage (inhibit) perseverance on tasks on which success is not immediately forthcoming, often because they tacitly assume that the tasks are too difficult, given their abilities. Individuals may rationalize this lack of persistence by reasoning that one should know when to exercise self-discipline and avoid escalating commitment to a lost cause. Unlike people who persist, people who avoid or quit early thus afford themselves less opportunity to develop or to enhance their skills through continued if not more intensive practice, experience, study, and learning.

In sum, the trait of fear of failure involves individuals' engaging in both direct and indirect behaviors designed to reduce apprehension (anxiety, fear) about failing; these behaviors include acts that dampen, inhibit, or replace approach tendencies. Simple avoidance of achievement-oriented goals is the most direct behavioral indicator of fear of failure. However, avoidance may not be socially desirable or even possible, in which case subtle, inhibitory behaviors such as overly conservative decisions, diffusion of responsibility, and counterproductive strategies may occur. These latter manifestations of the trait of fear of failure can be devastating to businesses.

A Caveat of Multiple Causation

The preceding discussion should not be construed to suggest that personality traits such as achievement motivation and fear of failure are the only individually based causes of performance. Depending on the context, other types of traits, such as critical intellectual skills, also influence performance. Nevertheless, taking multiple causation as a given, we must consider that intellectual potential to accomplish high-press-for-achievement objectives is realized only when effort (intensity, persistence) is applied to the task. It is difficult, if not impossible, for an individual to perform successfully on most demanding tasks unless he or she approaches the task and then devotes intense and persistent effort to its accomplishment. Moreover, factors such as fear, anxiety, and apprehension adversely affect performance even if a person's intellectual potential is above average. Thus, although they are neither exclusive nor exhaustive, motivational traits contribute significantly and substantially to performance.

Causes of Traits: Needs (Motives)

To say that a person is "achievement motivated" or high in the trait of achievement motivation means that he or she consistently, over time and evocative situations, directs intense and persistent effort toward accomplishing demanding tasks. Note that we are describing this person's behavior. Now suppose that we ask, *Why* does this person approach (select) demanding tasks and then devote intense and persistent effort toward accomplishing them? In other words, why does he or she behave in ways that we describe as achievement motivated?

The Need to Achieve

An answer to this question appears to be that people who aim intense and persistent effort at achieving demanding objectives have a strong need (motive, desire) "to do things better" (McClelland, 1985b, chaps. 5, 7). A need to do things better involves a desire to experience the challenge, enthusiasm, and involvement that ensue from pitting oneself against a difficult and important task and demonstrating that one is capable of mastering it. Extrinsic factors such as competition and recognition from peers are not unimportant. However, the natural incentives for the need or motive to achieve are "intrinsic" to the act of attempting to achieve. That is to say, the incentives for achievement focus on the "thrill of the chase," especially when achievement behaviors such as approach, intensity, and persistence are associated with positive emotions, such as the experience of challenge, excitement, enthusiasm, and involvement. Additional incentives for the need to achieve involve the sense of pride and the feelings of accomplishment and mastery that accompany accomplishment of a demanding task (see Atkinson, 1957, 1978; McClelland, 1985a, 1985b; McClelland, Koestner, & Weinberger, 1989; Raynor, 1978).

We may thus say that some people are attracted to high-press-for-achievement goals and tasks, and are willing to devote intense and persistent effort to accomplishing these goals and tasks, because they have a need (motive, desire) to show that they are capable of mastering challenging tasks. The need to achieve derives its potency or forcefulness from the natural incentives of positive emotions or feelings, wherein the pursuit of demanding tasks is associated with enthusiasm, excitement, and involvement. Pride in having demonstrated mastery is also to be considered, as is winning approval and recognition for having competed successfully, given that many achievement-oriented tasks involve competition with others.

The Need to Avoid Failure

What, then, causes some people to experience considerable anxiety or fear over failing and to engage in avoidance or other forms of inhibitory behaviors? Consider that one of the reasons an achievement-oriented objective is considered an "achievement" is that it is "difficult." People fail out of college or are not accepted into graduate school. It is not uncommon to be passed over for promotion at least once in one's lifetime. A majority of new business ventures fail. One may practice unrelentingly for an athletic event and yet still fail to win or even place among the top finishers. Basically, striving to achieve carries with it a degree of uncertainty, a risk that the venture may be unsuccessful. This sense of uncertainty is strongest when the probability of success is approximately 5 in 10, for it is in such situations that an individual is least able to predict the outcome and thus is most likely to experience apprehension about the result (Atkinson, 1978).

Uncertainty and risk suggest that even though an achievement-oriented opportunity may trigger the need to achieve and anticipations of the thrill of the chase, it is also likely to stimulate an opposing or antagonistic need that performs a *self-protective function*. This need is a form of safety mechanism designed to protect individuals from engaging in activities that will cause them psychological damage. The protective mechanism consists of a natural proclivity to consider the downside of achievement striving, which is failure and the resulting humiliation, embarrassment, and sense of incompetence that follow failing. The need is therefore referred to as the *need* (or *motive) to avoid failure.* Everyone who cognizes normally has some concern with avoidance of failure. Nevertheless, people vary in the strength of their need to avoid failure. Those who have an intense aversion to uncertainty and are strongly concerned with protecting themselves from failure are predisposed to experience considerable fear of failure (e.g., apprehension, anxiety, dread, worry) when faced with high-press-for-achievement goals or tasks (see Atkinson, 1957, 1978; Nicholls, 1984; Rothbaum, Weisz, & Snyder, 1982; Schlenker & Leary, 1982).

Resultant Achievement-Oriented Tendency and Relative Motive Strength

Basically, people have a need to avoid failing in order to protect themselves from humiliation, shame, and embarrassment. When an individual is presented with an achievement-oriented opportunity, the need to avoid failing acts to counterbalance the need to achieve by stimulating concerns about the ramifications of attempting to succeed and falling short. The opposing forces of the need to achieve and the need to avoid failing create what we referred to earlier as approach-avoidance conflicts.

Individuals' attempts to resolve approach-avoidance conflicts when faced with achievement-oriented goals or tasks involve what Atkinson (1978) refers to as the "resultant achievement-oriented tendency," or simply the "resultant tendency" (p. 16). The resultant tendency varies, ranging on a continuum from a high probability of approach to a high probability of avoidance for a given task. These probabilities are determined in part by which of the two needs is stronger and by the degree of this dominance.

For some people, the resultant tendency is an "approach" or "excitatory" tendency, because the motive to achieve is stronger than the motive to avoid failure. When the need to achieve is strong and the need to avoid failure is only modest or weak, the excitatory tendency or probability of approach is quite high. Indeed, when an individual's strong need to achieve dominates a modest or weak need to avoid failure, that person tends not only to resolve approach-avoidance conflicts by engaging in achievement activities but to devote intense and persistent effort to succeeding at these activities. As a pattern of approach and effort expenditure recurs over time and situations, an individual who exhibits the pattern is identified as achievement motivated, or is said to possess the trait of achievement motivation.

For other people, the need to avoid failure is stronger than the need to achieve. These people are prone to avoid or at least to dampen their enthusiasm for achievement-oriented activities in an attempt to relieve anxiety and apprehension (i.e., fear of failure). These individuals are thus said to possess an "avoidant" or "inhibitory" resultant tendency (Atkinson, 1978, p. 16). When a strong need to avoid failure dominates a modest or weak need to achieve, the inhibitory tendency is quite high. People with this motive pattern consistently tend to resolve approach-avoidance conflicts by avoiding achievement-related activities or by engaging in one or more of the inhibitory behaviors described earlier (e.g., unnecessary diffusion of responsibility). People who consistently experience fear of failure and exhibit inhibitory tendencies over time and situations are described as possessing the trait of fear of failure.

Research has demonstrated that most people can be classified as having either a clearly dominant need or at least a tendency to favor one of the two needs (James, 1998). The resultant tendency is thus a function of a scale anchored by a dominant need to achieve on one end and a dominant need to avoid failure on the other. Between these anchors are gradations in the relative strengths of the needs. For example, just below a dominant need to achieve is a preference for the need to achieve over the need to avoid failure. The need to achieve does not always prevail over the need to avoid failure in this case. Nonetheless, on the average, individuals in this range have a relatively high probability of approaching demanding tasks. This probability is, however, lower than that for individuals for whom the need to achieve is clearly dominant.

Residing at the middle of the scale are the approximately 10% of all people who are classified as "indeterminate" because neither need dominates (James, 1998). Indeterminacy could result from various patterns, including high (need to achieve)-high (need to avoid failure), moderate-moderate, and low-low. The psychological dynamics are different among these possible combinations. For example, a high-high pattern and, to a less pronounced degree, a moderate-moderate pattern suggest intense approach-avoidance conflicts. In contrast, a low-low pattern suggests indifference to achievement-oriented events. The behavioral outcome is similar, however, for all of the patterns. Indeterminacy is likely to engender vacillation, equivocation, and hesitancy. Moreover, the final choice of whether to approach or to avoid is likely to be based on factors other than resultant tendency.

How Do Needs Influence Traits?

If we were to follow the traditional path of discussion of personality in organizational settings, we would now briefly describe research studies that illustrate relationships between needs, as represented by resultant tendencies, and behaviors that are indicative of the traits of achievement motivation and fear of failure. For example, we would note that managers who are promoted more rapidly than others tend to have resultant tendencies in which the need to achieve exceeds the need to avoid failure. A similar pattern of needs is predictive of entrepreneurial activity (see McClelland, 1985b). We would also note that lack of persistence on demanding tasks following an initial setback is positively related to an inhibitory resultant tendency in which the need to avoid failure dominates the need to achieve (see Nicholls, 1984; Rothbaum et al., 1982; Schlenker & Leary, 1982).

Here, however, we shall depart from traditional treatments of personality in which traits are seen as products of needs. Our departure is not meant to reflect disagreement with the need-to-trait (behavior) causal link. Rather, our divergence is the result of our desire to study this link in greater depth by asking, How do needs influence traits (behaviors)? We have chosen to seek greater depth because (a) psychological researchers have made great strides in the recent past in advancing our understanding of how motives influence traits and (b) both research and practice in organizational settings are likely to benefit from these advances.

The truth of the matter is that what follows is an attempt to integrate what Cervone (1991) describes as "the two disciplines of personality psychology" (p. 371). These two disciplines are the *trait* perspective and the *social cognitive perspective*. Heretofore in this chapter, we have focused on individual differences in behaviors and the basic causes of these behaviors—namely, needs (motives). This is typical of a trait view of personality. By seeking to understand how motives engender the behaviors that define traits, we enter the social cognitive domain of personality. It is our belief that a complete account of personality requires discussion of both perspectives, with emphasis placed on how the approaches *unite and synthesize* to explain behavior. We cannot hope to provide a complete or exhaustive discussion of what is an evolving endeavor. We therefore focus on what we believe are the primary functions that operate in the progression from needs to social cognitions to traits.

The Mediating Role of Social Cognition in Need-Trait Relationships

Let us begin by revisiting the definition of personality. In Chapter 1, we defined personality as a dynamic organization of mental (i.e., cognitive) structures and coordinated mental (cognitive) processes that determine individuals' emotional and behavioral adjustments to their environments. If we think of traits such as achievement motivation and fear of failure as behavioral adjustments to environments, then cognitive structures and processes are, according to this definition, key causes of these environmental adjustments. Cognitive structures consist of the enduring mental components—for example, knowledge, beliefs, cognitive schemata (see below), implicit reasoning propensities, values, emotional repertoires, self-concepts, goals, and expectancies—on which individuals rely in giving meaning to their environments and in thinking and feeling. Cognitive processes are the actual mental operations of perceiving, thinking, and feeling.

Cognitive structures and processes are the principal components of "social cognition," which Cervone (1991) defines as the "cognitive processes and structures (e.g., self-conceptions, standards, goals) through which individuals assign personal meaning to events, plan courses of action, and regulate their motivation, emotion, and interpersonal behavior" (p. 372). Our objective here is first to understand how key aspects of social cognition affect characteristic behavioral adjustments to environments (i.e., traits). We shall then endeavor to understand how motives influence social cognition. Basically, we shall build a model wherein social cognition serves to mediate the effects of motives on traits. The important contribution of such a model is that social cognition helps to explain the mental processes by which motives influence traits. The mediation model takes the following form:

$$\text{Motives} \rightarrow \text{Social Cognition} \rightarrow \text{Traits}$$

Beginning with the Social Cognition → Traits link, we shall continue to draw on resultant achievement motivation as an exemplar of the influences of cognitive structures and processes on behavioral adjustments. Consider that whether one approaches or avoids a personally evocative and demanding goal or task is largely determined by how one responds to questions such as the following:

- What is a reasonable estimate of the probability of my succeeding (or failing) at this task or accomplishing this goal?
- To what extent will success be determined by how intensely I work and by my willingness to persist over what may be a long period of time?
- Have motivated and talented people burned out trying to accomplish this goal or task in the past?
- To what extent is success on this task subject to external influences (e.g., suppliers, organizational regulations and policies, support of top management)?
- How long should I persist at this task before I consider it impossibly difficult? When does perseverance become obsessiveness?
- What effect will attempting this task have on other aspects of my life, such as on relationships with my family and my health?
- How is success (failure) on this task related to my career goals and aspirations?

An individual must process information cognitively—specifically, frame and analyze—to answer these questions. For example, the person must interpret what such things as a demanding task, success, intensity, and persistence mean to him or her. This is "framing," and it is indicated by the adjectives that an individual uses to interpret (perceive, assign meaning to) events. To illustrate, some people frame working hard on a demanding task as "being overloaded and stressed," whereas others frame it as being "intrinsically motivated and job involved."

To frame an event is to place the event in an interpretative category, or what some psychologists refer to as a *cognitive schema* (e.g., people high in fear of failure place demanding tasks in the interpretative category of "stressful" because this is what demanding tasks mean to them). Cognitive schemata are thus the internal prisms through which external stimuli pass, and in passing they are translated into interpretative adjectives that indicate personal meaning. Cognitive schemata reside in cognitive structures, and a particular individual tends to draw on the same cognitive schemata repeatedly to give meaning to events. Recurring use of the same schemata gives rise to the idea of "framing proclivities," which are dispositions to use only certain adjectives to interpret the same or similar events. It is these framing proclivities that determine how an individual will interpret the questions posed above, and thus it is framing proclivities that determine the input into the mental analyses through which the questions are ultimately answered.

The individual's objective in performing mental analyses is to draw inferences about such things as the probability of succeeding or failing, the amount of personal control he or she has over success and failure, the influence achievement striving will have on his or her lifestyle, and the effects success and failure might have on his or her career. These analyses are often grounded in "implicit assumptions," which are unconscious hypotheses and theories that shape and guide reasoning, the products of which are experienced as rational thinking and decision making.

For example, some individuals possess an implicit or unconscious proclivity to assume that internal causes are more important than external causes when they make attributions about the causes of performance. Their analyses to determine the causes of success or failure on actual tasks are unknowingly shaped and guided by this implicit assumption. This means that these individuals are unconsciously biased toward finding that internal factors (e.g., intensity, commitment) are the primary causes of performance. The result is that these individuals arrive at conscious judgments that success or failure was largely a function of internal factors such as how hard an individual was willing to work. If asked, these individuals would affirm that their reasoning is purely rational. They are unaware of their implicit disposition to favor internal attributions when they reason about the causes of performance.

Other people may evidence in their reasoning an unconscious proclivity to assume that external forces are the primary causes of success or failure on demanding tasks. This unconscious proclivity will unknowingly orient their conscious reasoning toward judging that factors such as resources and leadership are the principal causes of performance on demanding tasks. These individuals will also believe that their reasoning is purely rational. The unconscious or implicit tendency to favor external explanations is neither recognized nor available to introspection (e.g., self-analysis).

Like cognitive schemata and framing proclivities, many implicit assumptions are permanent fixtures of cognitive structure. This means that individuals use them repeatedly to guide their analysis and thinking. That people are not aware of these influences on their reasoning is indicated by the fact that they are often referred to as *implicit social cognitions* (see Greenwald & Banaji, 1995). In general terms, implicit social cognition is the operation of framing proclivities and implicit assumptions that are beyond the awareness of, or are not accessible to introspection by, the individual (see Epstein, 1994; Erdelyi, 1992; Greenwald & Banaji, 1995; Kilstrom, 1999; Nisbett & Wilson, 1977; Westen, 1990, 1991; Winter, John, Stewart, Klohnen, & Duncan, 1998).

We are now ready to introduce the Motives $\rightarrow$ Social Cognition link of the Motives $\rightarrow$ Social Cognition $\rightarrow$ Traits model. Assignment of meaning based on framing proclivities, followed by analysis based on both framing proclivities and implicit assumptions, is a reasoning process. Two especially interesting features of this process are as follows: (a) People whose need to achieve dominates their need to avoid failure often answer the questions posed above (e.g., Will I be successful?) *differently* than do people whose need to avoid failure dominates their need to achieve, and (b) irrespective of which need is dominant, almost every individual believes that his or her particular reasoning is rational and objective as opposed to irrational, subjective, or foolish.

When people with a strong need to achieve reason differently than people with a strong need to avoid failure, reasoning is "conditional" on the personalities of the reasoners (James, 1998; James & McIntyre, 2000). In Chapter 1, we defined *conditional reasoning* as reasoning that is dependent on personality, which occasions when framing and analyses are dependent on the particular motives, framing proclivities, and implicit assumptions of the reasoner. We illustrated the concept thus: Whether framing and analysis will identify aggression or social adaptiveness as being a sensible behavioral adjustment to an environment is conditional (i.e., dependent) on whether the person doing the reasoning is aggressive or socially adaptive.

In the present context, we are concerned with the following issue in relation to conditional reasoning: Whether framing and analysis will identify approach or avoidance as being the most reasonable behavioral adjustment to a demanding task is conditional (i.e., dependent) on whether the person doing the reasoning is motivated more by achievement motivation or by fear of failure. Thus what are considered to be the most reasonable answers to the questions posed above are conditional on who is doing the reasoning, a person whose need to achieve is dominant or a person whose need to avoid failure is dominant. (People for whom neither need is dominant tend to vacillate between rationales.)

Below, we explore some differences in reasoning between people with different need configurations. To facilitate this discussion, we adopt a form of shorthand: We refer to persons for whom the need to achieve dominates the need to avoid failure as AMs; by contrast, we refer to people for whom the need to avoid failure dominates the need to achieve as FFs.

Conditional Reasoning as a
Product of Justification Mechanisms

Basically, people with opposing needs often behave differently in the same environment, in part because they have different ideas about what constitute reasonable adjustments to that environment. Let us now delve a bit deeper into why reasoning is conditional on whether the person doing the reasoning is an AM or an FF. To justify engaging in their respective desired behaviors, both AMs and FFs depend on implicit biases in reasoning that are designed to enhance the rational appeal of their respective desired behaviors. In Chapter 1, we introduced the term *justification mechanism* (JM) to refer to implicit biases whose purpose is to define, shape, and otherwise influence reasoning so as to enhance the rational appeal of behaving in a manner consistent with a disposition or motive (the operative disposition being aggression in Chapter 1). We shall now extend this discussion to justification mechanisms for AMs and FFs.

Justification mechanisms are unknowingly mapped into conscious thought through the following process: (a) They implicitly influence the cognitive schemata (interpretative categories) that AMs and FFs, respectively, use to frame events (JMs define and shape many of the framing proclivities used by AMs and FFs); and (b) they shape and define many of the analyses that AMs and FFs, respectively, use in determining whether to approach or to avoid demanding tasks. The products of justification mechanisms are unrecognized slants and biases in (a) how AMs and FFs, respectively, interpret achievement and success; and (b) what AMs and FFs, respectively, believe to be rational decision making about whether to approach or to avoid a demanding task.

Justification mechanisms for AMs are defined as implicit biases whose purpose is to define, shape, and otherwise influence reasoning so as to enhance the rational appeal of approach behaviors. Justification mechanisms for FFs are defined as implicit biases whose purpose is to define, shape, and otherwise influence reasoning so as to enhance the rational appeal of avoidance (or inhibitory) behaviors.

Some of the more salient justification mechanisms for AMs are described below; these are followed by some of the more salient JMs for FFs (this presentation is based on a recent article by James, 1998). It is important to reiterate that the individuals who rely on these justification mechanisms are unaware of the conditional nature of their reasoning and the biases in their thinking. To them, their analyses involve natural framing and sensible assumptions that offer logical guides for inferences about the effects of behaviors (e.g., approach to or avoidance of demanding tasks) on such things as success/failure at work, health, relationships with others, and a general sense of emotional well-being (see Wegner & Vallacher, 1977).

Justification Mechanisms of AMs

AMs have an unrecognized tendency to attribute behavior to personal responsibility (see Bandura, 1986; Hall, 1971; Jones, 1973; McClelland & Boyatzis, 1982; Weiner, 1979, 1990, 1991). They are predisposed to reason from the perspective that people should, if the opportunity arises, take initiative and be responsible for decisions and strategies. They are also predisposed to reason from the perspective that people should be held personally accountable for the success or failure of their own endeavors. This implicit hypothesis that people should be held personally accountable for success/failure on demanding tasks engenders a tendency to favor internal attributions (initiative, perseverance, conscientiousness) as explanations for performance in achievement situations. The predilection to invoke internal attributions (explanations) indicates a lack of inclination to use external attributions (e.g., helpful coworkers contributed to success when one's performance is good, inadequate resources restricted performance when one fails) for explanatory purposes.

Note that an exclusively rational analysis might uncover reasonable support for *both* internal (e.g., effort, skills) and external (e.g., leadership, resources) explanations for performance. Highly motivated individuals, however, are predisposed to reason from the perspective (i.e., have an implicit assumption) that success/failure on demanding tasks is largely a function of personal initiative, intensity, and persistence (i.e., internal attributions). Thus, in their attempts to justify approach to demanding goals and objectives and the pursuit of achievement, AMs are inclined to give greater emphasis to internal factors than is perhaps deserved (see Weiner, 1979, 1990, 1991). This is what is meant by an *unconscious bias.*

Bias does not denote error, for internal factors constitute one plausible explanation for performance. But a purely rational model calls for a dialectic, in which both personal and external factors are viable as causes of performance. The connotation of bias is thus a predilection to favor one side of a dialectic when a rational analysis can identify two (or more) alternative, often conflicting, plausible explanations, and there is no logical basis for favoring one explanation over any other.

AMs may well subscribe *consciously* to the idea of a dialectic, and may even express strong belief in the validity of explanatory models that espouse both internal and external causes. However, when asked to analyze specific events and to determine causes of success/failure rationally, AMs consistently favor internal causes as rational explanations.

AMs tend unconsciously to favor explanations based on personal responsibility because (a) they want to believe that success on demanding tasks is not only possible but also controllable through their efforts, and (b) attributing success to personally controllable factors such as initiative and perseverance suggests that they are competent, self-reliant, and talented. It is also noteworthy that a predilection to attribute success on demanding tasks to internal, personal agents fosters an optimistic view of the likelihood of one's success, which is to say the likelihood that demanding goals and tasks will succumb to one's intense and persistent efforts.

This, then, is a form of unconscious bias, although not necessarily error (see Funder, 1987), whose purpose is to enhance the logical appeal of approach behaviors. It illustrates the presence of a justification mechanism—namely, Personal Responsibility Bias—in framing and analysis. Reasoning that has been unconsciously shaped, defined, and guided by the Personal Responsibility Bias is said to be conditional because framing and analysis are dependent on the reasoner's having a strong motive to achieve. An individual's reasoning is said to be conditional on his or her personality when this reasoning is shaped by a motive to achieve in the first place and relies on one or more JMs to enhance

Table 2.1   Illustrative Justification Mechanisms for Achievement Motivation

1. *Personal Responsibility Bias:*   A tendency to favor personal factors such as initiative, intensity, and persistence as the most important causes of performance on demanding tasks.

2. *Opportunity Bias:*   A tendency to frame demanding tasks on which success is uncertain as "challenges" that offer "opportunities" to demonstrate present skills, to learn new skills, and to make a contribution.

3. *Positive Connotation of Achievement Striving Bias:*   A tendency to associate effort (intensity, persistence) on demanding tasks with "dedication," "concentration," "commitment," and "involvement."

4. *Malleability of Skills Bias:*   A tendency to assume that the skills necessary to master demanding tasks can, if necessary, be learned or developed through training, practice, and experience.

5. *Efficacy of Persistence Bias:*   A tendency to assume that continued effort and commitment will overcome obstacles or any initial failures that might occur on a demanding task.

6. *Identification With Achievers Bias:*   A tendency to empathize with the sense of enthusiasm, intensity, and striving that characterizes those who succeed in demanding situations. Includes a selective focus on positive incentives that accrue from succeeding.

the logical plausibility of engaging, and persisting, in achievement-oriented behaviors.

We can see the full scope of conditional reasoning by contrasting the reasoning of AMs with the reasoning of FFs. Arguments that champion approach over avoidance, or vice versa, as the most reasonable adjustment to a demanding task highlight the conditionality of reasoning on individual differences in the personalities of the persons doing the reasoning. We will address this issue shortly.

An implicit affinity for personal responsibility is just one illustration of how justification mechanisms shape, define, and otherwise influence the framing and analyses of AMs. Other JMs for AMs are listed in Table 2.1. Included in this set is the Positive Connotation of Achievement Striving Bias. This JM often affects AMs' framing of working long hours, which is often accompanied by minimal rest and reduced attention to other facets of their lives. AMs frame or interpret sustained and single-minded concentration on the attainment of a demanding goal as a demonstration of dedication, intensity, commitment, involvement, or tenacity. Tacit in this framing is an unrecognized predilection on the part of AMs to ignore or to discount the many forms of stress (e.g., overload, conflict between work and nonwork roles) that they are likely to encounter in their quest to achieve (McClelland, 1985b; Spence & Helmreich, 1983).

One of the reasons AMs do not frame working on demanding tasks as stressful is that they tend to regard these tasks as "challenges" or "opportunities" (Spence & Helmreich, 1983). This framing is reflective of an implicit bias (i.e., JM) to assume that demanding activities are opportunities to take on important objectives, to demonstrate noteworthy skills, and to make contributions in areas that count. This is the JM known as Opportunity Bias.

Note how this framing contrasts with that of FFs. The essence of being an FF is to associate threat and anxiety with the same demanding tasks that AMs perceive as challenges and opportunities. AMs are able to take this perspective because they expect to succeed. Indeed, unlike FFs, who fixate on the downside of achievement striving, AMs attend selectively to the upside. This orientation is manifested by a selective focus on the positive incentives that accrue to successful achievers, both material (e.g., promotion) and emotional (e.g., involvement, excitement, a sense of efficacy). (In Chapter 3, we formally extend the discussion of justification mechanisms to include biases in cognitive processes, such as selective attention.)

Another important JM for AMs is the Efficacy of Persistence Bias. A hallmark of being an AM is the tendency to reason from the perspective that continued effort and perseverance will ultimately result in successful accomplishment of achievement-oriented objectives (McClelland, 1985b; McClelland et al., 1989; Revelle & Michaels, 1976; Weiner, 1979). The Efficacy of Persistence Bias is especially likely to influence reasoning when an AM must overcome obstacles and transitory failures. Examples include (a) a scientist who views a failed experiment as a learning experience and moves on to continue experimentation, (b) an entrepreneur who begins anew after a business failure with even greater determination to build a successful enterprise, (c) an athlete who persists in training and intensifies her practice sessions after having failed to meet her own standards in competition, and (d) an aspiring author who, like Alex Haley, continues to submit manuscripts even though they are rejected repeatedly.

An alternative explanation could have been invoked by the individual involved in each of these illustrations. A number of these alternative explanations could have resulted in these persons' abandoning their objectives (e.g., attributions to uncontrollable outside forces). However, an unrecognized willingness to invoke reasoning that justifies persisting in work on a task demonstrates the Efficacy of Persistence Bias and the dominant motivational force—that is, the need to achieve—that this JM serves. It is also noteworthy that the tendency of AMs to slant their reasoning to favor the efficacy of persistence is often accompanied by a corollary and supporting tendency to think that, if necessary, an individual can learn or develop the skills necessary to accomplish a demanding task through training, practice, and experience (see Dweck & Leggett, 1988). This reasoning is often at least partially influenced by the JM labeled the Malleability of Skills Bias.

In sum, JMs serve AMs' need to achieve by implicitly shaping, defining, and guiding the reasoning that AMs use to enhance the rational appeal of approaching demanding tasks. It is thus JMs that make it possible for AMs to approach and to persevere on personally challenging tasks without experiencing debilitating anxiety about the uncertainty of success or being intimidated by the risk to security that often accompanies failure on important tasks. Indeed, the conscious reasoning engendered by JMs encourages AMs to engage in steadfast pursuit of difficult objectives because this reasoning frames the objectives as opportunities worth commitment and sacrifice, where willingness to expend intense and persistent effort will eventually produce success.

Justification Mechanisms of FFs

Achievement commands respect in our culture, and demanding tasks that herald achievement are imbued with considerable valence. As we have seen, this valence triggers approach tendencies on the part of AMs. For AMs, approach is corroborated and sanctioned as being rational by a set of JMs that lionize demanding goals and render success as primarily a function of dedication and commitment. FFs are also aware of the importance of achievement and the rewards that accrue to those who succeed on difficult tasks. However, this knowledge does not engender the attraction to such tasks experienced by AMs. Rather, for FFs the recognized significance of doing well on difficult tasks stimulates fear and anxiety about the consequences of not doing well, the primary concern being whether they will be perceived as incompetent. Basically, the types of goals and tasks that serve as challenges and opportunities for AMs create psychological hazards (e.g., apprehension, debilitating anxiety, threat) for FFs.

FFs seek relief from their fear of failing by avoiding the achievement-oriented activities on which they see themselves as likely to fail. As we have discussed, avoidance (and other nondestructive types of inhibitory behaviors) is often viewed as a self-protective process, or "coping mechanism," for FFs (see Atkinson, 1957, 1978; Kuhl, 1978; Nicholls, 1984; Rothbaum et al., 1982; Schlenker & Leary, 1982; Sorrentino & Short, 1986). Especially important ingredients of this coping process are means to justify avoiding the tasks, goals, problems, and environments in which failure is perceived as probable. FFs believe that the avoidance/inhibitory behaviors in which they engage to relieve their anxiety about failing are reasonable and will produce the desired results. The framing and inferences employed by FFs to justify avoidance behaviors are often based on some aspects of the justification mechanisms summarized in Table 2.2. We describe several of these JMs in greater detail below.

FFs often reason that engaging in achievement striving is stressful (see Atkinson, 1957, 1978; McClelland, 1985b; Nicholls, 1984; Rothbaum et al., 1982; Schlenker & Leary, 1982). Such reasoning is often implicitly shaped by the JM called Negative Connotation of Achievement Striving Bias. Basically, FFs are unknowingly predisposed to frame achievement striving in negative terms. Illustrative occasions in which this JM is revealed include FFs' framing of achievement-oriented activities such as intensity and persistence as "overloading" and "sources of potential burnout." These are the same activities that AMs regard as indicators of perseverance and commitment. Dedication for AMs becomes mental or physical overload for FFs, from which spring feelings of anxiousness, strain, and tension.

A corollary to framing demanding tasks as stressful is FFs' predilection to see AMs' intense and persistent efforts to achieve as signs of compulsiveness and obsessiveness. The flip side of this corollary is that FFs tend to reason that people who take a more relaxed approach to work are less likely to demonstrate symptoms of stress, such as exhaustion, illness, burnout, and chronic anxiety about how one's career is progressing (Crocker, 1981; Crocker & Major, 1989; Raynor, 1978; Schlenker & Leary, 1982; Taylor & Brown, 1988; Taylor & Lobel, 1989; Wood, 1989). Such reasoning is also a product of an implicit tendency

Table 2.2   Illustrative Justification Mechanisms for Fear of Failure

1. *External Attribution Bias:*   A tendency to favor external factors such as lack of resources, situational constraints, intractable material, and biased evaluations as the most important causes of performance on demanding tasks.

2. *Liability Bias:*   A tendency to frame demanding tasks as personal liabilities or "threats" because one may fail and be seen as incompetent. Perceptions of threat are euphemistically expressed through terms such as *risky, costly,* and *venturesome.*

3. *Negative Connotation of Achievement Striving Bias:*   A tendency to frame effort (intensity, persistence) on demanding tasks as "overloading" or "stressful." Perseverance on demanding tasks after setbacks or obstacles are encountered is associated with "compulsiveness" and "lack of self-discipline."

4. *Fixed Skills Bias:*   A tendency to assume that problem-solving skills are fixed and cannot be enhanced through experience, training, or dedication to learning. Thus if one is deficient in a skill, one should not attempt demanding tasks or should withdraw if one encounters initial failure.

5. *Leveling Bias:*   A tendency to discount a culturally valent but, for the reasoner, psychologically hazardous event (e.g., approaching a demanding situation) by associating that event with a dysfunctional and aversive outcome (e.g., cardiovascular disease).

6. *Identification With Failures Bias:*   A tendency to empathize with the fear and anxiety of those who fail in demanding situations. Includes a selective focus on negative outcomes that accrue from failing.

7. *Indirect Compensation Bias:*   A tendency to attempt to increase the logical appeal of replacing a threatening situation with a compensatory (i.e., less threatening) situation by imbuing the less threatening situation with positive, socially desirable qualities.

8. *Self-Handicapping Bias:*   A tendency to deflect explanations for failure away from incompetence in favor of self-induced impairments, such as not really trying or not being prepared (e.g., defensive lack of effort).

NOTE: A nonexhaustive but representative sampling of research domains that have contributed to the understanding of justification mechanisms includes attribution models and theories, defense mechanisms (from abnormal psychology), framing, heuristics in decision making, implicit (personality) theories, biases in person perception, cognitive mechanisms for self-protection and self-enhancement (from social psychology), object relations, many of the social comparison principles, social inference, and systematic biases in performance evaluation.

to justify avoidance of demanding tasks by invoking the Negative Connotation of Achievement Striving Bias.

Other JMs are also reflected in FFs' reasoning. For example, FFs have a strong predilection to conclude that the failure on which they have focused their attention is due to external agents that are beyond their control (e.g., lack of resources, societal inequities, poor leadership). Such reasoning often reveals an underlying JM called the External Attribution Bias (see Table 2.2; see also Crocker & Major, 1989; Hinshaw, 1992; Schlenker & Leary, 1982; Taylor, 1991). As a specific illustration of reasoning based on this JM, consider FF students who conclude that their low to moderate scores on an important, difficult exam were products of uncontrollable external agents such as lack of resources (e.g., inadequate study time), situational constraints (e.g., loud roommates), impregnable material, and biased professors. Thus, whereas AMs tend to reason from the perspective that they can improve on less-than-stellar performance through control of internal factors (e.g., increase study time), FFs tend to focus their reasoning on external factors over which they have no control and that will likely nullify whatever effort they expend to master material. It is also the case that FFs are less than enthusiastic about AMs' tendency to hold people personally accountable for performance on demanding tasks. To FFs, it hardly seems reasonable to be held personally responsible for failures that were caused by factors over which they had little or no control.

AMs' tendency to champion the efficacy of intense and persistent effort comes under logical attack by FFs from yet another perspective. Research has shown that people who concentrate their attention on failure and its aversive consequences also tend to conclude that basic cognitive problem-solving abilities and critical intellectual skills are fixed and cannot be enhanced through experience, training, or dedication to learning. This reasoning is frequently shaped by a JM designated the Fixed Skills Bias (see Crocker & Major, 1989; Dweck & Leggett, 1988; Nicholls, 1984; Taylor, 1991; Taylor & Brown, 1988; Taylor & Lobel, 1989; Weiner, 1979, 1990, 1991; Wood, 1989). Reasoning engendered by the Fixed Skills Bias contrasts sharply with the reasoning of AMs, who, as noted, tend to analyze behavior from the perspective that if an individual does not have the skills necessary to accomplish a demanding task at the onset of a difficult assignment, he or she can develop those skills through training, experience, and learning (i.e., effort) as the assignment progresses. FFs, by contrast, are skeptical of pursuing assignments for which they perceive themselves as having deficient critical skills (i.e., they experience an inhibitory or restraining tendency).

The preceding discussion paints a picture in which FFs logically associate achievement-oriented activities with such things as stress, uncontrollable agents, risk, intractable difficulties, and a sense of helplessness. These logical connections furnish FFs with excuses for avoiding demanding tasks. In place of high-press-for-achievement situations, FFs seek secure and safe environments where the futures of their jobs and careers are predictable and certain. Such jobs and careers are often not particularly glamorous or prestigious, which stimulates the implicit operation of the JM labeled the Indirect Compensation Bias. That is, FFs attempt to justify their replacing threatening goals and tasks (i.e., high-press-for-achievement objectives) with less threatening (i.e., compensatory) goals and tasks by imbuing the latter objectives with positive qualities (e.g., reasoning that emphasizes the valence of job security).

In sum, the JMs possessed by FFs encourage them to reason from the standpoint that venting inhibitory tendencies is feasible and sensible as opposed to unrealistic, defensive, or foolish. Framing and inferences based on these JMs help make it possible for FFs to avoid demanding tasks without seeing themselves as unmotivated, indecisive, untalented, risk avoidant, or lacking in initiative. In particular, JMs and the reasoning they shape, define, and sustain assist FFs in arriving at the conclusion that they are cautious and patient individuals who, in the interest of maintaining realistic, stable, and predictable lifestyles, make decisions and engage in behaviors that promote balance, security, lack of stress, and tranquillity.

The Five Themes of the Social
Cognitive Approach: A Further Attempt to
Integrate the Trait and Social Cognition Approaches

Knowledge of how AMs and FFs reason differently, which is to say conditionally, furnishes us with a foundation from which to explore how differences in needs affect the behaviors that define traits. Indeed, we have already embarked on this exploration. In our discussion of JMs for AMs and FFs above, we have addressed two of five basic themes that define the social cognitive approach to personality. The first of these themes is that individuals assign personal meaning to (i.e., frame) events that affect their lives (Cervone, 1991). We have seen that AMs frame achievement-oriented activities as opportunities and challenges, and that FFs frame such activities as threats and psychological liabilities.

The second defining theme of social cognition is that people make and justify decisions. Here we have seen that whether one decides to approach or to avoid a demanding task is often conditional on whether one is an AM or an FF. We have also discussed how different decisions are individually justified. Specifically, AMs and FFs base their framing and analyses on different implicit assumptions (i.e., JMs). For example, AMs, in contrast with FFs, expect to succeed on demanding tasks because they are implicitly disposed to place greater confidence in their ability to control outcomes through intense and persistent effort.

We discuss the third through fifth themes of social cognition below. The third theme is that both AMs and FFs plan courses of action and continually adjust and regulate their actions so as attain demanding objectives. The fourth theme is that environments, including work environments, are capable of influencing motivational processes. The fifth and final theme is that selectivity exists in regard to where and when the needs to achieve and to avoid failure are activated.

Developmental and Self-Regulatory Processes for AMs

We will use the model presented in Figure 2.1 as a basis for discussing the developmental and self-regulatory processes of AMs. The top part of the model is largely a review. An approach-avoidance conflict involving a personally evocative and demanding task activates the dominant need to achieve. The activated need is experienced consciously through emotions that anticipate the thrill of the chase (e.g., excitement, enthusiasm). The activated need triggers (stimulates, directs, sustains) conditional reasoning (reasoning implicitly shaped by JMs) that justifies a decision that it is sensible to heed the urge to approach the task. For example, the task is regarded as challenging yet surmountable if one commits to providing the necessary effort and is willing to learn the necessary skills.

The task is approached, which begins with the planning of a course of action that is expected to result in task accomplishment. Specific end goals are set for overall task accomplishment. Specific intermediate goals are also set for subtasks that should be completed at specific times. Successful completion of subtasks indicates progress toward overall task accomplishment (Latham & Locke, 1991; Locke, 1991). Standards or criteria are determined that will be used to judge whether the intermediate goals and end goals have been met (or the degree to which they have been satisfied).

Effort is then expended to accomplish the goals. We expect two general activities to accompany effort. First, the individual will experience

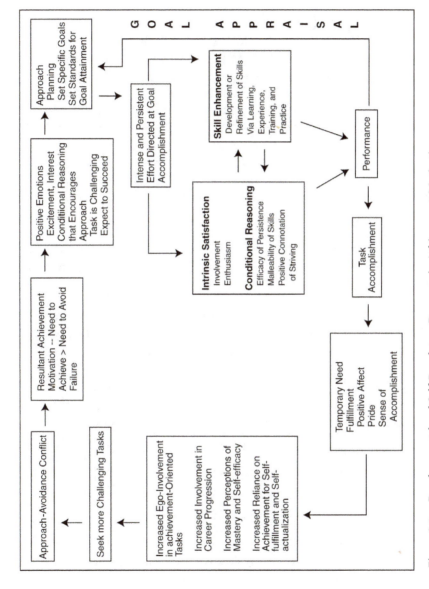

Figure 2.1. Developmental and Self-Regulatory Processes in Achievement Motivation

49

the intrinsic satisfaction that derives from attempting to accomplish an achievement-oriented goal. A sense of involvement and enthusiasm are illustrative. Accompanying these emotions will be conditional reasoning produced by JMs. For example, persistently working long hours will be framed as commitment, and it will be inferred (expected) that persistence will be efficacious in producing ultimate success on the task.

Second, effort may include attempts to learn or to develop new skills, or perhaps to improve skills that are already present, through training and practice. AMs, via their implicit belief in the malleability of skills, are likely to reason that skill enhancement is a natural component of motivation (Dweck & Leggett, 1988). In fact, the inference that skills can be enhanced through learning, training, and practice sets the foundation for AMs' expectation that perseverance will ultimately win the day. Consider the young amateur athlete who watches professional athletes perform exceptional feats. If the young athlete is an AM, what he sees as the difference between his present skills and the more profound skills of the professionals is the opportunity that the professionals have had to train and to practice. The actual act of reasoning—the inference that professionals are more proficient because they have had more training and practice—is conditional (i.e., it is reasoning dependent on personality). The unstated or tacit assumption that accompanies the conscious inference is that the young athlete can attain this same level of skill if he is motivated and willing to devote considerable effort to training and practice. Both the conscious inference and the unstated inference are implicitly shaped and guided by the Malleability of Skills Bias, which is a JM that orients reasoning toward inferring that skills can almost always be enhanced through effort.

To the extent that skills are truly subject to development, effort devoted to learning, training, and practice should produce skill enhancement. In turn, skill enhancement reinforces the conditional reasoning that engendered skill development in the first place (and thus the reciprocal causal arrows from skill enhancement back to emotions and cognitions in Figure 2.1). Two points are noteworthy here. First, motivation to achieve is an important cause of skill enhancement. Second, actual enhancement of skills reinforces and likely strengthens the conditional reasoning responsible for initiating skill development. We would expect AMs to pursue this sequence again—indeed, repeatedly. Thus motivation and skill development are seen as functionally related.

One feeds the other, and over time they become fused substantively and correlated statistically.

We do not mean to suggest that motivation and ability are indistinguishable or necessarily highly correlated. There are limits to how much skill individuals can develop no matter how much effort they exert, and it is not uncommon to find that AMs try to make up for lack of natural ability by ratcheting up their effort. Nonetheless, when viewed developmentally, achievement motivation and skills grow in functionally related sequences and are thus related, perhaps moderately so (Ackerman & Heggestad, 1997). Let us now turn to the next step in this sequence, which is performance.

We noted above that completing a demanding task typically involves successive attainment of specific intermediate goals for each stage of progression toward specific end goals. One meaning of performance is how an individual performs on one or more of the intermediate goals. At each point in the sequence, the individual appraises his or her performance against the standards that were set earlier in the planning stage. This appraisal process is indicated by a feedback loop in the model. Congruence between standards and goals reinforces a steady, stay-on-course response. Discrepancies between standards and performance indicate the need for adjustment. What adjustment is made depends on the attributions the individual makes for the discrepancies. For example, if performance is below standard and this result is attributed to insufficient effort (e.g., deficient practice or training), then an AM is disposed to increase effort expenditures.

The repeated appraisal of performance in relation to standards and the making of adjustments if indicated is referred to as *self-regulation of behavior* (Bandura, 1978, 1986, 1991; Latham & Locke, 1991; Kanfer & Kanfer, 1991; Mischel, 1973; Phillips, Hollenbeck, & Ilgen, 1996; Thomas & Mathieu, 1994). We shall assume here that the self-regulatory efforts are successful, resulting in accomplishment of the demanding task. The act of achievement temporarily fulfills the individual's need to achieve and produces positive affect, such as pride, happiness, and a sense of accomplishment.

The next stage of the model is especially important. When AMs achieve and they attribute that achievement in whole or in part to their efforts and skills, they have a tendency to enlarge their "ego involvement" in achievement-oriented activities (Hall, 1971). Expanded ego

involvement is indicated by such things as increased personal identification with the source of achievement, such as a job or career; an expanded sense of self-efficacy in relation to competencies that produced achievement; and, most important, an enlarged reliance on
achievement-oriented activities for self-definition and self-fulfillment.
Increased ego involvement in achievement-oriented activities suggests
an iterative process wherein individuals grow not only in competence,
self-efficacy, and reliance on achievement to define their self-identities,
but in their desire to maintain this growth through accomplishing successively more difficult tasks. It is the last of these, the desire to continue
to grow and to better oneself through accomplishing progressively
more difficult objectives, that appears to lie at the heart of achievement
motivation (see McClelland, 1985b).

We shall not attempt to present a parallel model for FFs, for we have
already discussed the basic ingredients of such a model. Basically, FFs
sustain and reinforce their fear of failure through framing and analysis
that encourage the avoidance of achievement-oriented tasks and the
seeking of compensatory jobs and careers. FFs' self-regulatory systems
focus on the reduction of anxiety and the maintenance of safe and secure environments. These systems are perturbed when FFs cannot
avoid high-press-for-achievement tasks, in which case they are likely to
engage in one of the inhibitory behaviors discussed earlier.

It is also noteworthy that by not engaging in and by not persisting at
demanding tasks, FFs often pay the price of low skill enhancement. That
is, one cannot enhance one's skills if one does not devote effort to training, development, and practice. Thus over time we would expect the differences in skill levels between AMs and FFs to magnify. The issue of ego
involvement in jobs and careers is a bit trickier. Safety and security can
be strong reinforcers for FFs, and it would be unwise to assume that because FFs are involved in compensatory jobs, they are less ego involved
than AMs. What we can say is that FFs are not prone to become ego involved in achievement-oriented activities.

Environmental Influences on Motivation:
The Person-by-Situation Interaction
and Person-Environment Fit

When faced with the demanding task of trying to get his work published, Alex Haley, our prototype AM, chose to approach and to perse-

vere for 7 years. In contrast, some FFs also wanted to publish but experienced great anxiety over the possibility of failing and chose to concede long before 7 years elapsed, perhaps before they had even written or submitted initial manuscripts. Variations on this theme are endemic to how AMs and FFs differ in responding to achievement-oriented tasks. That is, when a person is given a personally demanding and evocative task, whether he or she responds by approach or by avoidance is viewed as contingent on whether that person is an AM or an FF. In general terms, the response to a situational demand (i.e., achievement-oriented task) is contingent on the personality of the respondent (i.e., whether the respondent is an AM or an FF). We refer to such contingencies as *person-by-situation interactions,* or *P × S interactions.* The term *interaction* conveys that the effect of the situation is not the same for everyone, but instead is moderated by the personality of the respondent.

When relationships between situational demands and behavioral responses are moderated by personality, we tend to focus on P × S interactions to explain behavior. Concentrating on P × S interactions means that we will want to know the personality of an individual (whether he or she is an AM or an FF) before we attempt to predict what effect a situation (i.e., demanding task) will have on his or her behavior. This has proven to be a challenge for those investigators who wish to concentrate attention on traits as the primary causes of performance in work settings (see Schmidt, Hunter, & Outerbridge, 1986). It has also been a challenge for those who believe that situational attributes such as incentive systems, organizational structure, and leadership overwhelm the effects of traits on performance in organizational settings (see Davis-Blake & Pfeffer, 1989).

The simple fact is that when we deal with situations in which we expect personality to be influential—that is, with situations that are personally evocative to individuals and in which individuals are empowered to make decisions about how to behave—then P × S interactions are overwhelmingly the choice of most investigators as the best means to explain behavior (see Endler & Magnusson, 1976; House, Shane, & Herold, 1996; Kristof, 1996; Magnusson, 1990; Mischel, 1990; Pervin, 1990). Explanations of behavior are often done from the perspective of *person-by-environment (or situation) fit* (see Bretz & Judge, 1994; Cable & Judge, 1994, 1996, 1997; Chatman, 1989, 1991; Chatman & Barsade, 1995; Edwards & Harrison, 1993; Gustafson & Mumford, 1995; Hogan & Blake, 1996; Hogan, Hogan, & Roberts, 1996; Judge & Ferris, 1992;

ENVIRONMENTAL DEMAND

Resign from Salaried Job *Start Own Business*	*Remain in Salaried Job*
Many entrepreneurs have succeeded in the past. Opportunity to be self-reliant and to make own decisions. Most people who failed did not work hard enough. Those who succeeded put in many hours. Being successful will require commitment, sacrifice, and involvement in work. Will have setbacks, but setbacks will be learning experiences that eventually will produce a successful venture.	Not using skills or realizing potential; missing opportunities to grow and advance. Job is somewhat boring and unchallenging. Could make decisions better than they are now being made by supervisors. Most peers do not really care about getting ahead, doing things better than they are now being done.
Most new ventures fail. Will lose pension and security of monthly check. Can put in many hours and yet still fail for reasons beyond control, such as downturn in economy. Starting a business is stressful and could lead to problems with health. Will have to neglect children and friends. Funding will be tight, and even a minor setback could be disastrous.	Job is stable and provides a reliable income. Pension and retirement benefits are safe. Do not have to be obsessed with work; have time for other pursuits.

RESULTANT ACHIEVEMENT MOTIVATION — AM (top row) / FF (bottom row)

Figure 2.2   Conditional Reasoning Within a Person-Environment Fit Model

Kristof, 1996; O'Reilly, Chatman, & Caldwell, 1991; Rynes, Bretz, & Gerhart, 1991; Schaubroeck, Ganster, & Jones, 1998; Schneider, Goldstein, & Smith, 1995; Schneider, Smith, & Goldstein, 2000; Schneider, Smith, Taylor, & Fleenor, 1998; Turban & Keon, 1993). Person-by-environment fit, or P-E fit, models are specific applications of P × S interactions. The illustrative P-E fit model presented in Figure 2.2 addresses this point.

P-E Fit

The most basic issue of fit between individuals and work environments concerns individuals' decisions about which type of work environment is best for them. This is often a product of conditional reasoning—for example, AMs and FFs have different views about what constitutes the "best" environment. Figure 2.2 presents a decision that has been shown to trigger needs and approach-avoidance conflicts for AMs and FFs (McClelland, 1985b): the decision concerning whether (a) to start a business and attempt to become a successful entrepreneur or (b) to seek/remain in a salaried job in a secure organization. The word *secure* connotes a business that has not experienced large fluctuations in its workforce and that rewards commitment and loyalty. The entrepreneurial environment offers opportunity but also uncertainty about success, whereas the salaried job in a secure environment presents the individual with a "role" (Hogan & Roberts, 2000) that requires less risk, is generally less demanding, and is more stable, at least in the near future.

The triggering of needs is indicated consciously by the experience of emotions and conditional reasoning. Entrepreneurship, for example, evokes excitement and enthusiasm on the part of AMs, but anxiety and apprehension on the part of FFs. Justification mechanisms are activated to process information and to ponder which is the more reasonable decision, entrepreneurship or security. We shall draw on prior discussion to contrast the conditional reasoning engendered by the use of different JMs by AMs and FFs to frame and analyze each environment. A summary of this conditional reasoning is presented in Figure 2.2.

The two cells that deal with entrepreneurial activity—the left-hand side of the figure—are illustrations of AM and FF conditional reasoning when each personality type is faced with the same demanding task. AMs tend to build a justifiable case for approach, whereas FFs tend to build a justifiable case for avoidance. The beginnings of an interaction are also evident. How one frames the idea of starting a new business is conditional on one's need structure. From this fledgling interaction emerges the first hint of the meaning of "fit" between the person and the environment. There exists a fit or congruence between AMs and entrepreneurial activity because AMs frame starting one's own business as a reasonable activity that potentially could improve one's quality of life. A lack of fit between FFs and entrepreneurial enterprises is also evident. FFs frame initiating a new business as unreasonable because it is most likely to fail. And if by chance it were to succeed, one would still pay a heavy price in terms of stress, health problems, and deterioration of relationships with family and friends.

Turning to the right-hand side of Figure 2.2, we see that reasoning about a salaried job in a secure organization is also conditional on personality type. FFs judge a salaried job to be a good idea because it contributes to what they regard as salient determinants of a good quality of life (i.e., stability, security, time for nonwork pursuits). There is, therefore, a fit between FFs and a stable/secure work environment. In contrast, a lack of fit is indicated between AMs and salaried jobs in safe, secure work environments. Consider, as an example, an aspiring automobile mechanic who wants to open her own shop but for the present is working for a dealer. The dominant need to achieve is expressed through this person's conditional reasoning that she (a) is not living up to potential, (b) could do things better if she were making the decisions, and (c) could be successful as an entrepreneur because she is a good mechanic who is willing to commit whatever effort is needed to succeed.

The salience of P × S interaction and P-E fit is underscored if we simply ignore the contingencies in Figure 2.2 and attempt to make statements about the effects of work environments on "people in general." Suppose someone advocated that "the greater the challenge, the greater the satisfaction with one's job." According to this hypothesis, entrepreneurs are, on the average, more satisfied with their jobs than salaried employees because entrepreneurial activities are more challenging than the more standardized, formalized, and bounded activities of salaried employees, especially those in large organizations. Entrepreneurs are thus more able to experience the challenge of making decisions, whereas salaried employees often have the less demanding, and less rewarding, task of following orders.

One can easily disconfirm the hypothesis that challenging environments are more satisfying, however, by pointing to FFs' anxiety, apprehension, and fear of failing when confronted with demanding goals and tasks. Indeed, the hypothesis appears to have been formulated in innocence of the principles of individual differences in cognitive processes such as perception, wherein it is primarily AMs that evaluate demanding activities using terms such as *challenge*. FFs are more prone to frame these same demanding activities using terms such as *threat* and *risk*. We might also draw from prior discussion on the types of inhibitory behaviors that FFs are likely to invoke when they are faced with high-press-for-achievement environments. The simple hypothesis that challenging environments are more satisfying appears not to have contemplated the resulting organizational dysfunctions engendered by FF behaviors such as overly conservative decision making, unnecessary diffusion of responsibility, defensive lack of effort, stress-induced performance decrements, and lack of persistence. These are actions inspired by fear, even panic in some cases. They are not the behaviors of satisfied individuals.

Of course, the distinction between entrepreneurial activity and a salaried position in a secure organization is sufficiently large and evocative to dramatize the fallacy of making the assumption that "all" employees will like or benefit from becoming entrepreneurs. But what if we simply deal with "challenging activities" and consider only those options available to salaried employees? These options might include increased autonomy in deciding how a job should be done or enhanced empowerment to contribute to decisions regarding organizational governance. Would we see the fallacy in the omnibus hypothesis "The greater the challenge, the greater the satisfaction with one's job" so quickly? Apparently not, for major change efforts of the past have been based on just such a hypothesis (e.g., job enlargement, job enrichment, participative decision making). We now know that failure to consider individual differences and P × S interaction/P-E fit can cause considerable problems for change efforts (see Cascio, 1989). Hopefully, this is not a lesson that each new generation of organizational theorists has to learn for itself, although some are concerned that this may be so (see House et al., 1996).

The Attraction-Selection-Attrition (ASA) Model

Let us focus now on AMs who find entrepreneurship or at least entrepreneur-like activities enticing. Basically, AMs are attracted to work environments in which they have (a) opportunities to better themselves, to develop their full potential, to do something important, and to make a contribution; and (b) the power to make decisions that affect their work, which includes autonomy and sufficient influence to determine the nature of tasks, to act without consultation or permission, and to affect decisions made by managers (see Atkinson, 1957, 1978; Bandura, 1986; McClelland, 1985a; McClelland et al., 1989; Spence & Helmreich, 1983; Turban & Keon, 1993; Weiner, 1979, 1990, 1991).

A "nonrestrictive" type of organizational climate is most likely to offer such attributes. Nonrestrictive climates are characterized by managers who place confidence in employees, who value and emphasize independent accomplishment, and who encourage employees to develop their full potential to perform (see James, Demaree, Mulaik, & Ladd, 1992). These strategic values are operationalized by decentralization of overall authority structures, minimal formalization of communications and standardization of job requirements, reward and incentive systems based on individual merit, and a penchant to adopt innovative ideas for solving problems.

Companies that have adopted nonrestrictive climates are interested in people who will thrive in such environments. They tend, therefore, to seek out AMs in the selection process. Once selected, AMs tend to have good P-E fit with nonrestrictive climates. They are happy and productive (see the references cited above). They are therefore likely to stay, or to refrain from attrition. There are exceptions of course, such as when an AM leaves a nonrestrictive climate to begin his or her own company. And AMs can be drawn to other companies because they offer greater opportunities for achievement, as occurs frequently in the computer industry.

Nonetheless, the general trend is that if AMs are not pursuing entrepreneurial activities, then they are attracted to companies with nonrestrictive climates and self-select themselves into these work environments. The resulting compatibility between AMs and nonrestrictive climates is reinforcing for both AMs and the organizations. This compatibility encourages company policy makers to maintain the nonrestrictive climate and the selection process that attracts and picks AMs. It is also the case that AMs are likely to want to stay with nonrestrictive organizations.

On the other hand, FFs may find nonrestrictive climates a bit more strenuous than they desire. Or they may be uneasy with the personal responsibility and initiative required to perform in nonrestrictive environments. Personal responsibility, for example, suggests to FFs that they will be held accountable for any failures that may occur. FFs are further concerned with such things as stress and the possibilities of burnout from trying to succeed. FFs are thus prone to decide that nonrestrictive climates are not very appealing. Consequently, FFs are less likely than AMs to seek employment in nonrestrictive environments. If FFs accept employment in nonrestrictive climates by chance or because they lack viable alternatives, then they are more likely to leave than are AMs. All they may need is an excuse such as an offer of employment from a less demanding organization.

Schneider (1987; see also Schneider et al., 1995, 1998) refers to the processes described above as the "attraction-selection-attrition" model, or the ASA model. A key outcome of ASA processes is a continual narrowing of the applicant/employee pool by self-selection, selection by the organization, and attrition by those who fail to find good P-E fit. Basically, ASA processes produce increasing homogeneity of personality characteristics among organizational incumbents (Schneider et al., 1995). It is possible that, in some organizations at least, this homogenizing process can produce sufficient similarity among incumbents that the organization can be thought of as having a "modal personality type" (Schneider et al., 1998). An example of such an organization would be a scientific research center populated primarily by AM scientists.

A subtler implication of the ASA model is that personality affects the type of climate adopted and fostered by an organization. Organizations develop nonrestrictive climates for many reasons, one of which may be that the organization's founder was an AM (see Staw, 1991) who designed a climate that he or she found satisfying. Similar logic holds when management teams are made up primarily of AMs. Nonrestrictive climates may also emerge by trial and error, such as when organizations restructure until they find a system that attracts and retains AM employees. The basic point is that a personality variable—achievement motivation—influences organizational values, structure, and processes.

In turn, by encouraging AMs to approach demanding tasks and providing them with the freedom to make decisions about how those tasks should be mastered, nonrestrictive organizations offer AMs opportunities to satisfy their need to achieve. In fact, nonrestrictive organizations provide contexts in which the developmental model presented in Figure 2.1 can flourish. This suggests that, due in part to their working in nonrestrictive climates, AMs may satisfy their needs, develop their skills, increase their ego involvement in achievement-oriented tasks, and seek progressively more difficult tasks. Basically, the organizational environment becomes a source for sustaining if not intensifying the motive structure that defines an important component of personality.

In sum, personality has causal influences on situations, and situations have causal influences on personality. These "reciprocal" causal influences are referred to as *reciprocal interactions* (see Bandura, 1977, 1986; Bowers, 1973; Endler & Magnusson, 1976; Schneider, 1987). An important use of reciprocal interactions has been to identify fallacies in prior organizational theory and research. For example, if AM individuals work productively in an organization that promotes and reinforces initiative and personal responsibility, then it makes little sense to attempt to determine which is more important, the personality of the incumbents or the climate of the organization. Personality and climate mutually reinforce one another, and neither is more important than the other. Yet, despite warnings from several investigators (see Endler, 1975; James, Hater, Gent, & Bruni, 1978; Roberts, Hulin, & Rousseau, 1978), attempts to determine which is the more important cause of behavior, personality of incumbents or climate of the organization, have constituted the sport of choice of many organizational investigators. It is our hope that new generations of researchers will recognize the folly of such endeavors.

Cross-Situational Consistency, Situational Specificity, and Coherence

We have described a trait as a disposition (predilection, proclivity, tendency) to behave in a relatively consistent manner over time and *across different situations.* The qualifier "across different situations" has proven to be slippery and a source of confusion. Does the definition of trait suggest that people who are motivated to achieve in academics will also be motivated to achieve in business, or in the arts, or in athletics? Can achievement motivation be a trait if individuals who demonstrate AM characteristics in math generally fail to demonstrate those same characteristics in hockey? Questions such as these have generated great controversy in personality research over the past 30 years (see Buss, 1989; Epstein, 1979, 1983; Epstein & O'Brien, 1985; Funder & Colvin, 1991; Grote & James, 1991; Kenrick & Funder, 1988; Mischel, 1968; Mischel & Peake, 1982; Pervin, 1985, 1990; Wright & Mischel, 1987). A fragile truce currently exists among most of the parties to these controversies. We shall use a brief case study involving achievement motivation to define and illustrate the principal terms on which there is general agreement.

A Brief Case Study

Terence Cheng was born soon after his parents immigrated to San Francisco from Asia. His parents managed to bring sufficient funds with them to open a small restaurant. Terry began working in the restaurant as an adolescent. He started out washing dishes, progressed to busing tables, and then functioned as a waiter. Throughout this time, he and his family were committed to making a success of the restaurant. Everyone devoted many hours to work on a daily basis. The family members shared a sense of involvement and enthusiasm in first attempting to survive in the restaurant business and then, having endured, expanding both the size of their business and the number of clientele. They attributed their success to initiative, perseverance, willingness to learn how to succeed in a new culture, and confidence in their ultimate success.

Terry also obtained excellent grades in school. Above average in intelligence, he realized his academic potential through diligence and tenacity. He often studied for long hours after the restaurant closed and on weekend mornings. Here again, Terry framed his efforts as dedication to doing things well, and he often experienced a sense of enthusiasm as he mastered demanding material. Terry would also have liked to participate in after-school sports. Indeed, he was excited when his physical education class played basketball. Terry wanted to practice and to develop whatever athletic talent he had to play basketball. Unfortunately, working in the restaurant and studying exhausted his time and precluded his taking part in serious athletic pursuits. This was also true for drama, to which Terry was inexplicably drawn; he had no time to indulge his impulse to develop acting skills.

There were, of course, a number of other domains in which others achieved but for which Terry experienced no excitement or desire to join in the thrill of the chase. Included here were football, art, holding political office, philosophy, choir, chess, and video games. If asked, Terry could not explain why these activities failed to initiate a spark in him. He would note, however, that even if interested, he probably lacked the mental, physical, motivational, or social competencies to succeed in these endeavors. On the other hand, he was aware that the achievements of others in these domains were products of the same interests, intensity, and perseverance that fueled his attainments in the family business and in academics.

Terry attended college. It was a long and difficult process, completed at a community college where the flexibility of class offerings allowed him to work full-time at the restaurant while pursuing a degree. Terry majored in business and, over the course of his college years, constructed a strategic plan for using the family restaurant as a base for developing a chain of restaurants. Toward the end of his college career, his parents retired, leaving Terry in charge of the family business. Terry both thrived and learned from his experiences as a manager. After 3 years of learning and developing managerial skills, which he used to refine his expansion plan, Terry spearheaded the opening of a second restaurant. It was exacting work, but this restaurant, like the first, soon prospered. Over the next 10 years, Terry directed the opening of 15 more restaurants. At present, Terry is the chief executive officer (CEO) of a family-owned company that is preparing to open restaurants throughout the western United States.

Temporal Stability

Let us look first at a basic task that Terry has expressed a desire to achieve. We shall draw a random sample of occasions of Terry's achievement-oriented behavior. An illustrative task is that of student in upper school, and the sample of occasions will be hours spent studying per week over a randomly selected 6-month period. This sample consists of approximately 26 weeks (occasions). For each of the 26 weeks, we measure the number of hours Terry studied. We examine these 26 "repeated measurements" to see if Terry's study behavior was consistent over occasions.

Terry is considered high in achievement motivation because he demonstrated a consistent tendency to study for relatively long periods of time on each of the 26 weeks. We thus conclude that Terry's disposition to behave in an achievement-oriented manner is *temporally stable,* by which we mean that a behavioral indicator of the trait (studying long hours) is manifested consistently over time when the task (situation) is the same.

We do not ascribe a trait to an individual unless he or she manifests behaviors representing that trait in a temporally stable manner. We must also consider that a trait can be manifested in different ways. To illustrate these points, let us turn momentarily to a classmate of Terry's named Karen. Karen's study time varied indiscriminately over the 26 weeks, being high in some weeks but low in others. This variety in behavior indicates that Karen does not manifest achievement-oriented behavior in regard to academic tasks *on a reliable basis.* Simply stated, she is inconsistent in her willingness to devote long hours to study. We would, therefore, conclude that data based on study time does not support an inference that Karen is achievement motivated.

Note that we do not conclude that Karen is unmotivated, for she may still have a high need to achieve. However, if indeed Karen has a high need to achieve, then this need is being manifested in an area other than academics.

The defining characteristic of temporal stability is that repeated measures taken on the same trait behavior over occasions from the same situation are roughly the same. Terry's history offers us a number of additional opportunities to assess the temporal stability of behaviors that reflect the trait of achievement motivation. We could look at the temporal stability of Terry's achievement motivation as a manager or as CEO of the family company. We could also look at the temporal stability of other academic pursuits, where separate estimates of time devoted to study could be obtained for middle school and college.

Cross-Situational Consistency

Let us now inquire whether Terry's achievement-oriented behaviors were consistent *across* educational levels. For example, we could investigate whether Terry's investitures of effort in studying were consistently above average for middle school, for upper school, and for college. Note that we do not ask whether Terry spent the same number of hours studying across educational levels. We expect that college requires more hours of study per credit hour than upper school, and that upper school requires more hours of study per credit hour than middle school. Our question is thus a *relative* one. In comparison to other students with the same or similar course loads, was Terry consistently above the norm (in the upper end of the distribution, in the upper part of the rank ordering) on study time over educational levels?

According to Terry's history, he consistently devoted more time to studying than did his peers across (i.e., in each of) the three educational levels. We would thus say that Terry's achievement motivation was *cross-situationally consistent* over different educational situations (i.e., levels). Technically, we should say that Terry's achievement motivation was *relatively* cross-situationally consistent over middle school, upper school, and college. However, it is generally understood that cross-situational consistency is relative to the norm within each situation, so the term *relative* is considered redundant here. Another way of saying the same thing is to ask whether Terry's place in the rank ordering of students in regard to study time was about the same across the three educational levels.

Functionally Equivalent Situations

Middle school, upper school, and college in Terry's case are what Wright and Mischel (1987) call "functionally equivalent classes of situations" (p. 1162). These authors suggest that situations are functionally equivalent if the pertinent mental, motivational, social, and physical "competencies" required of individuals to perform in the situations are the same or similar. The three levels of education did indeed make functionally equivalent, although progressively more challenging, mental and motivational demands on Terry's competencies. The fact that Terry consistently devoted an above-average number of hours to study across these three functionally equivalent situations increases our confidence that he possesses the trait of achievement motivation. Here again, as with temporal stability, Terry behaved reliably in an achievement-oriented manner. He *consistently* attempted to achieve.

Functional equivalence of situational demands assists in the determination of whether a person possesses a trait for two related reasons. First, a personal disposition to behave in a systematic way is indicated when repeated measurements taken on the same behavior across functionally equivalent situations are, relative to others in those situations, consistent. Should a person's behavior vary over functionally equivalent situations, we are less confident about making a trait attribution because the person is unreliable (inconsistent) in how he or she responds to equivalent situations. Thus his or her behavior in a new but functionally equivalent situation (e.g., graduate school) could not be predicted with any certainty. It is only when past behaviors provide reliable guides for predicting future behaviors in new but functionally equivalent situations that we infer the presence of a dispositional tendency or trait.

Second, if behavior is inconsistent over situations but the situations vary in terms of mental, motivational, social, or physical demands, then it might be argued that differences in situations engendered the differences in behaviors. One tacit supposition here is that a person may possess a trait, but his or her disposition to behave in a consistent way across situations may be overwhelmed by idiosyncratic situational demands. However, no such explanation for cross-situational disparities in behavior is possible if the situations make functionally equivalent demands. Functionally equivalent situations thus simplify the task of determining whether or not a person possesses a trait. When behavior is consistent across functionally equivalent situations, one has a reasonably clear case that a trait such as achievement motivation is present.

A critic might suggest at this point that functionally equivalent situations engender consistent behavior. The implication here is that behavior is simply under the control of situational influences. The problem with this criticism is that it cannot explain why people behave differently in the same situation. For example, unlike Terry, not all students study diligently and persistently in upper school. Moreover, these differences occur repeatedly and reliably over functionally equivalent situations. Behavior cannot be totally under the control of situational influences if people in the same situations behave differently and these differences are both temporally stable and cross-situationally consistent.

Different Situations

Suppose that we compare Terry's academic performance in upper school with his performance as a waiter in the family restaurant. The intense and persistent effort evidenced in both situations indicates (relative) cross-situational consistency of achievement motivation. Yet restaurants and schools are not functionally equivalent situations. Although both require individuals to work hard to be successful, the mental, social, and physical demands of the two situations are quite different. Thus, there must be more to cross-situational consistency than similarities in relevant competencies. Moreover, Terry's progression from service tasks to managerial tasks, and from managerial tasks to entrepreneur, developer, and CEO of a corporation, represents major changes in occupational demands and therefore situations. The mental and social competencies required to succeed as a waiter are quite different from those required to succeed as a CEO.

Needs and Values

McClelland et al. (1989), Locke (1991), and Winter et al. (1998) offer an explanation for cross-situational consistency of achievement motivation even though situations differ. The explanation is based on the distinction between needs and values. Needs indicate general affective, cognitive, and behavioral tendencies and predict spontaneous behavioral trends over time. We shall stipulate that Terry is an AM and thus has a general tendency to do well and is prepared to work intensely and persistently to be successful. The fact that Terry is an AM also indicates a general tendency to reason (conditionally) in ways that attribute achievement to such things as initiative, the efficacy of persistence, and willingness to commit and become involved, irrespective of specific task (James, 1998). But being an AM with a strong need to achieve does not indicate the specific activity or activities in which Terry will attempt to satisfy his intense need.

Values give direction to, or "channel" (Winter et al., 1998), the expression of needs. Values determine the specific activity or activities that an AM will employ to attempt to satisfy his or her desire to achieve. Values represent an individual's conscious or self-ascribed interests, desires, goals, preferred modes of conduct, preferred rewards and incentives, expectations, and plans. A person such as Terry not only consciously values achievement, but is aware of the areas in which he or she would like to achieve.

In part, this awareness may be a product of the underlying need to achieve in the sense that one is aware that one experiences positive emotions (excitement, a craving, an urge to approach) when certain types of tasks and goals are made salient. However, values are also products of socialization, learning, instruction, initiation, and internalization of cultural, parental, and peer norms and ideologies (see Mischel & Shoda, 1999). As part of this learning, an AM like Terry develops a sense of the specific situations in which he or she would like to succeed, in some cases perhaps situations in which he or she should try to succeed (e.g., a parent's goal), and whether he or she has the skills, or is capable of developing the skills, to succeed.

Thus Terry simultaneously attempted to achieve as a waiter in the family business and as a student in upper school because (a) he had a strong need to achieve and (b) he valued achievement in *both* the family restaurant and academics. Terry progressed through more difficult jobs in the restaurant business because he valued developing and expanding the family business. Terry also had urges to attempt to achieve in other activities along the way, such as in basketball in upper school. However, even though the need to achieve was activated by an athletic event, priorities already prescribed by values determined that Terry had no time left to pursue an intrinsic interest in basketball. Thus the trait of achievement-oriented behavior was not cross-situationally consistent with respect to basketball even though the need to achieve was activated. One now begins to see why cross-situational consistency based on behavior is not well understood, and why it is a source of controversy. There is also a message here about the use of behavior, or the lack thereof, to infer underlying needs. We revisit the issue of how values channel the expression of needs in Chapter 5.

Situational Discriminativeness

We can expand the above discussion to explain Terry's lack of cross-situationally consistent, achievement-oriented behavior in regard to areas such as art, holding political office, and playing video games. Terry's need to achieve was not activated by these activities as it was in the case of basketball. For example, Terry experienced no impulse to approach these activities, which indicates that he experienced no sense of excitement or urge to become accomplished in them. Moreover, Terry placed no value on these activities, which means that he had no practical reason to pursue them. Terry was engaging in what is often referred to as *situational discriminativeness* (see Mischel & Peake, 1982). That is, Terry relied on his needs, as experienced by his emotions, and his values to distinguish among (a) those situations that offer no visceral attraction or pragmatic interest (e.g., artistic tasks), (b) those situations that are attractive but for practical reasons cannot be pursued (basketball), and (c) those situations that are attractive, valued, and will be approached (e.g., academic tasks).

There is no (or at least very little) anxiety, apprehension, or fear of failing with respect to situations that are not sufficiently evocative to Terry to activate either his need to achieve or his need to avoid failing. Suppose, however, that Terry does experience apprehension about engaging in some activities, such as parasailing. Indeed, he perceives himself as lacking in prerequisite skills (e.g., knowledge of the aerodynamics of flight), and he fears the outcome of attempting to parasail and failing. Does this suggest that Terry has latent FF tendencies? No, it does not indicate fear of failure as we have been using that term in this chapter. Most people are apprehensive about parasailing, and a sizable contingent of these folks would infer that being apprehensive about parasailing is more a question of judgment than one of personality. More to the point, however, is that fear of failure occurs when an individual experiences a desire to approach an activity (e.g., publishing) but is apprehensive about being humiliated by failure and that apprehension dampens his or her enthusiasm to such a point that an approach-avoidance conflict ensues, ultimately producing avoidance. The key to fear of failure, and being an FF, is avoidance of personally demanding tasks. Even more telling is a temporally stable and cross-situationally consistent dispositional tendency to avoid such tasks.

Coherence

Based on the preceding discussion, we can construct a profile of Terry's achievement-oriented behavior across diverse situations. This pattern will indicate an enduring tendency to call forth achievement behaviors in some situations (e.g., to attempt to achieve in the classroom and the restaurant business) and to hold back attempts to achieve in other situations (e.g., basketball or art). This pattern of engagement-nonengagement is referred to as a *cross-situational profile.* It will repeat itself many times, which indicates a lawfulness and consistency to behavior (see Magnusson, 1976). The term *coherence* is used to indicate the stability or replicability of cross-situational profiles (see Grote & James, 1991).

It is coherence that is the key to describing behavior over diverse situations. But this is only part of the story, for *coherence* refers only to behavioral indicators of a trait. As we have noted, *trait* refers only to behavior—existence of a trait does not explain why the behavior occurs. To understand and explain coherence, we must investigate why an individual manifests a behavior in a stable and consistent manner in some situations but not in others. And this requires that we delve into needs, justification mechanisms, conditional reasoning, and environmental contexts, including various forms of P × S interactions. We cannot determine why behaviors are or are not cross-situationally consistent as long as we focus only on behavior. It is only when we delve into the causes of behavior that we begin to unravel the issues of cross-situational consistency and coherence.

Concluding Comments

In this chapter we have introduced many of the fundamental concepts that contribute to an understanding of personality in organizational settings. We have made a concerted effort to integrate the concepts of needs, social cognitions, and traits. We have also tried to communicate (a) the sense of patterning and coordination that exists among needs, traits, and social cognitions; and (b) the interactions among these components of personality and organizational environments. In these endeavors we have used the same personality variables, achievement motivation and fear of failure, throughout the chapter.

It is often suggested that a worthwhile approach to learning about personality is that of immersion in the details and nuances of a particular theory or approach. The intent is for the reader to develop a sense of the depth, patterning, coordination, interactions, and, yes, complexity of personality by focusing first on the mental, behavioral, and environmental networks surrounding a particular personality variable or two. This knowledge then serves as a foundation for extending learning to include other personality variables. As the reader's knowledge expands, he or she will come to understand that the initial variables to which he or she has been exposed, such as achievement motivation and fear of failure, serve as exemplars. The addition of new personality variables requires the reader to make adjustments and changes to such things as trait behaviors, needs, justification mechanisms, and the variables that are salient for person-environment interactions and studies of coherence.

However, the important point is that the reader will know what to look for in seeking understanding of a new personality variable. How is the trait defined behaviorally? What needs and social cognitions cause the trait behaviors to occur? What environmental conditions moderate the manifestation of the trait behaviors, and why? What is the expected pattern of coherence for one who possesses the requisite needs and social cognitions? These are fundamental questions that are triggered by the concepts and processes described in this chapter, and they apply irrespective of the specific personality variable of concern.

3 Personality Variables

We defined personality in Chapter 1 as the cognitive structures and coordinated cognitive processes that determine a person's behavioral adjustments to his or her environment (see Allport, 1937; Millon, 1990). We devoted Chapter 2 to a description of how needs, social cognitions—that is, cognitive structures and cognitive processes—and characteristic behavioral adjustments (or traits) are functionally related. Our objective in this chapter is to identify the key variables in each of the primary components of personality. We begin by introducing a broad taxonomy of characteristic behavioral adjustments. Key traits are clustered or organized around five broad dimensions of behavior. We then turn our attention to identifying broad categories of the key social cognitions that govern individual differences in behavioral adjustments.

Prominent Traits in Contemporary Personality

Buss and Finn noted in 1987 that "several generations of research on personality have yielded numerous traits in a confusing array that begs for organization" (p. 432). Recently, researchers have made Herculean efforts to remedy this problem by identifying pivotal traits. They then employ these pivotal traits as general categories onto which are mapped a large number of specific traits. In this section we describe the efforts researchers have undertaken to develop this categorical structure, or hierarchical organization, of traits. We begin with a brief account of the origin of the meaning of the concept of "trait" and early attempts to classify traits. We proceed historically to the early empirical attempts to categorize traits. These endeavors, like current attempts to organize traits, were generally founded on a statistical process known as factor analysis. We offer a brief, nontechnical overview of how to go about interpreting a factor analysis, our objective being to assist readers in interpreting illustrative tables rather than to diverge into statistical dialogue. Following an overview of the highlights of early attempts to classify traits, the discussion turns to a recently developed, controversial, but nonetheless well-received organizational system for personality traits. This system is known as the *five-factor model.*

The Etiology of "Trait"

Allport and the Idiographic Versus Nomothetic Approach to Traits

Gordon Allport (1937) is considered to be the guiding light and chief advocate of contemporary thinking about traits. Allport promoted an *idiographic* approach to the study of personality. In this approach, every individual is regarded as an integrated system that is worthy of independent scientific analysis. More specifically, one individual is to be examined in great depth, without concern for the establishment of general laws of behavior that apply beyond that particular individual.

An idiographic approach to analysis may be contrasted with a *nomothetic* approach, in which the same attribute or set of attributes is studied in multiple individuals, the intent being to use comparative differences (e.g., rank ordering of achievement motivation) among individuals to discern general laws or principles of human behavior (e.g., more motivated students get higher grades than do less motivated students). Like many psychologists, Allport wanted to adopt an idiographic approach when describing specific individuals, yet realized that a new science of traits could not be constructed for every individual. Furthermore, he understood that scientific progress for trait psychology was rooted in a nomothetic approach. Thus he employed nomothetically derived traits to describe people, but cautioned that nomothetic analyses (i.e., comparisons with other individuals) provide only approximations of what specific individuals are like.

Allport (1937, 1961) employed traits as the primary basis on which to describe people. He defined a trait as a "neuropsychic structure having the capacity to render many stimuli functionally equivalent, and to initiate and guide equivalent (meaningfully consistent) forms of adaptive and expressive behavior" (1961, p. 347). Allport assumed that traits are real, which is to say that they actually exist as part of the person. A contrasting view is that traits are convenient hypothetical constructs that exist primarily in the minds of psychologists as means to explain behavior. Allport recommended that some traits be considered "stylistic," meaning that they are behavioral tendencies without specification of motivational or causal content. An example would be a person's tendency to turn right when exiting a building. Allport believed that other traits, such as ambition, have motivational content, which is to say that they initiate and guide behavior (see Pervin, 1990).

As we have noted, Allport's philosophical underpinning was that each person's traits are distinctive and need to be assessed uniquely. As part of this idiographic process, he believed that a person's traits are classifiable according to the extent to which they pervade the individual's personality. He referred to the most pervasive traits as "cardinal dispositions." Although such traits occur rarely, a cardinal disposition dominates the behavior of the individual if indeed it is present. An example would be the trait of aggressiveness for persons classified as "aggressive personalities."

More typical of most individuals is behavior attributable to what Allport called "central dispositions," which comprise a relatively small number of traits (between 3 and 10) that, as a set, are pervasive for a given person. Allport noted that the characteristics a person would use when writing a letter of recommendation for someone would be illustrative of central dispositions. "Secondary dispositions" are more situationally specific traits (e.g., food preferences). Allport argued that each person's pattern of cardinal (if present), central, and secondary traits is unique, and that one can understand a person only by examining this unique pattern. This, then, is the idiographic approach, which is characterized by the use of a unique set of traits to describe each individual.

Allport's idiographic stance made the comparison of individuals with different cardinal, central, and secondary traits very difficult. For example, it would not be possible to compare individuals on a trait such as achievement motivation if this trait is cardinal or central for only a subset of individuals. Allport did, however, concede that certain "common traits" guide or are descriptive of the behavior of individuals in general. Examples of common traits include achievement motivation, submissiveness, sociability, and self-discipline. People vary in terms of how much of a common trait they possess, and these comparative differences are both quantifiable and measurable. Individuals may thus be compared on a trait such as self-discipline, and general statements can be made, such as the extent to which variation on this trait covaries with variation on other attributes, such as punctuality. A "personality trait" is thus construed to be a predisposition to respond in a particular way to situations, persons, and objects.

Allport, in conjunction with Odbert, attempted to apprehend the potential domain of common traits by identifying 17,953 words in the English language that refer to characteristics of personality (Allport & Odbert, 1936). To reduce this large number of characteristics to a smaller number, Allport and Odbert determined the frequency with which each characteristic was used in everyday language. This "lexical" aspect of their research was predicated on the assumption that the more important a disposition is, the more often it will be referred to in everyday language. Allport was also one of the first investigators to measure common traits. His study assessing the common trait of dominance-submissiveness using subjects' self-descriptions of how they expected to act in a variety of situations (Allport & Allport, 1928) is considered a classic.

Murray and the Concepts of Need and Press

Allport's colleague at Harvard, Henry Murray, was also influential in the development of the trait concept. Allport and Murray agreed on some aspects of trait theory and disagreed on others (for a review, see Pervin, 1990). We will focus here on a point of disagreement between them. As we have noted above, Allport attributed motivational (causal) status to some traits. Murray, however, distinguished between *needs* and *traits,* much as we have in Chapter 2. In Murray's (1938) view, traits have no motivational content. Traits are consistencies or regularities in behavior that suggest predispositions to behave in particular ways in given situations and toward given persons and objects. Needs, on the other hand, are a source of motivational content. Needs serve to activate, direct, and sustain the behaviors that operationally define traits. We adopted Murray's approach in our discussion in Chapter 2.

Murray was a member of a large, heterogeneous contingent of psychologists who became intensely interested in studying the forces that motivate people. These studies took diverse and often conflicting directions. Murray was concerned with the motivational forces of personality and asked questions such as the following: Is there a specific set of common human motives that are readily measurable? Do general motives influence behavior? Does variation in individual motivation cause people to think, feel, and act differently?

Thinking and research on questions such as these set the foundation for "needs theorists," who are distinguished by their belief that needs provide the motives that influence thought and action. Although not the first to suggest that underlying needs are fundamental to personality, Murray is acknowledged as the father of modern needs theory. This should not be construed to mean that Murray focused strictly on the internal functioning of individuals as the exclusive, or even the principal, causal source of trait behavior. In fact, Murray was one of the first psychologists to emphasize that one must consider the individual and the environment together when analyzing personality. As recounted by Pervin (1990), Murray believed that because "at every moment an organism is within an environment, the organism and its milieu *must be considered together*" (p. 9; emphasis added).

Murray's belief that persons and contexts should be studied jointly was based on the idea that individuals are driven to lessen tensions generated by forces that are both internal (*needs*) and external (*press*) to them. Murray defined a need as an internal force that transmits into an action in a given direction in an existing situation. Needs direct behavioral choices, influence the intensity of chosen behaviors, and sustain continued behavior over time and situations. *Press* refers to various environmental stimuli that activate needs, such as perceived opportunities for need expression. Environmental factors that may restrict or constrain need expression are also included in press. It is when a given need repeatedly interacts with a specific press over an extended period of time that one arrives at what Murray called a "thema." Themas are reflected in observed regularities or consistencies in behavior and are analogous to our definition of trait in Chapter 2 as a disposition or tendency to behave in a relatively consistent manner over time and across diverse situations.

Murray believed that basic physiological and psychological needs are located within all organisms. A list of the psychological needs that Murray considered most important to personality is presented in Table 3.1. Included among these needs are achievement, autonomy, and understanding. Murray postulated that some aspects of needs are "manifest" (conscious or observable by the individual), whereas others are "latent" (unconscious, not observable by the individual). An example of a manifest component of a need would be a conscious desire to have friendships with others. An example of a latent aspect of a need would be an unexplainable impulse to meet a particular person whom one has just encountered. Murray believed that the strength of a need has to be assessed in both manifest and latent forms. To measure manifest needs, he recommended the following four criteria: (a) frequency of action or count, (b) duration of action or time, (c) intensity of action based on a grading of strength of responses to an action, and (d) readiness to act, as indicated by speed of response.

Measuring latent (aspects of) needs is much more complicated. An early methodology for measuring latent needs involved probing a person's fantasies. This was the foundation for a projective technique, known as the Thematic Apperception Test (TAT), that Murray developed. The first version of the instrument was published in 1935; the current version is the second revision (Murray, 1943). We provide detailed discussion of the TAT in Chapter 4. The relevance of the instrument stems from Murray's supposition that people may or may not be willing to disclose underlying tendencies, or may not be able to express their impulses because the bases for the impulses are unconscious. The TAT gained popularity among diagnosticians due to its capability to assist them in determining individuals' unconscious needs, as well as emotions, conflicts, and perceived external pressures (i.e., press). As we shall see in Chapter 4, however, modern measurement theorists have shown less than unabated enthusiasm for projective techniques like the TAT.

Murray emphasized the point that two people could have the same need, such as a need for achievement, and yet, due to differences in other

Table 3.1 List and Descriptions of Murray's Needs

Need	Description
Abasement	To submit passively to external force. To accept injury, blame, criticism, punishment. To surrender. To become resigned to fate. To admit inferiority, error, wrongdoing, or defeat. To confess and atone. To blame, belittle, or mutilate the self. To seek and enjoy pain, punishment, illness, and misfortune.
Achievement	To accomplish something difficult. To master, manipulate, or organize physical objects, human beings, or ideas. To do this as rapidly and as independently as possible. To overcome obstacles and attain a high standard. To excel oneself. To rival and surpass others. To increase self-regard by the successful exercise of talent.
Affiliation	To form friendships and associations. To greet, join, and live with others. To cooperate and converse sociably with others. To love. To join groups.
Aggression	To overcome opposition forcefully. To fight. To revenge an injury. To attack, injure, or kill another. To oppose forcefully or punish another.
Autonomy	To get free, shake off restraint, break out of confinement. To resist coercion and restriction. To avoid or quit activities prescribed by domineering authorities. To be independent and free to act according to impulse. To be unattached, unconditioned, irresponsible. To defy convention.
Blamavoidance	To avoid blame, ostracism, or punishment by inhibiting asocial or unconventional impulses. To be well behaved and obey the law.
Counteraction	Proudly to refuse the admission of defeat by restriving and retaliating. To select the hardest tasks. To defend one's honor in action.
Defendence	To defend oneself against blame or belittlement. To justify one's actions. To offer extenuations, explanations, and excuses. To resist "probing."
Deference	To admire and support a superior other. To praise, honor, or eulogize. To yield eagerly to the influence of an allied other. To emulate an exemplar. To conform to custom.
Dominance	To influence or control others. To persuade, prohibit, dictate. To lead and direct. To restrain. To organize the behavior of the group.
Exhibition	To make an impression. To be seen and heard. To excite, amaze, fascinate, entertain, shock, intrigue, amuse, or entice others.
Harmavoidance	To avoid pain, physical injury, illness, and death. To escape from a dangerous situation. To take precautionary measures.
Infavoidance	To avoid humiliation. To quit embarrassing situations or avoid conditions that may lead to belittlement; the scorn, derision, or indifference of others. To refrain from action because of the fear of failure.
Nurturance	To nourish, aid, or protect a helpless other. To express sympathy. To "mother" a child.

(continued)

Table 3.1   List and Descriptions of Murray's Needs

Need	Description
Order	To put things in order. To achieve cleanliness, arrangement, organization, balance, neatness, tidiness, and precision.
Play	To relax, amuse oneself, seek diversion and entertainment. To "have fun," to play games. To laugh, joke, and be merry. To avoid serious tension.
Rejection	To snub, ignore, or exclude another. To remain aloof and indifferent. To be discriminating.
Sentience	To seek and enjoy sensuous impressions.
Sex	To form and further an erotic relationship. To have sexual intercourse.
Succorance	To seek aid, protection, or sympathy. To cry for help. To plead for mercy. To adhere to an affectionate, nurturant parent. To be dependent.
Understanding	To analyze experience, to abstract, to discriminate among concepts, to define relations, to synthesize ideas.

NOTE: This list of needs was compiled by the authors from Murray (1938, 1966).

needs, aptitudes, skills, or environmental presses, manifest this need through different behaviors (traits). Analogously, two people could emit the same behavior for different reasons. This signifies the potential danger of inferring needs from behavior. Although aware of these caveats, psychologists nonetheless sought to establish a homology between the needs listed in Table 3.1 and the behaviors engendered by these needs. Over time, the distinction between needs (e.g., a need for achievement) and the behaviors presumably produced by these needs (e.g., academic achievement) became hazy. In fact, the names given to needs were usurped and used to designate trait behaviors. This remains a popular exercise today, as we shall see below.

The Organization of Traits

Cattell and the Use of Factor Analysis to Cluster Traits

Cattell (1950, 1965) pioneered the idea that the large numbers of traits proposed by Allport and others could be categorized into a small number of clusters or dimensions. Cattell used a statistical technique known as factor analysis to determine (a) the number of categories required to cluster all or most traits, and then (b) which traits went into which categories. The categories of traits are referred to as *factors*. The degree to which a trait is represented by a given factor is determined by a *factor loading*. Each trait has a factor loading on each factor. The factor loadings vary from +1.0 to –1.0. Moderate to high *absolute* loadings of .40 or greater—that is, +.40 to +1.00 and –.40 to –1.00—indicate that the trait belongs on a factor. The meanings of positive and negative with respect to a loading depend on the designation given to the factor. For example, if the factor is designated Motivation, then a loading of +.85 for the trait of "persistence" indicates that this trait is on the positive end or "pole" of the factor. A loading of –.80 by the trait of "lethargy" on this same factor indicates that inactivity and sluggishness are on the negative pole of Motivation.

Factors may also be thought of as having scales. The pattern of positive and negative loadings then suggests characteristic/noncharacteristic behaviors. To illustrate, people with a high score on the Motivation factor would be characterized by traits in the positive pole (e.g., persistence). Traits in the negative pole (e.g., lethargy) represent noncharacteristic behaviors for people with high scores on the factor. Analogously, people with low scores on the Motivation factor would be characterized as having the traits in the negative pole but not in the positive pole. Thus unmotivated people would be characterized as lethargic and lacking in persistence.

Factor loadings between +.39 and –.39 (some people use +.29 and –.29), especially those hovering around .00, suggest that a trait should not be clustered—or does not "load"—on the factor in question.

The clustering of traits through factor analysis is predicated on observations that some traits are correlated. That is, the behaviors defining the traits tend to appear in recurring patterns. For example, if a person is persevering, then he or she is also likely to be stable, responsible, and attentive as opposed to frivolous or neglectful.

An illustration of the results of a factor analysis is presented in Table 3.2. On the left-hand side of the table are listed 14 traits that describe various behaviors. These traits are clustered into two factors. Factor I is labeled Conscientiousness because the seven traits that load highly on it share a common theme of either the presence or absence of a sense of duty, dedication, and faithfulness. The positive pole of this factor includes high positive factor loadings on the traits of industriousness, order, self-discipline, and reliability. This pattern denotes that a high score on Conscientiousness is obtained by people who are industrious, orderly, self-disciplined, and reliable. In contrast, people are said to lack

Table 3.2 Illustrative Factor Loadings of 14 Traits on Two Factors

| Trait | Factor | |
	I. Conscientiousness	II. Agreeableness
Industriousness	.85	.01
Order	.80	.04
Self-discipline	.75	−.06
Reliability	.70	−.01
Negligence	−.80	.11
Rebelliousness	−.70	.03
Intemperance	−.55	.09
Trust	.00	.87
Amiability	.08	.79
Generosity	−.04	.72
Tolerance	.10	.65
Vindictiveness	−.06	−.80
Criticism	.04	−.71
Antagonism	.13	−.58

SOURCE: Based loosely on results reported by Goldberg (1990).

Conscientiousness if they are negligent, rebellious, and intemperate. Lack of Conscientiousness is indicated by the moderate to high negative factor loadings on the traits of negligence, rebelliousness, and intemperance. These traits define the negative pole of Factor I.

Factor II is designated Agreeableness. Seven traits, different from the traits that loaded on Conscientiousness, have high absolute loadings on this factor. Four of these traits (trust, amiability, generosity, and tolerance) are included in the positive pole of Factor II (i.e., these traits have high positive loadings), whereas the other three traits (vindictiveness, criticism, and antagonism) are included in the negative pole of this factor. The pattern of loadings suggests that agreeable people tend to be trusting, amiable, generous, and tolerant. They are not characterized as being vindictive, critical, or antagonistic. Conversely, disagreeable people tend to be characterized by vindictiveness, criticism, and antagonism. They would generally not be described as trusting, amiable, generous, or tolerant.

The seven traits that load on Conscientiousness are basically unrelated to Factor II. Analogously, the seven variables that load on Agreeableness are unrelated to Factor I. These results suggest that the factors of Conscientiousness and Agreeableness are essentially unrelated. This means that all of the following combinations are possible: (a) people who are conscientious and agreeable, (b) people who are neither con-scientious nor agreeable, (c) people who are conscientious but not agreeable, and (d) people who are agreeable but not conscientious. Lack of relationship between factors is a common finding produced by factor analysis. The basic logic is that if two factors are uncorrelated, then knowledge of a person's position on one such factor should not be used to predict his or her standing on the other factor.

As suggested above, the objective of factor analysis is to reduce a large number of traits to a manageable set of underlying dimensions of per-sonality. In pursuit of this objective, Cattell (1947) submitted Allport's list of almost 18,000 traits to a series of analyses that culminated with a series of factor analyses. He obtained self-descriptions from several samples of persons on the 17,953 personality-descriptive adjectives col-lected by Allport and Odbert (1936). He then used rational and statisti-cal analyses to reduce these terms to 4,504 "real" traits, and then to 171 trait names. Cattell then asked college students to rate their friends on these 171 terms; it is these ratings that he factor analyzed. The factor analyses produced 16 factors that Cattell (1957) referred to as the "source traits," or primary factors, for personality. These 16 traits are described in Table 3.3. They form the basis for an inventory to measure personality known as the 16PF.

Cattell's early use of factor analysis to identify the principal underly-ing factors of personality traits served as a prototype for research that followed. The ensuing research often deviated from Cattell's approach in that self-reports (rather than peer reports) were frequently used to collect data on key adjectives or items that provided more specific por-traits of behavior. Moreover, different subsets of trait variables were sub-jected to factor analyses, samples other than students were employed, and different mathematical approaches to factor analysis were used. A long-term product was that the seminal set of factors thought to be nec-essary to capture the essence of personality was judged to be less than 16, as we shall soon see. Nonetheless, the 16PF is still in use, and Cattell is widely recognized as a major figure in contemporary personality the-ory. (The 16PF can also now be scored in terms of 5 general factors.)

Other Factor-Analysis-Based Personality Inventories

The Eysenck Personality Inventory (Eysenck, 1952, 1965, 1981) is a somewhat more Spartan measure of personality than the 16PF.

Table 3.3. Historical Comparison of 16PF Factor Names and Descriptors

Descriptors of Low Range	Primary Factors	Descriptors of High Range
Reserved, Impersonal, Distant Cool, reserved, impersonal, detached, formal, aloof. *Sizothymia*	Warmth (A)	**Warm, Outgoing, Attentive to Others** Warm, outgoing, kindly, easygoing, participating, likes people. *Affectothymia*
Concrete Concrete-thinking, lower general mental capacity, less intelligent, unable to handle abstract problems. *Lower Scholastic Mental Capacity*	Reasoning (B)	**Abstract** Abstract-thinking, more intelligent, bright, higher general mental capacity, fast-learner. *Higher Scholastic Mental Capacity*
Reactive, Emotionally Changeable Affected by feelings, emotionally less stable, easily upset, changeable. *Lower Ego Strength*	Emotionally Stability (C)	**Emotionally Stable, Adaptive, Mature** Emotionally stable, mature, faces reality, calm. *Higher Ego Strength*
Deferential, Cooperative, Avoids Conflict Submissive, humble, obedient, easily led, docile, accommodating. *Submissiveness*	Dominance (E)	**Dominant, Forceful, Assertive** Dominant, assertive, aggressive, competitive, stubborn, bossy. *Dominance*
Serious, Restrained, Careful Sober, serious, restrained, prudent, taciturn, introspective, silent. *Desurgency*	Liveliness (F)	**Lively, Animated, Spontaneous** Enthusiastic, spontaneous, happy-go-lucky, cheerful, expressive, impulsive, talkative. *Surgency*
Expedient, Nonconforming Expedient, disregards rules, self-indulgent. *Low Superego Strength*	Rule-Consciousness (G)	**Rule-Conscious, Dutiful** Conscientious, conforming, moralistic, staid, rule-bound. *High Superego Strength*
Shy, Threat-Sensitive, Timid Shy, threat-sensitive, timid, hesitant, intimidated. *Threctia*	Social Boldness (H)	**Socially Bold, Venturesome, Thick-Skinned** Bold, venturesome, uninhibited, can take stress, thick-skinned. *Parmia*
Utilitarian, Objective, Unsentimental Tough-minded, self-reliant, no-nonsense, rough, realistic, unsentimental. *Harria*	Sensitivity (I)	**Sensitive, Aesthetic, Sentimental** Tender-minded, sensitive, intuitive, refined, dependent. *Premsia*
Trusting, Unsuspecting, Accepting Trusting, accepting conditions, easy to get on with *Alaxia*	Vigilance (L)	**Vigilant, Suspicious, Skeptical, Wary** Suspicious, hard-to-fool, skeptical, distrustful, oppositional. *Protension*
Grounded, Practical, Solution-Oriented Practical, concerned with down-to-earth issues, steady, prosaic, conventional. *Praxernia*	Abstractedness (M)	**Abstracted, Imaginative, Idea-Oriented** Imaginative, absent-minded, absorbed in ideas, impractical. *Autia*

Descriptors of Low Range	Primary Factors	Descriptors of High Range
Forthright, Genuine, Artless Forthright, genuine, artless, open, unpretentious, naive, warmly emotionally involved. *Artlessness*	Privateness (N)	**Private, Discreet, Non-Disclosing** Shrewd, polished, socially aware, worldly, astute, diplomatic, calculating, emotionally detached, wears a social mask. *Shrewdness*
Self-Assured, Unworried, Complacent Self-assured, untroubled, secure, feels free of guilt, self-satisfied, confident. *Untroubled*	Apprehension (O)	**Apprehensive, Self-Doubting, Worried** Apprehensive, self-blaming, guilt-prone, insecure, worrying. *Guilt Proneness*
Traditional, Attached To Familiar Conservative, respecting traditional ideas. *Conservatism*	Openness to Change (Q1)	**Open To Change, Experimenting** Experimenting, liberal, analytical, critical, free-thinking, open-to-change. *Radicalism*
Group-Oriented, Affiliative Group-oriented, a joiner & sound follower, group dependent. *Group Adherence*	Self-Reliance (Q2)	**Self-Reliant, Solitary, Individualistic** Self-sufficient, resourceful, prefers own decisions. *Self-Sufficiency*
Tolerates Disorder, Unexacting, Flexible Undisciplined, self-conflict, lax, follows own urges, uncontrolled, careless of social rules, low self sentiment integration. *Low Integration*	Perfectionism (Q3)	**Perfectionism, Organized, Self-Disciplined** Following self-image, socially precise, self-disciplined, compulsive, exacting will power, control, high strength of self sentiment. *High Self-Concept Control*
Relaxed, Placid, Patient Relaxed, tranquil, composed, has low drive, unfrustrated, torpid. *Low Ergic Tension*	Tension (Q4)	**Tense, High Energy, Impatient, Driven** Tense, driven, frustrated, over-wrought, has high drive. *High Ergic Tension*

NOTE: Fifth Edition factor names and descriptors are in bold type; earlier edition descriptors are in unbolded type; and R.B. Cattell's original names are in italics. Copyright © 1994 by the Institute for Personality and Ability Testing, Inc. Reproduced with permission. "16PF" is a trademark belonging to IPAT.

Eysenck's theory is parsimonious in that it comprises but three traits: Neuroticism (N), which includes moodiness, nervousness, and irritability; Extraversion (E), which involves sociability, outgoingness, and liveliness; and Psychoticism (P), characterized by insensitivity to others, uncaring, and solitariness. In addition to these three traits, Eysenck's inventory measures lying (L). The dimensions of Neuroticism and Extraversion resulted from Eysenck's early factor-analytic research.

Guilford (1940; Guilford & Martin, 1943) began research and development on personality in the late 1930s and early 1940s. He adopted the strategy of correlating assessments based on a new personality inventory with assessments based on earlier inventories designed to measure the same psychological traits. He was thus able to ascertain the extent to which new instruments measured similar as well as unique aspects of personality in comparison with the older instruments. Moreover, Guilford determined the interrelationships among a wide variety of personality traits from different personality inventories. He then factor analyzed these data to determine the underlying dimensions (i.e., factors) of personality that were common to the multiple inventories.

Guilford's research resulted in several published personality inventories. Three of these were later collapsed into a single composite inventory that came to be known as the Guilford-Zimmerman Temperament Survey (GZTS; Guilford & Zimmerman, 1956). The 10 traits measured by this instrument are general activity, restraint, ascendance, sociability, emotional stability, objectivity, friendliness, thoughtfulness, personal relations, and masculinity.

The pioneering works of Cattell, Eysenck, and Guilford served as exemplars for later development of a number of currently popular personality inventories. Included here are the California Personality Inventory (Gough, 1987), the Hogan Personality Inventory (Hogan, 1986), the NEO Personality Inventory (Costa & McCrae, 1985), the Multidimensional Personality Questionnaire (Tellegen, 1982), and the Personality Research Form (Jackson, 1967). The development of each of these inventories involved factor analysis. This is not to suggest, however, that a consensus exists as to what is to be measured by personality inventories. John (1990) characterizes the extant knowledge of personality traits as follows:

> The number of personality concepts, and of scales designed to measure them, has escalated without an end in sight (Goldberg, 1971). Researchers, as well as practitioners in the field of personality assessment, are faced with a bewildering array of personality scales from which to choose, with little guidance and no overall rationale at hand. Even worse, scales with the same name often measure concepts that are not the same, and scales with quite different names overlap considerably in their item content. Although diversity and scientific pluralism can be useful, the systematic accumulation of findings and the communication among researchers continues to be difficult in the present-day Babel of concepts and scales. (p. 66)

John (1990) and Digman (1990) argue strongly for an integration of the vast array of traits measured by the different personality inventories. What is needed, they concur, is a unified theory of personality. A crucial step in the development of a unified theory is the building of a "taxonomy" of personality traits in which a parsimonious set of primary or overarching domains of personality are first identified and then used to categorize the large number of specific traits. More specifically, a taxonomy (a) proposes a general set of themes that are common to all or most personality inventories, and then (b) uses each theme as a common denominator for clustering together a large number of related traits. Although perhaps not a theory in the sense that it stipulates functional relationships among the various traits, a taxonomy at least proposes a means for organizing traits into a general framework. A common framework promotes use of the same language by different people when working in the domain of personality (John, 1990). This is a major advance, in our opinion.

A Taxonomy of Personality Based on the Five-Factor Model

A taxonomy of personality has evolved over the past 30 years or so, although this organizing framework has reached prominence only in the past decade. The impetus for the development of this taxonomy was furnished by concerns that Cattell's 16 factors are too complex (Banks, 1948) and/or not empirically replicable by independent factor analyses (Fiske, 1949; Tupes, 1957; Tupes & Christal, 1961). Investigators found that only *five* factors were needed to summarize a large number of traits. Tupes and Christal (1961), basing their work on reanalyses of both Cattell's and Fiske's earlier work, suggested the five personality factors of Surgency, Agreeableness, Dependability, Emotional Stability, and Culture.

Most personality researchers were unaware of the technical report published by Tupes and Christal proposing the five factors of personality. An exception was Norman (1963), who proceeded to replicate the five-factor model. This replication turned out to be the first in a string of corroborating studies (see Borgatta, 1964; Costa & McCrae, 1985; Smith, 1967). In general, over a number of studies, considerable agreement was found that five factors were sufficient to construct a taxonomy of personality. There has been less than perfect agreement, however, concerning how these five factors should be named. Digman (1990) used prior work by Goldberg (1981), Hogan (1983), Brand (1984), Digman (1988), and John (1989) to propose how the factors found by different investigators might be synthesized to provide a common, overarching set of names for the five factors. Digman's summary of how factors from different studies might be integrated into a common framework is reproduced in Table 3.4. The five factors of personality that Digman proposed, or what has come to be known as the five-factor model (FFM), are presented below.

- Factor I. Extraversion versus Introversion

  Traits loading on positive pole (+I):   talkative, assertive, active, energetic, outgoing, sociable, enthusiastic, spirited, gregarious, playful, expressive, spontaneous, unrestrained, animated, outspoken, dominant, forceful, adventurous, noisy

  Traits loading on negative pole (–I):   quiet, modest, withdrawn, reserved, shy, retiring, lethargic, silent, aloof, inhibited, unaggressive, passive, pessimistic

- Factor II. Agreeableness

  Positive pole (+II):   trusting, sympathetic, kind, amiable, generous, affectionate, tolerant, cooperative, empathic, lenient, courteous, flexible, modest, moral, warm, natural, appreciative, softhearted, helpful, forgiving, pleasant, good-natured, friendly, gentle, unselfish, sensitive

  Negative pole (–II):   critical, vindictive, unfriendly, aggressive, hard-hearted, cold, antagonistic, faultfinding, quarrelsome, unkind, cruel, stern, thankless, stingy, belligerent, bossy, rude, pompous, irritable, conceited, stubborn, distrustful, selfish, callous

- Factor III. Conscientiousness

  Positive pole (+III):   industrious, organized, achievement oriented, self-disciplined, reliable, efficient, dependable, precise, persistent, cautious, punctual, decisive, dignified, predictable, thrifty, conventional, planful, responsible, practical, deliberate

  Negative pole (–III):   slipshod, careless, nonambitious, negligent, inconsistent, inefficient, disorderly, frivolous, irresponsible, unreliable, undependable, forgetful, disorganized, reckless, aimless, slothful, indecisive

- Factor IV. Emotional Stability versus Neuroticism

  Positive pole (+IV):   stable, calm, durable, self-reliant, poised, placid, contented, steady, self-confident, assured

  Negative pole (–IV):   tense, anxious, nervous, insecure, temperamental, fearful, unstable, emotional, envious, gullible, moody, touchy, high-strung, self-pitying, self-punishing, despondent

Table 3.4 The Five Robust Dimensions of Personality from Fiske (1949) to the Present

Author	I	II	III	IV	V
Fiske (1949)	Social adaptability	Conformity	Will to achieve	Emotional control	Inquiring intellect
Eysenck (1970)	Extraversion	Psychoticism	Psychoticism	Neuroticism	
Tupes & Christal (1961)	Surgency	Agreeableness	Dependability	Emotionality	Culture
Norman (1963)	Surgency	Agreeableness	Conscientiousness	Emotionality	Culture
Borgatta (1964)	Assertiveness	Likability	Task interest	Emotionality	Intelligence
Cattell (1957)	Exvia	Cortertia	Superego strength	Anxiety	Intelligence
Guilford (1940)	Social activity	Paranoid disposition	Thinking introversion	Emotional stability	
Digman (1988)	Extraversion	Friendly compliance	Will to achieve	Neuroticism	Intellect
Hogan (1986)	Sociability and ambition	Likability	Prudence	Adjustment	Intellectance
Costa & McCrae (1985)	Extraversion	Agreeableness	Conscientiousness	Neuroticism	Openness
Peabody & Goldberg (1989)	Power	Love	Work	Affect	Intellect
Buss & Plomin (1984)	Activity	Sociability	Impulsivity	Emotionality	
Tellegen (1985)	Positive emotionality		Constraint	Negative emotionality	
Lor (1986)	Interpersonal involvement	Level of socialization	Self-control	Emotional stability	Independence

SOURCE: Digman (1990). Reproduced with permission from the *Annual Review of Psychology*, Volume 41, copyright © 1990 by Annual Reviews, www.annualreviews.org

Table 3.5　Designations for the Big Five

Factor	Digman (1990)	Costa and McCrae (1985)	Goldberg (1990)
I	Extraversion vs. Introversion	Extraversion	Surgency
II	Agreeableness	Agreeableness	Agreeableness
III	Conscientiousness	Conscientiousness	Conscientiousness
IV	Emotionalism vs. Neuroticism	Neuroticism	Neuroticism
V	Intellect	Openness	Intellect

- Factor V. Intellect

  Positive pole (+V):　wide interests, imaginative, wise, objective, knowledgeable, insightful, original, curious, sophisticated, artistic, clever, inventive, sharp-witted, ingenious, witty, resourceful, creative

  Negative pole (−V):　narrow interests, unimaginative, unintelligent, simple, shallow, imperceptive, commonplace

Digman's names and the designations given to these same five factors by prominent investigators of the FFM (Costa & McCrae, 1985; Goldberg, 1990) are displayed in Table 3.5. What differences there are in names appear insignificant. It might be noted, however, that the order of the factors (e.g., which factor is designated Factor III) may vary from investigator to investigator. Thus, for the present, one must be circumspect about referencing factors in terms of numbers. It is preferable to use designations (e.g., it is better to report that someone is high on Agreeableness than that he or she is high on Factor II).

The FFM constitutes a taxonomy of personality traits. For easy reference, we summarize this taxonomy in Table 3.6, which shows the designation given to each factor and a sampling of the traits that clearly cluster into it. The traits sampled for each factor, both in this table and in the presentation above of the FFM, are based on research reported by Goldberg (1990) and John (1990).

It is generally accepted that the FFM identifies fundamental domains of personality. The principal traits for each factor have long histories of research in personality. The FFM is not without its critics, however. For example, some have argued that (a) the FFM should be based on six factors or perhaps as many as nine factors (e.g., achievement motivation could serve as a separate factor), (b) one of the traits subsumed under an FFM factor is actually the primary concern (e.g., achievement orien-

Table 3.6 A Taxonomy of Personality Traits Based on the FFM

Factor I: Extraversion vs. Introversion	
Positive Pole (+I)	*Negative Pole (−I)*
Talkative	Quiet
Assertive	Modest
Active	Withdrawn
Energetic	Reserved
Outgoing	Shy
Sociable	Retiring
Enthusiastic	Lethargic

Factor II: Agreeableness	
Positive Pole (+II)	*Negative Pole (−II)*
Trusting	Critical
Sympathetic	Vindictive
Kind	Unfriendly
Amiable	Aggressive
Generous	Hard-hearted
Affectionate	Cold

Factor III: Conscientiousness	
Positive Pole (+III)	*Negative Pole (−III)*
Industrious	Slipshod
Organized	Careless
Achievement oriented	Nonambitious
Self-disciplined	Negligent
Reliable	Inconsistent
Efficient	Inefficient

Factor IV: Emotional Stability vs. Neuroticism	
Positive Pole (+IV)	*Negative Pole (−IV)*
Stable	Tense
Calm	Anxious
Durable	Nervous
Self-reliant	Insecure
Poised	Temperamental

Factor V: Intellect	
Positive Pole (+V)	*Negative Pole (−V)*
Wide interests	Narrow interests
Imaginative	Unimaginative
Wise	Unintelligent
Objective	Simple
Knowledgeable	Shallow
Insightful	Imperceptive

tation rather than conscientiousness is the chief concern in Factor III), (c) some traits have been missed altogether (e.g., independence), (d) different traits have been forced into the same factor (e.g., assertiveness and sociableness in Factor I), and (e) the FFM is more reflective of laypersons' implicit theories of what personality is than of a sophisticated psychological analysis of the determinants of behavior (see Block, 1995; Goldberg & Saucier, 1995; Hogan, 1983; Hogan & Hogan, 1995; McAdams, 1992; McCrae & Costa, 1994; Pervin, 1994; Schneider & Hough, 1995; Tellegen, 1993). Each of these arguments has some validity, and we should note that the composition and structure of the FFM are being studied intensely at the present time. It is reasonable to expect at least some modifications in the future.

In fairness, we should also note that for the first time, a common framework and language exist for the study of personality. Recent trends have found many personality researchers using the FFM as common ground for discussing and investigating personality. This appears to be a reasonable exercise, given that the FFM continues to demonstrate resilience or robustness with respect to time, people, and variables. For example, research has shown that the factors constituting the FFM generalize across subjects (Digman & Takemoto-Chock, 1981; Norman, 1963; Peabody & Goldberg, 1989), across observers (Fiske, 1949; Tupes & Christal, 1961), across languages (Church & Katigbak, 1989), and across diverse sets of traits (Borkenau & Ostendorf, 1990; McCrae & Costa, 1987; McCrae, Costa, & Busch, 1986). We review research on the FFM in organizational research in Chapter 4.

In sum, a recently derived and empirically robust taxonomy suggests that a very large number of traits fit into one of five categories. We consider measurement procedures for the FFM in the next chapter. First, however, we shall attempt to delineate broad categories of cognitive structures and cognitive processes. The cognitive functions of interest here are those that people use to justify the characteristic behavioral adjustments that make up the traits in the FFM.

Broad Categories of the Social Cognitions That Are Used to Justify Characteristic Behavioral Adjustments

It is generally assumed that a number of gradations exist between the positive pole and the negative pole for each factor in the FFM. The actual distribution of the population at large on any factor, or any given trait within a factor, is dependent on the factor or trait in question. For example, people may distribute normally on a scale that ranges from *Talkative* to *Quiet*. The distribution of these same people may be decidedly lumped toward *Dependable* on a scale that varies between *Dependable* and *Undependable*. Whatever the distribution, the clustering of traits into positive and negative poles has a very clear and salient implication. Within an environment that is evocative and that offers behavioral choices, individuals are likely to differ in how they behave. In other words, different people make different behavioral adjustments to the same environment.

For example, in a social situation involving new people, extraverts are talkative, outgoing, and sociable, whereas introverts are reserved, shy, and quiet (the +I and –I poles of Factor I). When people are asked to contribute their time to worthy social causes, agreeable people tend to be sympathetic and generous, whereas disagreeable people tend to be hard-hearted and cold (+II and –II). A work deadline requiring maximum effort and perseverance engenders industriousness, achievement motivation, and reliability on the part of conscientious individuals, and carelessness, lack of attention, and inconsistency among nonconscientious individuals (+III and –III). A personal crisis engenders a calm reaction that focuses on self-reliant solutions for emotionally stable people, but anxiety, nervousness, and a sense of uncontrollable, impending doom for neurotic people (+IV and –IV). A potentially creative solution to a problem stimulates interest and perceptive thoughts of long-range and indirect consequences in intelligent, open-minded individuals, whereas less intelligent, closed-minded individuals dislike change and fail to see beyond obvious, short-range, and self-focused consequences (+V and –V).

In Chapter 2 we discussed how individual differences in behavior adjustments to the same environment are governed by individual differences in social cognitions. We noted that even though people behave differently, each individual believes that his or her particular behavior is reasonable as opposed to irrational, subjective, or foolish. Thus when quiet people and talkative people react differently to the same social context, both quiet and talkative persons believe their respective behavior to be reasonable. As in previous chapters, we use the term *conditional reasoning* here to refer to occasions in which what is considered adaptable or justifiable behavior is contingent (dependent, conditional) on the personality of the individual who is doing the reasoning.

Our task here is to provide an overview of aspects of social cognitions that are known to contribute to individual differences in behavioral adjustments. We shall focus on the framing and analytic processes that produce variations in judgments of what is justifiable behavior in the same situational context. In concert with our discussion in Chapters 1 and 2, we suggest that people with different personalities (e.g., talkative versus quiet, achievement oriented versus avoidant) reason differently, or conditionally, because their respective analyses are intended to justify different behaviors.

To review briefly, conditionality of reasoning is seen in differences in how people frame an environment and in the inferences they make about how best to adapt to that environment. *Framing* per se refers to valuations of attributes and events in terms of their "meaning" (substance, intent, psychological significance) to the individual. A framing proclivity consists of the adjectives that a person habitually uses to frame events (e.g., is persistence on a challenging task typically perceived as "commitment" or "compulsiveness"?). Inferences come from reasoning about cause-effect that the individual believes offers (a) rational explanations for why behavior occurred (is personal effort a strong cause of success or is effort often overshadowed by personally uncontrollable situational factors such as unsupportive managers?) and (b) reasonable grounds for predictions (e.g., if I work hard then I will be successful versus no matter how hard I work I cannot overcome the lack of resources).

Framing and inference are often partially grounded in veridical perceptions and valid premises and assumptions. However, framing and inference tend also to be shaped by slants or biases that are designed to enhance the logical appeal of the trait-based or characteristic behavioral preferences of the reasoner. These biases are typically unrecognized by the reasoner—that is, they are implicit or unconscious. In Chapters 1 and 2 we have referred to these reasoning biases as justification mechanisms, or JMs. A general definition of a JM is as follows: an implicit bias that defines, shapes, and otherwise influences reasoning so as to enhance the rational appeal of motive-based or dispositional behavior.

We focus on JMs in this chapter because JMs are basic cognitive elements of personality as personality is represented in framing and thinking about what is a justifiable behavioral adjustment in an environment. We provided illustrations of JMs and the conditional reasoning produced by JMs for aggressive versus socially adaptive individuals in Chapter 1, and for people with high versus low relative motive strength in Chapter 2. These illustrative JMs were drawn from general categories of JMs, or, more specifically, the general categories of implicit (reasoning) biases that give rise to JMs. We present these general categories of implicit biases below, focusing on identifying the types of implicit biases that constitute JMs and how these biases affect the content of what individuals perceive and infer (i.e., reasoning content).

Following this presentation, we consider how JMs also influence the types of reasoning that individuals do (i.e., reasoning strategies). Included among these strategies are confirmatory biases and selective attention. To set the stage for these overviews, we first want to distinguish more fully between JMs as they relate to reasoning content and JMs as they relate to reasoning strategy.

Justification mechanisms comprise implicit biases that, unknown to the reasoner, shape, define, and guide the perceptions, understandings, hypotheses, causal explanations, and expectancies the reasoner employs to give meaning to events and to reason about how best to adjust to an environment. The biases are designed to enhance the rational appeal of motive or dispositionally based behavior. Thus, for example, highly motivated individuals are implicitly biased to reason that achievement is largely a product of initiative, intensity, and persistence as opposed to being dictated by outside, uncontrollable forces. Although partially accurate, such reasoning involves a JM that we have referred to as Personal Responsibility Bias (see Table 2.1 in Chapter 2), which is an unrecognized proclivity to arrive at the conclusion that one has more control over personal success/failure than may be true.

Note that JMs have content; they involve identifiable assumptions that produce reasoning that attempts to enhance the logical appeal of specific behaviors. JMs may also influence the strategies that individuals use to reason. For example, a bias toward personal responsibility is likely to stimulate a "directed search process" wherein the reasoner seeks occasions on which initiative, intensity, and persistence did in fact lead to success. Such a directed search represents a strategy in how one reasons that is known as a confirmatory bias. The term *confirmatory* denotes that the reasoner selectively seeks out only information (evidence, data, historical events) that supports his or her underlying JM.

Reasoning strategies are temporary mental actions that serve JMs, but are not themselves associated with indigenous content. A particular process such as a directed search for confirming evidence may serve any number of JMs. Thus we do not think of reasoning strategies as JMs, but rather as implicit biases in reasoning that are shaped and directed by JMs.

Unfortunately, no taxonomy exists for either JMs or reasoning strategies. This is largely because researchers are currently actively attempting to chart an ever-expanding social cognitive terrain. The best that can be offered now are overviews of what appear to be promising domains of (a) the types of implicit biases that comprise JMs and (b) reasoning strategies that are affected by JMs.

The overviews presented below are drawn primarily from the (implicit) social cognition literature. In the past 20 years or so, substantial advances have been made in the identification of cognitively and/or motivationally inspired biases, many of which operate unconsciously, that affect the analyses, judgments, explanations, models, and inferences that constitute reasoning in everyday social contexts. A nonexhaustive but representative sampling of research domains that have recently contributed to the understanding of reasoning biases includes attribution models and theories, framing, heuristics in decision making, implicit (personality) theories, biases in person perception, cognitive mechanisms for self-protection and self-enhancement, object relations, many of the social comparison principles, social inference, and systematic biases in performance evaluation (see Baumeister, 1982; Baumeister & Scher, 1988; Brewin, 1989; Cooper, 1981; Crocker & Major, 1989; Dweck & Leggett, 1988; Einhorn & Hogarth, 1978; Epstein, 1994; Erdelyi, 1992; Feldman, 1981; Fiske & Taylor, 1984, 1991; Funder, 1987; Greenwald & Banaji, 1995; Hogarth, 1987; Holmes, 1978, 1981; Jussim, 1991; Kahneman & Tversky, 1973, 1984; Kilstrom, 1999; Klayman & Ha, 1987; Kruglanski, 1989; Kruglanski & Ajzen, 1983; Kruglanski & Klar, 1987; Kunda, 1990; Miller, 1987; Nisbett & Wilson, 1977; Pyszczynski & Greenberg, 1987; Ross, 1977; Schlenker & Leary, 1982; Schneider, 1991; Sherwood, 1981; Shrauger & Osberg, 1981; Skowronski & Carlston, 1989; Taylor, 1991; Taylor & Brown, 1988; Taylor & Lobel, 1989; Trope, 1986; Tversky & Kahneman, 1973, 1974, 1981, 1983; Wegner & Vallacher, 1977; Weiner, 1979, 1991; Westen, 1991; Winter, John, Stewart, Klohnen, & Duncan, 1998; Wood, 1989). Fiske and Taylor (1984, 1991) provide excellent reviews of most of these subjects.

Types of Implicit Biases That Give Rise to Justification Mechanisms

We present an overview below of nine categories of implicit biases that make up JMs. Some of these domains have long histories in research and theorizing about human cognition (e.g., halo, rationalization) and are treated in many of the works cited immediately above. Others have shorter but often illustrious histories (e.g., attribution biases; see Weiner, 1991). Still others are essentially new, having been identified in recent research, including that on conditional reasoning (e.g., differential framing, leveling; James, 1998). We suspect that new domains of implicit biases and JMs will be added to this list as research continues to accumulate on biases in social cognition. We should note that we make no attempt here to track the histories of the biases to their possible roots in such things as defense mechanisms (see Cramer, 2000). Although salient, most of the knowledge of social cognitive processes that has been used to identify/develop JMs is a product of the past 20 years and is addressed in the works cited above.

Differential Framing

Differential framing refers to qualitative disparities in the meanings imputed to (i.e., the adjectives used to describe) the same attributes or event(s) by different individuals (James, 1998). For example, FFs tend to frame perseverance on a demanding task following initial failure as "compulsiveness," whereas AMs tend to frame this same perseverance after failure as "dedication."

As we discussed in Chapter 2, to frame an event is to place that event in an interpretative category, or *cognitive schema* (e.g., people high in fear of failure place demanding tasks in the interpretative category of "stressful"). Cognitive schemata are internal prisms through which external stimuli pass and in passing are translated into interpretative adjectives that indicate personal meaning. Individuals draw repeatedly on the same cognitive schemata to give meaning to events. It is the recurring use of the same schemata to give meaning to events that determines a *framing proclivity,* which is a disposition to use only certain schemata and adjectives to interpret the same or similar events.

Differential framing often involves unrecognized tendencies to frame behaviors and/or behavioral objectives in ways that encourage or discourage specific actions. For example, AMs implicitly believe that demanding tasks provide "challenges" that offer them "opportunities" to demonstrate present skills, learn new skills, and make a contribution (see Opportunity Bias in Table 2.1). AMs also tend to impute positive connotations to effort, seeing intensity and persistence as forms of "dedication," "concentration," and "involvement." These perceptions are based on an underlying tendency to slant the meaning of effort toward perceptions that enhance the rational appeal of approaching demanding tasks.

In contrast, FFs are predisposed to slant framing toward dampening the logical appeal of approach to challenging tasks. For example, FFs unknowingly tend to frame demanding tasks as "threats" that create "risk" and impute to these tasks negative connotations such as "overloading" and "stressful." Such framing reveals an unconscious tendency to seek out negative connotations in achievement striving (see the third JM in Table 2.2).

Unrecognized biases that enhance or dampen the attractiveness of trait-related behaviors are prevalent throughout other traits in the FFM. Consider, for example, the Potency Bias that shapes the framing of aggressive individuals. This bias involves a tendency to frame and analyze other people using the contrast of strength versus weakness. People with a strong Potency Bias tend to frame others on a continuum ranging from strong, assertive, powerful, daring, fearless, and brave to weak, impotent, submissive, timid, sheepish, compliant, conforming, and cowardly. They use this bias to justify aggression through arguments such as (a) aggression (e.g., confrontations with teachers, fights with coworkers) results in one's being "respected" by others, and (b) weakness/submissiveness invites aggression because it shows that one is willing to submit.

Nonaggressive, socially adaptive individuals tend not to perceive others through a prism of potency. In place of the Potency Bias, they tend to perceive others through a prism that frames them on a continuum ranging from likely to be a friend, companion, confidante, partner, or colleague to likely to be part of only a neutral, unemotional, or uninvolved relationship.

Additional examples of personality-based differences in framing—that is, differential framing—abound. For example, extraverts are predisposed to frame occasions where they meet new people as opportunities for making new friends, whereas introverts tend to frame such occasions as being associated with discomfort and potential embarrassment. Emotionally stable people perceive the delaying of decision making until information is obtained as careful and cautious, whereas emotionally unstable, impatient people frame these same delays as indicators of indecisiveness and timidity. Agreeable, trusting individuals are inclined to frame interactions with authority figures such as the police from the perspective of one who is being defended and protected. Disagreeable, aggressive people are prone to frame these same interactions from the perspective of one who is being tyrannized and oppressed. As a final illustration, consider intelligent people who frame the consequences of their behaviors from the perspectives of both their short-term and long-term effects. Unintelligent people tend to focus only on the short-term, "bottom-line" implications of their actions.

Framing proclivities and differential framing set the stage for the analysis and hypothesizing that we often think of as reasoning. Consider that how events are framed often shapes and bounds people's thinking and inferences about these events. Thus differential framing is viewed as the first stage of the conditional reasoning process.

Attribution Biases

Attribution biases are predilections to ascribe behavior to causal factors that implicitly justify motives or behavioral dispositions. Following differential framing, attribution biases are perhaps the single most prevalent source of implicit social cognitions aimed at justification. In Chapter 1, we described the Hostile Attribution Bias, which is a tendency on the part of aggressive individuals to arrive at the conclusion that the targets of their aggression acted malevolently and with harmful intent toward them, thus triggering and justifying their aggressive responses.

In Chapter 2, we discussed how AMs (i.e., people whose relative motive strength favors achievement motivation) favor initiative, intensity, and persistence as the most important causes of success in performance on demanding tasks. This bias toward ascribing performance to "personal responsibility" is a manifestation of a more general proclivity known as the Personal Responsibility Bias. Opposing this bias is the External Attribution Bias. People whose relative motive strength favors fear of failure (i.e., FFs) are prone to invoke external factors such as lack of resources, situational constraints, intractable material, and unfair evaluations as the most important causes of performance on demanding tasks (see Table 2.2). Such favoritism sets the stage for justifying avoidance because the inevitable failure will not be one's fault.

Other forms of attribution biases pertain to such things as whether causes of a behavior are judged to be (a) more stable or unstable than is factual, or (b) more controllable or uncontrollable than is factual (see Weiner, 1990). An illustration of an overattribution to controllability is an extravert who presumes that he or she has greater mastery over social situations than is authentic, whereas an example of an underattribution to controllability is an introvert who reasons that his or her life is dominated by capricious social forces. A bias favoring stability is one reason an intelligent person who is in pursuit of deeper explanations fails to appreciate the effects of random shocks on behavior. A bias favoring instability is illustrated by the imperceptive person who fails to recognize an underlying pattern in what to him or her appear to be unrelated events.

Halo

Halo (also known as implicit or illusionary correlation) involves a tendency to associate behavior in one area with behavior in a different area. For example, an individual who demonstrates conscientiousness is expected also to be stable, agreeable, wise, and sociable. Or an individual who is demonstrably undependable is expected, based on this evidence alone, to be anxious, unintelligent, disagreeable, and withdrawn as well. A related kind of halo occurs when a judge forms a general impression of a target and this general impression influences all or most of the judge's ratings of the target across multiple traits (Cooper, 1981).

Halo has been studied extensively by researchers in the field of performance evaluation (see Feldman, 1981; Ilgen, Barnes-Farrell, & McKellin, 1993; Landy & Farr, 1980; Murphy & Anhalt, 1992). Although many questions remain, this literature has consistently demonstrated a tendency for a judge's ratings on one category of behavior (e.g., creativity) to be correlated more highly than would be indicated by the facts with a different category of behavior (e.g., conscientiousness). Moreover, much of the systematic variance in ratings of ostensibly different behaviors tends to be accounted for by a single underlying factor. These results suggest that raters tend to form general impressions of others and tend to assume implicitly that behavior in one domain may be used to forecast, with reasonable accuracy, behavior in other domains.

Halo gives rise to JMs when individuals with different motives and dispositions forge different expectations based on the same stimulus behavior. For example, aggressive individuals are prone to associate lack of an aggressive manner with weakness or cowardice and to expect nonaggressive individuals to act in humble and deferential manners. These associations and expectations are products of halo and underlie the formation of the Potency Bias JM. In contrast, nonaggressive, socially adaptive people are likely to associate the same lack of aggressiveness with civility, courteousness, and good-naturedness. Expectations for future behavior flow from these associations.

Identification

Identification is a tendency to empathize with the plights, experiences, perceptions, emotions, and behavioral dispositions of specific types of persons. Identification often reflects a person's own predilections and experiences. For example, FFs tend to empathize with the fear and anxiety of those who fail in achievement situations because they themselves experience fear and anxiety in such situations. AMs tend to identify with the sense of enthusiasm, intensity, and striving that characterize those who succeed in demanding situations. Here again, identification mirrors the tendencies of AMs to be excited, intense, and enthused in achievement situations.

Other illustrations of identification include occasions in which agreeable people feel a sense of bonding with those who are kind, amiable, generous, and trusting. Disagreeable people tend to identify with people they believe to be assertive, nonvulnerable, realistic, and strong.

Indirect Compensation

Indirect compensation refers to a tacit or typically unrecognized attempt to increase the logical appeal of replacing a threatening situation with a compensatory (i.e., less threatening) situation by imbuing the compensatory situation with positive, socially desirable qualities. For example, FFs tend to place greater value on job security than on opportunities for advancement, learning, and rewards. Introverts rank peace and quiet over affectionate and warm interpersonal relationships. Unimaginative people prefer practical and bottom-line-oriented transactions to in-depth and abstract explanations.

Discounting

Discounting is a predilection to invoke evidence, assumptions, and explanations that dispute, reject, or invalidate critiques of one's justifications for favored behaviors. For example, AMs are predisposed to discount FFs' use of indirect compensation to impute socially desirable qualities (e.g., job security) to non-achievement-oriented tasks. AMs devalue such tasks by characterizing them as routine, boring, uninteresting, or dull. In like manner, FFs discount AMs' interest in achievement-oriented tasks by characterizing them as risky, uncertain, or stressful.

Leveling

Leveling is a special form of discounting in which the reasoner devalues a culturally valent but, for the reasoner, psychologically hazardous event by associating that event with a dysfunctional and aversive outcome. For example, FFs tend to associate approach to achievement-oriented situations with increased risk of cardiovascular disease. This is an example of reasoning in which the unrecognized desire to devalue achievement striving engenders a potentially false causal inference, perhaps fueled by correlational data such as that showing that business executives have an above-average frequency of heart-related health problems. Another example of leveling is when shy individuals associate attempts to initiate social interaction with being rebuffed and embarrassed.

Positive and Negative Leniency

Some individuals have an unrecognized tendency to overestimate their proficiencies (positive leniency) or to underestimate their proficiencies (negative leniency) in a behavioral domain. Examples of positive leniency include overconfidence on the part of AMs when approaching difficult tasks (i.e., their belief that they have a greater likelihood of success than they actually do), highly intelligent persons' benevolent self-perceptions that they possess keen insight, and aggressive individuals' overestimates of their ability to intimidate others. Negative leniency is illustrated by FFs' partially unwarranted lack of confidence in their likelihood of success on demanding tasks, introverts' lack of confidence in their social skills, and anxious individuals' perceptions of their inability to cope with evocative situations.

Rationalization

Rationalization involves the use of superficially rational arguments, assertions, explanations, hypotheses, or premises to justify dispositional behaviors. One might suppose that all JMs are forms of rationalization, given that JMs are defined as "reasoning biases" intended to enhance the logical appeal of reasoners' behaviors. This is not necessarily true, however, because although they are purveyors of bias, not all JMs are "superficially rational." Consider the discussion presented in Chapter 2 regarding the JM called the Personal Responsibility Bias for AMs:

> Note that an exclusively rational analysis might uncover reasonable support for *both* internal (e.g., effort, skills) and external (e.g., leadership, resources) explanations for performance. Highly motivated individuals, however, are predisposed to assume that success/failure on demanding tasks is largely a function of personal initiative, intensity, and persistence (i.e., internal attributions). Thus, in their attempts to justify approach to demanding goals and objectives and the pursuit of achievement, AMs are inclined to give greater emphasis to internal factors than is perhaps deserved (see Weiner, 1979, 1990, 1991).

This JM thus represents a slant toward or overemphasis on personal causes of performance, but the reasoning is not "superficial."

On the other hand, some JMs are indeed forms of rationalization because they are based on superficially rational reasoning. For example, the FF JM that we call the Self-Handicapping Bias involves attempts to deflect explanations for failure away from incompetence in favor of self-induced impairments, such as not really trying or not being prepared (e.g., a defensive lack of effort). Rationalization also tends to occur in attempts to justify socially unacceptable or antisocial behaviors such as aggression and unreliability. We presented an illustrative JM that is also a rationalization for aggression in Chapter 1. This JM is labeled Retribution Bias and consists of an attempt to sanction logically an unrecognized desire to cause harm to others. An example of the Retribution Bias at work is the rationalization that causing harm to a target is justified because the target provoked the aggression and thus the aggressor is only defending him- or herself.

To conclude, this overview of implicit biases is meant to be illustrative of potential sources of JMs. The specific JMs constructed for a trait or traits, such as those described in Table 2.1 for AMs and Table 2.2 for FFs, must be predicated on the types of reasoning biases that pervade the framing and analyses that people use to defend the manifestation of traits. Potential domains of implicit biases and the JMs they engender are still being identified, and readers with an interest in pursuing this area are advised to review the social cognition literature on a regular basis.

How JMs Influence Reasoning Strategies

We begin this subsection by asking how people judge whether their behavior is rational or sensible. To judge, people often attempt to do the following:

1. Discriminate among degrees of truth and falsity of assumptions about what is the best course of action
2. Identify unstated premises in advocacy for different behavioral adjustments
3. Distinguish among degrees of relevance and irrelevance of information (evidence, data, historical events, testimony) in regard to decision making and judgment
4. Make valid inferences or generalizations based on what are often incomplete data (e.g., what the likely or expected outcome of a behavioral choice may be)

Justification mechanisms may be mapped directly into these reasoning processes. To illustrate, FFs may map an External Attributional Bias (e.g., professors are biased against me) into a query about the controllability of a specific event (e.g., grade on a particular test). In this case, reasoning (inference about grade) is given content by a JM. That is, the JM implicitly shapes the inference that a low grade should be expected because the professor is biased. This was the subject of the preceding discussion.

Alternatively, JMs may be mapped onto reasoning through their influences on the strategies by which one reasons. For example, we mentioned earlier that a Personal Responsibility Bias may direct a search for information that confirms expectations that success is due largely to effort. In such a situation, a JM influences the strategy one uses to reason (i.e., to search for corroborative evidence), which in this case is referred to as a confirmatory bias. Below, we review the confirmatory bias along with other salient and identifiable reasoning strategies that are likely to be harnessed to serve JMs. Our intent here is to identify key categories of reasoning strategies that serve personality. We make no attempt to be exhaustive in this discussion; interested readers may find extended treatments of these strategies in many of the works cited earlier on implicit social cognition.

Confirmatory and Disconfirmatory Biases

A confirmatory bias involves a directed search designed to seek out information (evidence, data, historical events) that corroborates what the individual considers to be justified behavioral adjustments. The example given above involves AMs searching for information that confirms their bias to attribute performance on achievement-oriented tasks to internal factors such as effort. Other examples of confirmatory biases include extraverts who seek out evidence that confirms their belief in their mastery over social situations and disagreeable individuals who search for evidence that supports their belief in cynical explanations for behavior.

A disconfirmatory bias involves a directed search designed to seek out information that discredits displeasing (e.g., opposing, conflicting, contrasting, critical) arguments about what constitute justifiable behavioral adjustments. For example, FFs may seek out cases in which lack of resources or other uncontrollable factors engendered failure on demanding tasks. They then use this evidence to discount AMs' reasoning that success on demanding tasks is largely a function of personal effort. FFs would generally be unaware that an External Attribution Bias stimulated the directed search for evidence that failure is often beyond personal control.

Primary versus Peripheral Relevance of Evidence

Many individuals have unrecognized predilections to judge evidence as (a) primary or relevant if it supports personally favored biases, but (b) peripheral or irrelevant if it is critical of what they consider reasonable or offers alternatives to their conclusions. For example, data from a small sample of 50 subjects may indicate that intellectually open people are more satisfied with their lives and tend to live longer than intellectually closed people. Intellectually open people are likely to respond favorably to new evidence that their lifestyle engenders happiness and longevity (the evidence is likely consistent with a halo bias). While recognizing that results on a small sample may be capricious, they nonetheless are willing to consider the data as at least indicative of tenable trends, although in need of further validation.

Evidence that they are less satisfied and live shorter lives is not likely to be well received by intellectually closed individuals. Indeed, such evidence is likely to trigger protective mechanisms such as discounting bias. A probable result is a reasoned judgment on the part of these individuals that the results of the study are the product of chance and sampling error produced by a small sample and are nongeneralizable.

Individuals may also regard evidence based on such things as low base rates and single evocative events as relevant or peripheral depending on their implicit biases. The "reasonableness" or "validity" of data is thus less than totally objective in at least some cases. Frequently, the judged validity of the data is itself a function of the role that the data play in the broader context of justification of behaviors.

Selective Attention

Selective attention refers to a tendency for individuals to attend principally in their perception to evidence that corroborates their JMs. Selective *in*attentiveness implies an analogous tendency in which evidence that is inconsistent with a person's JMs fails to reach the threshold of consciousness. An example of selective attention is AMs' proclivity to attend primarily to positive incentives resulting from a promotion, such as greater decision-making power and greater rewards. Accompanying this focused mindfulness is inattentiveness to potential negative outcomes, such as the enhanced stress that accompanies more consequential decision making. It should be noted that selective attention is a passive process in which receptiveness to information in perception is the issue. Confirmatory and disconfirmatory biases are proactive processes in which people seek out information that confirms or disconfirms their reasoning.

This completes our overview of cognitive processes associated with justifying behavioral adjustments. We conclude the chapter with a brief discussion of the role of nonconscious biases in individuals' thinking and reasoning about their behavior.

Implicit Biases: Wanted or Unwanted

We have attempted to identify prominent domains of social cognitions that explain how and why different individuals make divergent behavioral adjustments in the same environment. Simply stated, people who behave differently think differently. Salient components of these differences in thinking are (a) differential framing of the same situational context and (b) reasoning that on the surface appears sensible to the reasoner (at least) but in reality is implicitly influenced by biasing mechanisms (i.e., JMs) whose purpose is to enhance the logical plausibility, and thereby justifiability, of that reasoner's behavioral dispositions.

Interestingly, in constructing rationales for their behaviors, individuals often try to overcome their self-perceptions of their biases by employing what they believe to be principles of reasoning (see Einhorn & Hogarth, 1978; Feldman & Lindell, 1989). Their conviction that they have been successful in their pursuit of objectivity may be at least partially true. What individuals fail to realize, however, is that the arguments they have carefully constructed through reasoned judgments are subject to biasing processes of which they are unaware and over which they have no control. Their reasoning may thus be characterized as conditional; that is, the probability that a person will judge a behavior to be reasonable is dependent on the strength of that person's disposition to engage in the behavior. A related connotation of the term *conditional reasoning* is that what one considers a reasonable behavioral adjustment to a given context is often dependent on one's underlying personality.

The unrecognized, indeed unconscious, nature of justification processes may seem a vexing problem to those who wish to believe that their behavioral adjustments are based on truly objective reasoning. To these individuals we note that a large and accumulating body of research indicates that the justification processes discussed in this chapter are not likely to be recognized even by highly skilled reasoners who search for logical fallacies in their own reasoning (see Atkinson, 1978; Brewin, 1989; Kagan, 1988; Kunda, 1990; McClelland, 1985b; Nisbett & Ross, 1989; Nisbett & Wilson, 1977; Pyszczynski & Greenberg, 1987; Shrauger & Osberg, 1981; Westen, 1991). As we have remarked several times, the simple fact is that JMs are unknowingly mapped onto conscious thought through the adjectives that individuals employ to describe themselves and their environments, the hypotheses they use to offer ostensibly rational explanations for their behavior, the statistics they select to support (or to discount) premises about appropriate behavioral adjustments, and the experts and testimony that they consider (un)biased.

It is also noteworthy that justification processes are especially likely to occur when conditional reasoning opportunities are evocative and trigger latent motives or needs, such as the individual's needs to protect/enhance his or her self-concept, to be secure, to be accepted, and to achieve a reasonable degree of success (and to avoid demonstrating incompetence). For example, as discussed in Chapter 2, unrecognized biases in reasoning have a self-protective function in the sense that they are forms of safety mechanisms that protect FFs from engaging in high-press-for-achievement activities that might cause them psychological damage. Thus, unless biases in reasoning are being used to rationalize illegal and/or pathological behavior, it is perhaps best to think of them as a natural part of human functioning. People want to believe that their choices of behavior are justified, which is to say rational or sensible as opposed to irrational or foolish. It is often, although not always, functional and healthy psychologically for individuals to engage in nonconscious processes that assist them in realizing this belief.

 **4** The Measurement
of Personality in
Organizational Settings

In this chapter, we illustrate some strategies for measuring personality in organizational settings. We begin with a brief overview of the standards or criteria that are used to determine whether an instrument designed to measure personality is useful. We introduce and define the concepts of *validity* and *reliability* and then employ these standards to select and/or evaluate examples of the measurement instruments currently in use in organizations to measure personality. The review of personality measurement instruments here is highly selective, our intent being to present exemplars of techniques currently in use to measure traits, needs, affect, and conditional reasoning associated with the five-factor model (FFM) of personality. We present illustrations of measurement techniques for each of three broad categories: self-report measures, projective techniques, and conditional reasoning measures. Space limitations prevent our including a number of other techniques, such as assessment centers, clinical interviews, conjoint measurement, supervisory ratings of trait behaviors, and Q sorts.

Criteria for Evaluating Measurement Procedures

How does one tell whether or not a measure of personality is actually measuring what it claims to measure? For example, when respondents are told that they are "emotionally stable" or "conscientious" based on their responses to a self-report instrument such as the Hogan Personality Inventory (Hogan & Hogan, 1995) or the NEO Personality Inventory (Costa & McCrae, 1992a), how do we know that they have been accurately described? A domain of psychology known as *psychometrics* has evolved that specializes in research and statistical techniques that attempt to answer this question. According to psychometrics, the two key standards for judging whether a measurement instrument is accurately assessing what it purports to measure are reliability and validity (see Messick, 1988). We discuss these standards below.

Reliability

Our initial concern with measuring an attribute of personality is whether that attribute is reasonably stable and consistent. Suppose, for example, that we desired to measure the factor of Extraversion versus Introversion from the FFM. This desire is reasonable only if (a) some people exhibit stable (over time) and consistent (over situations) behavioral dispositions to be talkative, active, energetic, outgoing, and sociable, whereas (b) different people exhibit stable and consistent behavioral dispositions to be quiet, withdrawn, reserved, shy, and retiring. One sense of *reliable,* then, is that stable (over time) and consistent (over situations) individual differences must exist on the personality attribute in question in order to make measurement of the attribute possible.

If the attribute is stable and consistent, then we can ask whether the personality instrument designed to measure the attribute captures its stability and consistency. The trait Extraversion versus Introversion could be highly reliable (stable and consistent), but the instrument developed to measure it could be poorly designed and subject to random influences such as variations in the moods of respondents, sampling of behaviors that are not related to Extraversion versus Introversion, and divergences in the states of alertness of respondents at the times of measurement (see Nunnally & Bernstein, 1994). Random influences, collectively referred to as *random measurement error,* detract from the ability of the measurement instrument to assess the personality attribute. Freedom from random measurement error is thus another meaning of an instrument's "being reliable."

The preceding discussion suggests the following definition for reliability: A measurement instrument is reliable if the scores it furnishes accurately capture stable and consistent individual differences in an attribute with minimal random measurement error. Note that if a measurement instrument evidences low reliability, it could be because (a) the personality attribute is unstable or inconsistent or (b) the attribute is stable/consistent but the scores provided by the measurement instrument are seriously compromised by random measurement error. Or both factors could be present, such as when a poor instrument is developed to assess an unstable attribute.

A number of techniques are available for estimating reliability, each of which is sensitive to one or more salient components of reliability. We describe below the principal types of estimators used in contemporary personality research and their respective sensitivities.

Test-retest reliability.   The same measurement instrument, generically referred to in psychometrics as a *test,* is administered to the same sample of individuals at two different points in time, usually at least a few weeks apart and up to several months apart. Scores from Time 1 are then correlated with scores from Time 2. This estimator is sensitive primarily to the *stability* over time of the rank ordering of scores.

Parallel-form reliability.   At least two forms of a test are constructed with the objective that an individual will get the same score irrespective of which form of the test he or she takes. Forms that reasonably satisfy this objective are said to be parallel. Parallel-form reliability is typically estimated using the same design as test-retest reliability, the exception being that at Time 2, a parallel form is administered rather than the same form of the test as that used at Time 1. Estimates of reliability based on parallel-form reliability tend to be lower than those for test-retest reliability because parallel-form reliability is sensitive not only to *stability* over time in the rank ordering of scores, but also to the *equivalence* of the forms of the test. Lack of perfect equivalence, or perfect parallelness, may result in some differences in rank ordering of scores over time even though the trait is stable. If this occurs, then the actual stability of the personality attribute is underestimated by parallel-form reliability.

Internal consistency reliability. Measurements are taken at just one point in time, typically based on a set of self-report items that are designed to measure the same personality attribute (e.g., respondents complete an inventory containing 20 items that describe different behavioral indicators of achievement motivation). The average correlation (or interitem covariance) among scores on the items is then estimated. This statistic is employed to assess the degree to which the items collectively measure the same personality construct. Technically, a single estimate of reliability is computed and interpreted as the degree to which the items as a group have been sampled from the same "domain" of personality. In this sense, for the collective of items to be considered a domain or construct of personality, one must demonstrate that they are "internally consistent" indicators of the construct. To the extent that such measurements are correlated (an estimator of internal consistency) and collectively produce a reasonable reliability, one infers that an underlying domain exists and can be reliably measured. Basically, then, a high internal consistency reliability—typically estimated by "coefficient alpha" (Cronbach, 1951)—implies, or is sensitive to, the *cohesion* among a set of theoretically related measures of a personality construct.

Interrater reliability. The generic model for this type of reliability has two or more judges rating the same set of individuals on one or more traits. For example, each member of the clinical psychology faculty (the judges) rates each fourth-year clinical psychology graduate student (the targets) on emotional stability (the trait). The question addressed by interrater reliability is whether ratings given to the targets (students) by the different judges (faculty) are correlated (e.g., Do the judges rank order the students similarly?). Although estimation can be sophisticated statistically, interrater reliability can be calculated simply as follows. First, the ratings given by one judge are correlated with the ratings given by a different judge on the same sample of targets. This analysis is conducted for all unique pairs of judges, which results in $J(J-1)/2$ correlations, where J is the number of judges. These correlations are then averaged to estimate interrater reliability.

Desirable Reliabilities

Internal consistency estimators furnish lower-bound values of reliability, which means that estimated values tend to be a bit lower than parallel-form reliabilities, which in turn run a bit lower than test-retest reliabilities. These differences are not huge, and thus it is possible to make general statements about desirable magnitudes of reliability, including interrater reliabilities. For example, reliabilities of .70 or above are considered promising for a personality instrument that is still in the developmental phase. Reliabilities of .85 and higher are considered favorable for developed instruments. Preferably, several estimates of reliability should be available for a given instrument, including an estimate of internal consistency or interrater reliability and one of the estimators that takes stability into account.

Validity

Validity refers to "the degree to which evidence and theory support the interpretations of test scores entailed by proposed uses of tests. Validity is, therefore, the most fundamental consideration in developing and evaluating tests" (American Educational Research Association, 1999, p. 9). A number of different types of evidence can be accumulated about a test—technically, test scores—and each of these types of evidence may be used to support a specific type of interpretation of the test. In effect, one may think of the test as having different but not unrelated types of validity, each supporting a particular interpretation. We describe the principal types of validity found in contemporary research on personality in organizations below.

Construct validity. Construct validity concerns the assessment of the degree to which a personality instrument measures the construct of personality that it is theoretically meant to measure. This is the most encompassing form of validity, and other forms are derivatives of it. Many avenues exist through which one may test the inference that the scores on a "test" measure what they are purported to measure. One frequently employed approach to construct validation is factor analysis. The items that are believed to measure the same construct (or domain) are analyzed to see if they load on a single factor (see the brief introduction to factor analysis in Chapter 3). Another approach to construct validation is to ascertain whether a test alleged to measure a construct such as Conscientiousness is correlated reasonably highly with tests already known to measure that construct. This approach is referred to as *convergent validation*. Accompanying assessments of convergent validity are often appraisals of *discriminant validity*. Discriminant validity requires that scores on a measure of one construct (e.g., Conscientiousness) have low, or at most modest, correlations with scores on a measure of a different construct (e.g., Introversion/Extroversion).

Content validity.   Content validity concerns the assessment of the extent to which the items on a test are representative of a domain or construct of personality and, as a collective, span the entire domain of that construct. Clearly, content validity is crucial to construct validity. Content validity is also considered separately because the sampling of items (tasks, questions) to put in a measurement instrument determines the success or lack of such of the entire assessment process. The first step in content validation is the definition of the domain to be measured, including the breadth and depth of information that are required to assess whether a person possesses the personality attribute in question. The next step is the determination of the extent to which the actual items (tasks, questions) in the measurement instrument (a) are representative of the domain as defined and (b) provide coverage of the entire domain as defined. These determinations are typically made by a set of expert judges.

Criterion-related validity.   Criterion-related validity concerns the assessment of the extent to which scores on a measurement instrument are related to the external behaviors or outcome criteria that the instrument is intended to predict. For example, scores on a test designed to assess achievement motivation should be significantly related to outcome criteria of achievement, such as promotion rate for executives, grades for students, and number of patents for scientists. Criterion-related validity is said to be *predictive* if the time of personality assessment occurs before the time of outcome measurement. To illustrate, measures of achievement motivation are obtained at the start of a semester, and the outcome criterion is the final grade in a class at the end of that same semester. Criterion-related validity is said to be *concurrent* when the test and outcome criteria are measured at the same approximate time. For example, a self-report of anxiety and a measurement of blood pressure might be taken almost simultaneously.

Desirable Validities

Estimation of construct and content validity frequently involves complex judgmental processes that do not lend themselves to measurement using straightforward statistical yardsticks. Criterion-related validity is easier to capture. Basically, we want predictive and concurrent validities to be of high value—say, .40 and above. Almost inevitably, this desire is frustrated in personality research. For example, recent meta-analyses put the average, uncorrected validity between self-reports of personality and salient behavioral criteria in work settings (e.g., performance) at approximately .12, with a maximum rarely greater than .30 (see Barrick & Mount, 1991, 1993; Hough, 1992; Hough, Eaton, Dunnette, Kamp, & McCloy, 1990; Hurtz & Donovan, 2000; Salgado, 1997; Schmitt, Gooding, Noe, & Kirsch, 1984; Tett, Jackson, & Rothstein, 1991). Mischel (1968) reached similar conclusions, especially pertaining to the upper bound of .30, based on a review of general personality.

If we focus exclusively on theory-driven studies, which is to say on studies in which the investigators indicate a rationale for examining specific personality variables in relation to specific criteria on specific jobs, the average uncorrected validity between self-reports of personality and job performance climbs only to .13 (Tett et al., 1991). It appears reasonable to conclude, therefore, that personality measures tend to have significant but modest criterion-related validities. The lack of impressive criterion-related validities with salient behavioral criteria is the Achilles' heel of personality research (see Hurtz & Donovan, 2000).

Exemplars of Measurement Techniques for Personality

Self-Report Measures

Self-report inventories are the most popular method used by researchers attempting to measure personality in organizations. In Chapter 3, we reviewed several of the early and in some cases still prominent self-report inventories as part of our introduction to the five-factor model. These inventories, developed by Cattell, Eysenck, and Guilford, are referred to as *omnibus self-report personality inventories.* The term *omnibus* denotes that the inventories measure self-descriptions of multiple traits, needs, values, and characteristic levels of affect. Omnibus inventories are distinguished from a very large number of 5- to 30-item self-report inventories that have been constructed to measure specific attributes of personality. To make maximum use of limited space, we have chosen to focus here on a selection of omnibus personality inventories in our discussion of self-reports. Following descriptions of the selected inventories, we provide an overview of (a) the effectiveness of the FFM in predicting outcome criteria in organizational settings and (b) contamination of self-reports due to social desirability.

Omnibus Self-Report Personality Inventories

Researchers use omnibus self-report personality inventories when they want to gather the scores of respondents on a large number of personality traits, needs, values, and the like. We have selected three popular personality inventories to illustrate measurement by self-report. Each of these inventories is used extensively in industry, in part because each possesses a broad psychometric history that includes assessments of multiple types of reliability and validity. We have space here only to mention a small portion of these extensive psychometric histories (we summarize the validity of the FFM in organizations). Readers who desire more extensive reviews of these inventories or other measures that we do not illustrate may wish to consult the Buros *Mental Measurement Yearbooks* or texts devoted specifically to assessment and testing (e.g., Anastasi, 1982; Walsh & Betz, 1995). Test manuals for many inventories, including those described here, also contain reliability and validity information.

California Psychological Inventory.   Gough (1957, 1969, 1987) designed the California Psychological Inventory (CPI) to measure personality in normally adjusted individuals. The latest version of the CPI (revised in 1996) contains 434 true-false items. The central focus of the CPI is 20 folk scales. Gough refers to these 20 scales as "folk concepts" because they are thought to reflect attributes of personality that are common, enduring, and relevant to many different cultures. The 20 folk scales measured by the CPI are described briefly in Table 4.1. It is noteworthy that many of these scales are included as components of one of the factors of personality in the FFM (see Table 3.6 in Chapter 3).

Research has shown that the CPI's folk concept scales can be reduced to four or five major factors (see Bouchard, 1969; Crites, Bechtold, Goodstein, & Heilbrun, 1961; Gowan, 1958; Mitchell & Pierce-Jones, 1960; Springob & Streuning, 1964; Veldman & Pierce-Jones, 1964).

Table 4.1.   The 20 Folk Concept Scales and Their Intended Meanings

Measures of Poise, Self-Assurance, and Interpersonal Proclivities

Scale Name		Implications of Higher and Lower Scores
Do (Dominance)	Higher:	confident, assertive, dominant, task-oriented
	Lower:	cautious, quiet, hesitant to take the initiative
Cs (Capacity for Status)	Higher:	ambitious, wants to be a success, has many interests
	Lower:	unsure of self, dislikes direct competition, uncomfortable with uncertainty or complexity
Sy (Sociability)	Higher:	sociable, likes to be with people, outgoing
	Lower:	shy, often inhibited, prefers to stay in the background in social situations
Sp (Social Presence)	Higher:	self-assured, spontaneous; versatile; verbally fluent; pleasure-seeking
	Lower:	reserved, hesitant to express own views or opinions; self-denying
Sa (Self-acceptance)	Higher:	has good opinion of self; sees self as talented and personally attractive; talkative
	Lower:	self-doubting; readily assumes blame when things go wrong; often thinks others are better; gives in easily
In (Independence)	Higher:	self-sufficient, resourceful, detached; persistent in seeking goals, whether others agree or not
	Lower:	lacks self-confidence, seeks support from others; tries to avoid conflict; has difficulty in making decisions
Em (Empathy)	Higher:	comfortable about self and well-accepted by others; perceptive of social nuances, understands how others feel; optimistic
	Lower:	unempathic, skeptical about the intentions of others; defensive about own feelings and desires; has limited range of interests

Measures of Normative Orientation and Values

Scale Name		Implications of Higher and Lower Scores
Re (Responsibility)	Higher:	responsible, reliable, ethically perceptive; serious about duties and obligations
	Lower:	self-indulgent, undisciplined, careless; indifferent to personal obligations
So (Socialization)	Higher:	conscientious, well-organized; finds it easy to accept and conform to normative rules; seldom gets in trouble
	Lower:	resists rules, does not like to conform; often rebellious, gets into trouble easily; has unconventional views and attitudes
Sc (Self-Control)	Higher:	tries to control emotions and temper; suppresses hostile and erotic feelings; takes pride in being self-disciplined
	Lower:	has strong feelings and emotions, and makes little effort to hide them; has problems of undercontrol and impulsivity; likes adventure and new experience
Gi (Good Impression)	Higher:	wants to make a good impression; tries to do what will please others, sometimes to the point of being obsequious and sycophantic; short of this level, tends to be conventional, formal, and conservative
	Lower:	insists on being himself or herself, even if this causes friction or problems; dissatisfied in many situations, often complains; easily annoyed and irritated
Cm (Communality)	Higher:	fits in easily, reasonable, sees self as quite average person; makes little effort to change things
	Lower:	sees self as different from others; not conventional or conforming; often changeable and moody; extremely low scores suggest careless or random answering

(continued)

Table 4.1   Continued

Scale Name		Implications of Higher and Lower Scores
Wb (Well-being)	Higher:	feels self to be in good physical and mental health; optimistic about the future; cheerful
	Lower:	concerned about health and/or personal problems: tends to complain about being treated unfairly or inconsiderably; pessimistic
To (Tolerance)	Higher:	is tolerant of others' beliefs and values, even when different from or counter to own beliefs; fair-minded, reasonable, and tactful
	Lower:	distrustful, fault-finding, and extrapunitive; often has hostile and vindictive feelings

Measures of Cognitive and Intellectual Functioning

Scale Name		Implications of Higher and Lower Scores
Ac (Achievement via Conformance)	Higher:	has strong drive to do well; likes to work in settings where tasks and expectations are clearly defined; efficient and well organized
	Lower:	has difficulty in doing best work in settings that have strict rules and regulations; easily distracted; tends to stop working when things do not go well
Ai (Achievement via Independence)	Higher:	has strong drive to do well; likes to work in settings that encourage freedom and individual initiative; clear thinking and intelligent
	Lower:	has difficulty in doing best work in settings that are vague, poorly defined, and lacking in precise specifications; has limited interests in intellectual or cognitive endeavors
Ie (Intellectual Efficiency)	Higher:	efficient in use of intellectual abilities; can keep on at a task where others might give up or get discouraged; insightful and resourceful
	Lower:	has a hard time getting started on cognitive tasks, and seeing them through to completion; has difficulty in expressing ideas

Measures of Role and Personal Style

Scale Name		Implications of Higher and Lower Scores
Py (Psychological-mindedness)	Higher:	insightful and perceptive; understands the feelings of others, but is not necessarily supportive or nurturant
	Lower:	more interested in the practical and concrete than the abstract; looks more at what people do than how they feel or think; often apathetic and seemingly unmotivated
Fx (Flexibility)	Higher:	flexible; likes change and variety; easily bored by routine and everyday experience; may be impatient and even erratic; clever and imaginative, but also careless and loosely organized
	Lower:	not changeable; likes a steady pace and well-organized and predictable situations; conventional and conservative
F/M (Femininity/ Masculinity)	Higher:	among males, high-scores tend to be seen as high-strung, sensitive, and esthetically reactive; females with high scores tend to be seen as sympathetic, warm, and modest, but also dependent
	Lower:	decisive, action-oriented; shows initiative; not easily subdued; rather unsentimental; tough-minded

Attempts have also been made to categorize the CPI scales using a statistical technique known as smallest-space analysis (see Karni & Levin, 1972). Three "vectors" or bipolar continua have been identified using this approach. The first continuum is anchored by Extraversion (e.g., involvement, participative inclinations) on one end and Introversion (e.g., detachment, protective of privacy) on the other (this is analogous to Factor 1 of the FFM). The second continuum is anchored by Norm-Questioning dispositions (e.g., adventurous, unconventional) and Norm-Favoring inclinations (e.g., conscientious, rule respectful). The third continuum varies from strong to weak degrees of Self-Realization, Psychological Competence, and Ego Integration. These vector analyses represent an alternative attempt (in comparison to the FFM) to identify basic personality dimensions.

As an instrument, the CPI is an easily administered (to groups if desired) paper-and-pencil test (computer versions are available). The items ask respondents to provide information regarding their typical behavior patterns, ordinary opinions, and general attitudes relating to various family, social, and ethical concerns. Following are some illustrative true-false items from the Socialization (So) scale:

> Before I do something I try to consider how my friends will react to it. [True, or T, represents the positive pole or socialization.]
> I often think about how I look and what impression I am making upon others. [T]
> I have often gone against my parents' wishes. [False, or F]

Some exemplar items from the Independence (In) scale are as follows:

> I usually expect to succeed in things I do. [T]
> I would be willing to describe myself as a pretty "strong" personality. [T]

The Self-Control (Sc) scale contains items such as the following:

> I often act on the spur of the moment, without stopping to think. [F]
> Sometimes I feel like smashing things. [F]

Overall, the CPI is one of the most extensively researched personality tests on the market. Reviews of the CPI, especially recent ones, have been positive (see Bolton, 1992; Englehard, 1992). In regard to specifics, reliability estimates of both the stability of scale scores over time and the internal consistency of the majority of scales are acceptable. The alpha coefficients (Cronbach, 1951) were computed on a total sample of 6,000 persons (equally split between males and females). The range of the alphas for the folk scales varied from .62 on Psychological-mindedness (Py) to .84 on Well-Being (Wb), with a median of .77. For males only, the alpha coefficients ranged from .43 on Femininity/Masculinity (F/M) to .84 on Wb, with a median of .76. For females only, the alphas ranged from a low of .43 on F/M to a high of .85 on Wb, with a median of .76. Test-retest reliabilities for a sample of high school students ranged from a low of .51 for Communality (Cm) to a high of .84 for F/M, with a median retest correlation of .68.

The empirical validity coefficients for single scales can be quite low and nonsignificant. However, the CPI's usefulness as a predictor of criteria such as academic grades, delinquency, and job performance increases when scores from several scales are combined by means of multiple-regression equations. The CPI has been shown to be a significant predictor of high school and college achievement, grade point averages in medical school, effectiveness of police, and leadership and executive success (see Groth-Marnat, 1990; Hargrave & Hiatt, 1980). Silzer (1986) has reported the findings of two studies conducted by Personnel Decisions, Inc., during the 1970s and 1980s. In one, the Indicators of Management Success Study, several cognitive ability tests were administered together with the CPI to 1,749 managers (representative of all levels and functions of management). Of the then 18 CPI scales, 10 were correlated with management success. In the second study, the Assessment Research Study, a follow-up was conducted on 208 managers from two companies. The CPI again was found to contribute significantly to predictive effectiveness.

Campbell and Van Velsor (1985) have noted the predictability of the CPI in regard to effective leadership behaviors. The CPI was one of several instruments administered during a weeklong leadership development program at the Center for Creative Leadership. The researchers found that the CPI scores for managers who were highly rated as leaders differed significantly from the CPI scores for managers who had lower ratings as leaders. The evaluations of leadership effectiveness were based on the following dimensions: activity level, skills in leading discussions, ability to influence others, ability to analyze problems, task orientation, ability to motivate others, interpersonal skills, and verbal effectiveness. Evaluations were obtained from observers, peers, and self after each person participated in two group exercises. Managers who were rated highly had higher CPI scores than did lower-rated managers on the following CPI scales: Dominance, Self-Acceptance, Capacity for Status, Social Presence, Sociability, Achievement via Conformance, and Intellectual Efficiency.

As we have noted, we have space here only to illustrate a few studies for each instrument. The summary points for the CPI begin with the fact that respondents are asked to complete a ponderous number of items. In return, assessors are provided with measurements on traits that are generally reliable and offer significant empirical validities for a number of criteria. However, these validities, even those based on composite scales, are generally not of impressive magnitude. This suggests either that personality is not an especially important contributor to behavioral adjustment or that self-report measures capture only a portion of the causal influence of personality on behavioral adjustments. We return to this point later in this chapter.

NEO Personality Inventory (Revised).   The NEO Personality Inventory (Revised), or NEO-PI-R (see Costa & McCrae, 1985, 1992a), was developed primarily to measure the dimensions of the FFM described in Chapter 3 (see Table 3.6). The designations used in the NEO for the five factors in the FFM are Extraversion (E), Agreeableness (A), Conscientiousness (C), Neuroticism (N), and Openness to Experience (O). The items in the NEO address behaviors, interests, psychological well-being, and characteristic coping styles. The basic self-report inventory (Form S) requires a sixth-grade reading level and comprises 243 items. There are two other forms as well: Form R for observer ratings and a shorter version of Form S. All items are measured on a 5-point scale ranging from *strongly agree* to *strongly disagree.* Representative items are as follows:

I am not crafty or sly. [a measure of Agreeableness]

Some people think of me as cold and calculating. [Agreeableness; reverse coded]

I'm something of a "workaholic." [Conscientiousness]

Sometimes I'm not as dependable or reliable as I should be. [Conscientiousness; reverse coded]

When I do things, I do them vigorously. [Extraversion]

Many people think of me as somewhat cold and distant. [Extraversion; reverse coded]

In addition to the five primary personality dimensions, the NEO is designed to capture the six underlying facets of each dimension of the FFM. These facets are as follows:

1. *Extraversion:* Warmth, Gregariousness, Assertiveness, Activity, Excitement Seeking, and Positive Emotions
2. *Agreeableness:* Trust, Modesty, Compliance, Altruism, Straightforwardness, and Tender-Mindedness
3. *Conscientiousness:* Competence, Self-Discipline, Achievement Striving, Dutifulness, Order, and Deliberation
4. *Neuroticism:* Anxiety, Hostility, Depression, Self-Consciousness, Impulsiveness, and Vulnerability
5. *Openness to Experience:* Fantasy, Aesthetics, Feeling, Actions, Ideas, and Values

The NEO-PI-R is the result of more than 15 years of research using volunteer samples. With respect to psychometrics, test-retest reliabilities over a 6-month interval have ranged from .86 to .91 for the dimensions of the FFM and from .66 to .92 for the facets. Longer-term test-retest reliability estimates (i.e., 6 years) have been reported to be .80 for N, E, and O on Form S and .75 on Form R. Reviews of the instrument in *The Eleventh Mental Measurements Yearbook* (Kramer & Conoley, 1992) have been positive, noting that the NEO-PI-R scales have good convergent as well as discriminant validity (see Hess, 1992; Widiger, 1992). Convergent validity is evidenced by the fact that the NEO-PI-R facet scales correlate with alternative measures of similarly designated constructs (Costa & McCrae, 1988, 1992b; McCrae, Costa, & Piedmont, 1993). Discriminant validity is provided by evidence that the different facets of the NEO correlate differentially and as expected with alternative measures of the facets.

Additional research suggests that the Conscientiousness scale could be useful in assessing employee reliability (Barrick & Mount, 1991). A recent study supports this view; the researchers found that the Extraversion and Conscientiousness scales predicted absenteeism in a sample of 89 university employees (Judge, Martocchio, & Thoresen, 1997). Clinical research has shown that the NEO may have utility as part of a battery of instruments for assessing psychopathology (see Costa & Widiger, 1994). Although past research on normal, volunteer populations has not shown scores on the NEO to be noticeably distorted by social desirability (Costa & McCrae, 1985), the problem of self-presentation and socially desirable responding may well become an issue in applied settings. We return to the issue of validity for the NEO below, in our review of validities for the FFM.

Hogan Personality Inventory. The Hogan Personality Inventory (HPI) has been used in a variety of applied settings (e.g., military, health, insurance). It was developed in the context of socioanalytic theory (Hogan, 1983, 1986), which is based on the premises that individuals are motivated to engage in social interactions and that, over time, people develop social identities (i.e., agreed-upon trends in social behavior). Social identities are referred to as *reputations* in the Hogan model. Reputations provide a rich source for measurement inasmuch as they are often publicly visible, can be reliably assessed by the self or by others, and can be used to predict future behavior (see Emler, 1990).

Development of the HPI began in the late 1970s as part of a graduate class project on personality assessment. Hogan originally wrote items to reflect dimensions of the FFM. Research conducted as part of item development indicated that items in the subthemes or facets of the FFM clustered together. Hogan designated these groups of related items Homogeneous Item Clusters, or HICs. Items written for HICs were tested on undergraduate samples. After several iterations, 45 HICs, containing 420 items, were identified. These HICs were grouped into six basic dimensions or scales. The HICs and basic scales were further refined over a period of approximately 10 years, culminating in the 1992 HPI (revised edition). This HPI contains 206 true-false items that form the basis for 41 HICs and one validity scale. The 41 HICs are grouped into seven primary scales, which are as follows:

- *Adjustment:* assesses the degree to which an individual appears (a) calm versus tense and (b) self-accepting versus self-critical (37 items, alpha [internal consistency reliability] = .89) (Example item: "I keep calm in a crisis.")

- *Ambition:* measures the extent to which a person seems to be self-confident, active, and competitive (29 items, alpha = .86) (Example item: "I am a very self-confident person.")

- *Sociability:* assesses the degree to which an individual appears to need and/or like interacting with others (24 items, alpha = .83) (Example item: "I like to be the center of attention.")

- *Likability:* measures the extent to which a person perceives him- or herself to be tactful, perceptive, and socially astute (22 items, alpha = .71) (Example item: "I work well with other people.")
- *Prudence:* assesses the degree to which an individual appears to be conscientious, reliable, and conforming (31 items, alpha = .78) (Example item: "I do my job as well as I possibly can.")
- *Intellectance:* measures the extent to which a person seems to be discerning, creative, and attentive to intellectual matters (25 items, alpha = .78) (Example item: "I enjoy solving riddles.")
- *School Success:* assesses the degree to which an individual appears to enjoy academic activities and to value the pursuit of educational achievement (14 items, alpha = .75) (Example item: "I have a rather large vocabulary.")

The average alpha for the seven primary scales is .80; alphas for the HICs vary between .29 and .82. Test-retest reliabilities for the primary scales range from .74 (Prudence) to .86 (Adjustment). As noted above, the HPI contains a validity scale. This scale contains 14 items (alpha = .63) and is designed to detect careless or random responding.

Integral to the HPI is the assumption that various personal characteristics are predictive of job performance. This assumption has been corroborated by Hogan and Hogan (1986), who found the HPI to be correlated with job performance in a variety of settings (e.g., medical, military, insurance, and other occupational settings). Their report is based on 15 studies, which in turn were based on 24 samples (total $N =$ 2,227). Moreover, evidence has been found to support the idea that personality predictors vary depending on the job in question (see Hogan, Hogan, & Busch, 1984; Hogan, Hogan, & Roberts, 1996). Predictors such as Adjustment, Conscientiousness, and Agreeableness have been found to be positive indicators of job performance in "blue-collar" occupations. Conversely, constructs such as Imagination, Ambition, and Sociability are better predictors of job performance for managerial-level positions.

Hogan and Hogan (1995) have demonstrated that the HPI scales correlate in expected directions with other well-known psychological measures (e.g., cognitive ability, motives and interests, normal personality, and dysfunctional personality). They have also updated evidence to support the assumption that job performance is correlated with the HPI. Of further note regarding this well-researched and validated instrument is the HPI's ability to identify individuals who are likely to behave unreliably at work (Hogan & Hogan, 1989).

Effectiveness of the FFM in Predicting
Outcome Criteria in Organizational Settings

Recent meta-analytic results suggest that certain personality dimensions—especially Conscientiousness, which includes achievement striving and dependability—are significantly predictive of job performance criteria (Barrick & Mount, 1991; Hough et al., 1990; Hurtz & Donovan, 2000; Salgado, 1997; Schmidt & Hunter, 1998). The validities are not, however, of impressive magnitude (see Hurtz & Donovan, 2000). Average observed validities for Conscientiousness run less than .20. This means that less than 4% of the variance in job proficiency can be attributed to the best predictor among the personality variables. Even if the validities are corrected for statistical artifacts (unreliability, range restriction), the "corrected validities" for Conscientiousness average only .31 according to the most recent review (Schmidt & Hunter, 1998; the uncorrected coefficient was not reported). Meta-analytic results for the other dimensions of the FFM indicate that validities are lower on average against real-world job performance. For example, Hough et al. (1990) found that Adjustment (Emotional Stability, Factor 4 in the FFM; see Table 3.6) had a corrected coefficient of .23 against job proficiency (the uncorrected correlation was .13).

Irrespective of the somewhat disappointing results indicated by the meta-analyses, the past decade has witnessed renewed interest in the study of relationships between self-reports of personality, usually involving one or more of the FFM dimensions, and occupational outcomes. Research conducted by Gandy, Dye, and MacLane (1994) is illustrative. These investigators found that supervisory ratings of job performance were correlated significantly with NEO-PI-R scores in a national sample of more than 1,500 respondents. The Conscientiousness dimension exhibited the strongest pattern of correlations. It was found to relate to the quantity, quality, and accuracy of work as well as to overall judgments of competence. Furthermore, supervisory appraisals were also correlated with oral communication, written comprehension, reasoning, rule conformity, ability to overcome obstacles, and adaptability to changing work demands. Here again, however, validities were of low magnitude.

Also illustrative is a study by Piedmont and Weinstein (1994), who, in a subsequent analysis of their 1993 data, examined the degree to which scores on the NEO-PI-R predicted job performance ratings. Conscien-

tiousness and its subscales were the strongest predictors of job performance ([corrected] $rs = 0.15$ to 0.28). Extraversion correlated with suc-
cess ratings on Interpersonal Relations ($r = 0.20$), Task Orientation ($r = 0.16$), and Adaptive Capacity ($r = 0.19$). Neuroticism was negatively
correlated with Interpersonal Relations ($r = -0.16$) and Adaptive Ca-
pacity ($r = -0.17$).

As final illustrations, Barrick and Mount (1993) conclude that the degree of autonomy in the job moderates the relationship between the
personality dimensions and job performance. They found higher, albeit
modest, validities for Conscientiousness and Extraversion within jobs
involving a higher degree of autonomy than in jobs low in autonomy.
Dimensions from the FFM have also been shown to predict absenteeism. Judge et al. (1997) found that Extraversion (uncorrected $r = .26$)
and Conscientiousness ($r = -.23$) predicted this criterion.

Results such as those described above have led some authors (e.g.,
Barrick & Mount, 1991, 1993) to champion the FFM for predicting job
performance. Other investigators, such as Cortina, Doherty, Schmitt,
Kaufman, and Smith (1992), have voiced reservations about the FFM
(see also Hurtz & Donovan, 2000; Schmit & Ryan, 1993). Cortina et al.
tested utilization of the FFM in selection decisions without much success. These authors hypothesized that the history of validation research
for personality was unimpressive due to the lack of a well-accepted taxonomy for classifying personality variables. Their test of the FFM, however, did not provide evidence to support the notion that the FFM structure engenders increases in the predictive power of personality
variables. In a related vein, Tett et al. (1991) conducted a meta-analysis
of validities based only on those studies that used a confirmatory research design (e.g., tested a priori hypotheses regarding the relationship
between personality and job performance). They concluded that the
Agreeableness dimension had the greatest predictive potential, although all average validities were low and most had confidence inter-
vals that included zero.

The FFM and teams.   In a recent meta-analysis, Mount, Barrick, and
Stewart (1998) found that the dimensions of Conscientiousness, Agreeableness, and Emotional Stability were positively, albeit modestly (.10s
for uncorrected rs, .20s for corrected rs), related to performance in jobs
that involve interpersonal interactions. Furthermore, they found the
dimensions of Emotional Stability and Agreeableness to be related to

performance in jobs that require teamwork (where each employee interacts interdependently with team coworkers) versus in jobs involving only dyadic interactions with others (where each employee performs a direct service to clients—not involving other coworkers).

The proliferation of self-managed teams in work organizations has triggered interest in how the personalities of team members are related to group processes and outcomes. Using covariance structure modeling, Barry and Stewart (1997) found that Extraversion was in fact related significantly to group processes and outcomes. The relationships between Conscientiousness and these same criteria were nonsignificant, contrary to expectations. Barry and Stewart conclude that personality correlates of group performance might vary significantly from those that predict individual effectiveness on the job. One plausible explanation for this conclusion is that Conscientiousness may decrease in importance with team-based activities due to the ability of others to compensate for the lack of some conscientious group members.

In another study of team effectiveness, Barrick, Stewart, Neubert, and Mount (1998) found that team composition (i.e., ability and personality of team members) was operationalized in terms of (a) average scores of team members on ability and personality variables and (b) variation among team members on these same variables. Results demonstrated that teams higher in average General Mental Ability (GMA), Extraversion, Conscientiousness, Agreeableness, and Emotional Stability received higher supervisory ratings for their team performance. In addition, teams higher in average GMA, Extraversion, and Emotional Stability were perceived by their supervisors to have greater team viability. The researchers attributed this result to the belief that teams higher in Extraversion and Emotional Stability would be more likely to experience positive intragroup interactions.

Another interesting finding was a negative relationship between variation in Conscientiousness and team performance. Barrick et al. suggest that although higher average levels of Conscientiousness are desirable, the mixture of Conscientiousness within a team could be critical. A mixture of both conscientious and not-so-conscientious team members tended to lower team performance. The investigators infer that feelings of contribution inequity and/or the increase in workload on the more conscientious team members (who must not only perform their own work but also do or redo the work of less conscientious members) has a negative impact on overall team performance.

The FFM and vocational interests. Increased attention is being directed toward the relationships between personality dimensions and vocational or occupational interest. Research conducted by Matthews and Stanton (1994) has demonstrated that the 31 scales contained within the Occupational Personality Questionnaire (OPQ) are, following factor analysis, supportive of the FFM. Evidence has also been generated that indicates there is considerable overlap between measures of personality and measures of vocational interest. Costa, McCrae, and Holland (1984) correlated an early version of the NEO Personality Inventory (measuring only three dimensions of the FFM—Neuroticism, Extraversion, and Openness) with Holland's (1985b) Self-Directed Search measure. Neuroticism was not related to vocational interests. In contrast, Extraversion was strongly related to Social and Enterprising vocations, whereas Openness was negatively related to Conventional interests and positively related to Artistic and Investigative interests. Holland, Johnston, Hughey, and Asama (1991) replicated the finding that Openness is related to vocational interests, and demonstrated further that Openness is correlated with creativity.

In sum, there appears to be a reasonable relationship between at least some dimensions of the FFM and vocational interests. These results are consistent with our discussion in Chapter 2 in which we have suggested that values and interests give direction to needs. Using achievement motivation as an example, we showed that interests influence the specific activity or activities through which people high in achievement motivation (AMs) attempt to satisfy their strong desires to achieve. Specifically, vocational interests represent individuals' conscious or self-described desires, goals, preferred modes of conduct, preferred rewards and incentives, expectations, and plans. AMs would thus be expected to be interested in vocations that offer them challenges and opportunities to accomplish important tasks. This in turn suggests a significant relationship between needs as assessed by personality and interests as assessed by vocational inventories.

Debates regarding the predictive utility of the FFM.   Several researchers have argued that the FFM is too broad to have serious predictive utility (e.g., Briggs, 1989, 1992; McAdams, 1992; Tett et al., 1991). Some research has supported this premise. Hough (1992) has demonstrated that a nine-factor taxonomy produced higher validities in predicting job performance than did the five-factor model. Cellar, Miller, Dover-spike, and Klawsky (1996) recently championed a six-factor model using data from the NEO-PI-R. Others have noted that specific facets (e.g., Affiliation and Social Confidence) are more predictive of job performance than are the more global measures of the FFM (Saville, Nyfield, Sik, & Hackston, 1991). In like manner, Smither and Hogan (1993) found that subscales of the HPI related better to job criteria than did the major factor scales.

It has been suggested that the usefulness of the FFM may be limited because the factor structure of personality varies in different populations. McCrae and Costa (1987, 1989, 1990) argue against this supposition because the factor structure of the NEO is stable in samples of volunteers. Invariance of the factor structure in job applicant populations has yet to be firmly demonstrated for the NEO. There is reason to be concerned. Schmit and Ryan (1993), for example, examined the factor structure of the FFM in both applicant and nonapplicant populations. They found that the model fit the nonapplicant population better than it did the applicant population. This finding is consistent with the findings from earlier research conducted by Hogan and Hogan (1992) and McAdams (1992).

On the other hand, as reviewed earlier, meta-analyses by Barrick and Mount (1991) and Hough et al. (1990) indicate that at least one factor —Conscientiousness—is a modestly valid predictor across diverse occupational groups and multiple job-related criteria. Additional corroboration for this finding is provided by the Project A work in the U.S. Army Selection and Classification Study (McHenry, Hough, Toquam, Hanson, & Ashworth, 1990).

In sum, the cross-situational consistency of the factor structure and validity of the FFM is unresolved. Data are available to support either side of a dialectic. This is often indicative of a situation in which moderators are yet to be identified that explain when and where consistency is and is not likely to occur.

We close this section with a quote from a personal communication we received from B. Schneider (1997):

I am concerned . . . that the penchant for adopting the language and the constructs of the FFM as the answer to all of our questions regarding validity will result in the current interest in personality being just another fad in applied psychology. . . . Thus, although the FFM has been extremely useful as a unifying set of general constructs, it has not much improved the criterion-related validity coefficients being reported in the literature.

We agree.

Contamination of Self-Reports Due to Social Desirability

Generally speaking, individuals who complete self-report personality inventories to gain self-insight or to seek guidance will be motivated to give truthful answers. However, people also take self-report personality inventories as part of applying for or even keeping jobs. In this context, some individuals might consciously or unconsciously attempt to answer the items in ways that they think will make them appear to be desirable candidates or employees. One of the most serious and unresolved limitations of personality inventories is that of respondents' faking and/or providing socially desirable responses to personality items (Nunnally, 1978).

The general concern has been that some respondents consciously choose their answers so as to manage (i.e., influence, direct) the impressions that others have of them. Simply stated, they want others to view them in favorable ways, although occasionally respondents seek the opposite perception (e.g., unstable, disagreeable, unreliable). Hogan et al. (1996) refer to attempts to manage impressions as individuals' natural and functional attempt to manage their "reputations." It is also the case that even though some respondents may be willing to tell the truth about themselves, as they know it, they nonetheless unknowingly distort the truth and subsequently provide biased responses. Edwards (1957a), in fact, construes the social desirability variable to be analogous to a person's "putting up a good front," often unknowingly. Research in social cognition supports this view. Fiske and Taylor (1991), for example, have documented a number of unconscious biases that people employ to describe themselves and their behavior in ego-enhancing and/or ego-protective ways. Many of these biases are represented in the justification mechanisms we have discussed in Chapters 1 through 3.

Attempts to measure the tendency to respond in a socially desirable manner. A number of omnibus personality inventories, such as the CPI, are scored using special procedures that are designed to identify people who seek socially desirable responses. Generally, these "faking scales" are based on answers to items that are infrequently chosen by people who answer candidly. These answers are, however, preferred a significantly greater proportion of the time by those who are trying "to fake good" (and in some cases "fake bad") on the inventory. Other scales have been developed specifically to identify individuals who are drawn to socially desirable responses. These scales may be given separately or included in an omnibus instrument. For illustrative purposes, we will briefly describe two such scales: the Edwards Social Desirability Scale (SD) and the Marlowe-Crowne Social Desirability Scale (MCSD).

The Edwards Social Desirability Scale (Edwards, 1957b) is composed of 39 true-false items. Sample items are as follows (the socially desirable response is indicated for each):

I am happy most of the time. [T]

I sometimes feel that I am about to go to pieces. [F]

My hands and feet are usually warm enough. [T]

No one cares much what happens to you. [F]

Internal consistency reliabilities are in the acceptable range for this scale. Validity issues are addressed with the more frequently employed Marlowe-Crowne Social Desirability Scale.

The MCSD is the instrument that researchers usually choose to measure susceptibility to socially desirable responses. Crowne and Marlowe (1964) proposed this scale to assess the "need for approval." The MCSD is based on an instrument constructed in 1960 to measure socially desirable responding. Crowne and Marlowe (1960) constructed the MCSD to measure need for approval using a self-report instrument and to improve upon the Edwards (1957a) scale. Noting that Edwards's items were often founded in pathology, Crowne and Marlowe focused their items on common personal and interpersonal behaviors. They started with 50 true-false items, 33 of which survived various forms of reliability and validity analyses. The items in the MCSD are statements concerning personal attitudes and traits on (a) desirable but uncommon behaviors or (b) undesirable but common behaviors. Representative items include the following (keyed responses are in brackets):

Before voting I thoroughly investigate the qualifications of all the candidates. [T]

I sometimes try to get even, rather than forgive and forget. [F]

I like to gossip at times. [F]

I am always careful about my manner of dress. [T]

The higher the score on this scale, the greater the inferred need for approval. Crowne and Marlowe (1964) found satisfactory internal consistency coefficients, ranging from .73 to .88. In addition, they found a test-retest reliability of .88 over a 1-month interval. Fisher (1967) found a value of .84 for a test-retest reliability based on a 1-week interval. Based on several construct validity studies, Crowne and Marlowe (1964) proposed that high scorers on the MCSD prefer low-risk behaviors and avoid the evaluation of others. Indeed, high scorers on the MCSD share many of the characteristics we have described in Chapter 2 for people high in fear of failure. Reviewers have been fairly supportive of the need for approval construct (Millham & Jacobson, 1978; Strickland, 1977). The construct interpretation has shifted, however, to one of "avoiding disapproval" as opposed to the original connotation of seeking approval (Crowne, 1979). This again is reminiscent of fear of failure.

Validity evidence for socially desirable responding in self-report personality measures is "plentiful," according to Anastasi's (1982, p. 520) highly regarded book on testing. Nunnally (1967) concludes:

> There no longer is room for argument about the statistical importance of scales constructed to measure social desirability. They explain so much of the variance of individual differences in responses to self-inventories that statistical arguments concern whether or not there is enough independent variance in such inventories to continue investigating them. (p. 480)

This harsh judgment is mitigated by Hogan et al.'s cogent reminder that it is natural if not psychologically healthy for individuals to attempt to manage, both consciously and unconsciously, their reputations. Whereas socially desirable responding may reflect intentional misrepresentation, lack of insight, self-deception, and avoidance of owning up to faults, it may just as well indicate self-protection and coping with psychologically harmful events as well as individuals' attempts to conform to social mores, to satisfy need for social approval, and to perceive themselves in a favorable and self-accepting manner (Anastasi, 1982).

Recent research on faking in organizational settings continues to engender a dialectic regarding the prevalence of faking and, especially, the effects of faking on the accuracy and validity of scores on self-report personality instruments (Barrick & Mount, 1996; Becker & Colquitt, 1992; Douglas, McDaniel, & Snell, 1996; Hogan, 1991; Hough et al., 1990; Kluger, Reilly, & Russell, 1991; Ones, Viswesvaran, & Reiss, 1996; Paulhus, Bruce, & Trapnell, 1995; Rosse, Stecher, Miller, & Levin, 1998; Ryan & Sackett, 1987; Schmit, Ryan, Stierwalt, & Powell, 1995; Snell & McDaniel, 1998). One side of the argument, represented by Hough et al. (1990), Hough and Schneider (1996), and Ones et al. (1996), is that socially desirable responding (a) decreases accuracy of self-reports (e.g., scores on personality scales shift toward the socially desirable endpoint) but (b) does not affect the validity of self-reports in predicting behavioral criteria. Indeed, Hough and Schneider (1996) conclude that social desirability is a "mythical moderator" (p. 35; i.e., has no effect on empirical validities between self-reports and criteria).

Those on the other side of the argument, represented by Douglas et al. (1996), Kluger et al. (1991), Rosse et al. (1998), and Snell and McDaniel (1998), agree that socially desirable responding decreases the accuracy of self-reports of personality. These authors also contend that socially desirable responding detracts from the usefulness of self-reports for the valid prediction of job performance criteria.

In sum, essentially everyone agrees that socially desirable responding engenders conscious and nonconscious distortions in responses to personality inventories. Basically, many people, but not all (see Rosse et al., 1998), attempt to alter their scores on self-report personality measures. Whether response distortions moderate empirical validities for the self-report measures appears open to debate for now, but evidence appears to be mounting that validities are lowered in evocative contexts such as personnel selection.

Now let us add a third point. No one seems to mention that the observed validities, moderated or not, are low (i.e., fall below .30 with a mean of about .12). It is our belief that the ceiling of .30 provided by self-reports vastly underestimates the salient role that personality plays as a causal factor in behavior. We believe further that something should be done about this asymptote. Our suggestion is not to replace self-reports. Hogan is correct in noting that how one perceives oneself is an important component of personality irrespective of imperfections in the perceptions. In Chapter 5, we introduce two concepts new to personality research: *channeling hypotheses* and *integrating models*. Research based on these concepts has led to significant increases in validities for personality measures. Self-reports are included in these measures, but so are projective techniques. Thus, to set the stage for discussions of new and productive research paradigms, we now proceed to an overview of projective techniques.

Projective Techniques

Self-report inventories reflect respondents' ascriptions of behaviors, desires, intentions, goals, motives, and reasons for action to themselves based on their conscious perceptions (McClelland, Koestner, & Weinberger, 1989). Significant validities between self-reports of personality and behavioral outcomes suggest that these self-ascriptions are useful for understanding personality and for predicting behavioral adjustments to environments. However, self-report measures tend to be most effective in predicting short-term behavioral adjustments that require extensive cost-benefit analyses and comparisons of alternative models of behavior. They are less able to predict long-term behavioral trends or reactions to novel, especially evocative, stimulation. Several researchers consider long-term trends and responses to novel/evocative stimulation to be principally products of implicit or "latent" motives (see McClelland et al., 1989). We consider the concept of latent motive below in the context of achievement motivation and our prior discussion of the motive to achieve in Chapter 2.

In Chapter 2, we described the motive to achieve as latent, meaning having latent components, because people with a strong and dominant need to achieve (AMs) could not explain why they experienced positive feelings (e.g., excitement) toward approaching demanding tasks. Basically, AMs are not aware that an underlying force is partially responsible for energizing, selecting, and directing their actions toward devoting intense and persistent effort to demanding tasks (see McClelland, 1985a, 1985b; McClelland et al., 1989). What AMs are aware of are the end products of these processes, which are strong desires to do better than others, to take on challenging tasks, to compete with others and win, and to anticipate and then experience the thrill of the chase. They are also aware that they experience urges to approach high-press-for-achievement tasks because they inherently associate positive affect with these tasks (e.g., enthusiasm, recognition, excitement, pride). AMs cannot, however, explain why these associations occur (see Atkinson, 1957, 1978; McClelland, 1985a, 1985b; Raynor, 1978), nor can they control the strength of the positive affect. Most important, they cannot describe the respective strengths of their motives to achieve.

McClelland, Atkinson, Clark, and Lowell (1953/1976) have recommended use of the Thematic Apperception Test (TAT) to estimate the strength of the latent motive to achieve. The TAT is a "projective" measure, which in the present context means that the test is designed to stimulate respondents to reveal what for them are inaccessible motives by mapping—that is, projecting—their feelings, defenses, and justifications onto "fantasies" that they are asked to make up about ambiguous stimuli (i.e., pictures). (Projective measurement connotes that respondents are free to offer unstructured responses to vague stimuli.) Use of the TAT to measure the latent motive to achieve is perhaps the primary use of projective techniques in research on personality in organizational settings. We shall focus on this approach here.

The TAT was introduced in 1935 by Christina Morgan and Henry Murray. It was developed to provide a mechanism for measuring the needs and presses of Murray's need-press personality theory, described earlier (see Chapter 3; Table 3.1 displays a list of Murray's needs). The TAT is composed of a pool of 30 cards with black-and-white pictures plus one blank card. The picture on each card depicts an ambiguous situation. Which pictures any given respondent sees is determined by the need or set of needs to be measured. The selected pictures are presented to the respondent one at a time, accompanied by a request for the respondent to make up a plot or a story to go along with the picture.

More specifically, the respondent is asked to indicate what is happening in the picture at that given moment, what led up to the scene in the picture, and how the story ends. Card 1, for example, depicts a young, neatly dressed boy who is contemplating a violin that rests in front of him on a table. According to TAT experts (e.g., Bellak, 1986), Card 1 of the TAT tends to uncover an individual's relationships with parental figures. Within a middle-class American culture, the picture on this card is thought to be a prototype for achievement dramas. The violin and learning to play it are representative of achievement in general. The presence of a child in the picture tends to evoke personal childhood dilemmas from the respondent. Other persons are not included in the picture, enabling the subject to project early family surroundings onto the picture as well. A story that relates to achievement is thus expected.

Murray believed that respondents project their past experiences and present needs onto the fantasies or stories they construct for the TAT pictures. Respondents' stories for each of the cards presented are scored for the desired needs (and perceptions of environmental presses). Murray (1943) found that the average story length is about 300 words for adults and 150 words for children.

The TAT became a key methodology for some researchers who used it to measure important aspects of personality (e.g., Atkinson, 1981; Cramer & Blatt, 1990; McClelland, 1985b; Turner, 1970). Many of the needs identified by Murray (see Table 3.1) have been investigated using the TAT. In fact, more than 100 studies have used the TAT to assess the need for achievement (Birney, 1968; Winter, 1987). Many of these studies have been conducted by McClelland and/or his students. A synopsis of empirical validities for the need to achieve and other needs is presented in McClelland's 1985 book *Human Motivation* as well as in a later article by McClelland et al. (1989). Unfortunately, the validities are neither extensive nor of impressive magnitudes. Other needs that have been measured frequently via the TAT include affiliation and power (see Winter, 1987).

Murray's scoring system for the TAT is quite complex and is not widely used today, which is also true of other early scoring systems (see Bellack, Parsquarelli, & Branerman, 1949; Rotter, 1946; Tomkins, 1947). The half dozen administration and scoring systems in use today involve both oral and written response formats (see Vane, 1981). The McClelland-Atkinson approach involves exposing subjects to motive-arousing experiences prior to elicitation of stories from selected TAT pictures (Atkinson, 1958; Atkinson & McClelland, 1948; McClelland et al., 1953/1976). Nevertheless, the scoring protocols for the TAT are based on content analyses and remain quite subjective. Many psychologists are apprehensive about using projective tests. A number of psychometricians are less circumspect in their criticism of the TAT and other projective techniques, as we shall see below.

Psychometric Evaluation

Despite arguments to the contrary by McClelland (see 1985b), interrater reliabilities and construct validity of the scoring systems designed to score the free-response, fantasy-based projective tests have long been, and continue to be, of concern to psychometricians (Aiken, 1994; Anastasi, 1982; Cohen, Montague, Nathenson, & Swerdlik, 1988;

Groth-Marnat, 1984; Kaplan, 1982). A particularly disquieting feature is that scores on the TAT rely on subjective content analyses of completely unstructured responses to evocative pictures. Not only may a respondent be inconsistent in his or her fantasies on different occasions, but the highly subjective scoring of a particular respondent may be a function of who does the scoring and whether responses are in oral or written form (see Dana, 1982). The following summaries of recent reviews are reflective of the general opinions of test experts regarding the use of projective techniques, and the TAT in particular:

> Among their shortcomings are inadequacies of administration, scoring, and standardization. The lack of objectivity in scoring and the paucity and deficiency of representative normative data are particularly bothersome to specialists in psychometrics. (Aiken, 1994)

> Aside from their questionable theoretical rationale, projective techniques are clearly found wanting with regard to standardization of administration and scoring procedures, adequacy of norms, reliability, and validity. (Anastasi, 1982)

> Many experts consider the TAT, like the Rorschach, to be psychometrically unsound. With the unstandardized procedures for administration, scoring, and interpretation, it is easy to understand why psychometric evaluations have produced inconsistent, unclear, and conflicting findings. (Kaplan, 1982)

> Apparently most projective techniques do a rather poor job of measuring personality traits, tend to have unacceptably low reliabilities, are rather unstandardized, and are psychometrically unsound vehicles for measuring anything. (Nunnally, 1978)

> Although the TAT was relatively well received, its psychometric adequacy was, and still is, questioned. (Keiser & Prather, 1990)

In sum, the popularity of one of the most important projective tests, the TAT, increased rapidly during the late 1930s and early 1940s. This may have been due, in part, to some disillusionment with structured personality tests (Dahlstrom, 1969). In more recent times, projective techniques have fallen into disfavor. In regard to the TAT, there has been a decrease in its application (Piotrowski & Heller, 1989; Piotrowski & Lubin, 1990) as well as in research involving it (Polyson, Norris, & Ott, 1985). One cannot help but believe that critiques such as the above contributed to the general demise of whatever interest there once was in projective tests.

Conditional Reasoning Measures

Schwarz (1999) recently buttressed a point we made earlier in this chapter, that self-report inventories serve as the primary source of data for personality research. The subject matter for self-reports concentrates on individuals' *conscious cognitions,* including but not limited to their self-ascribed motives, values, beliefs, goals, interests, and behavioral dispositions (see Greenwald & Banaji, 1995; McClelland et al., 1989). In Chapters 1 through 3, we discussed the mounting evidence that *implicit or unconscious social cognitions* provide an additional, important, and often unique (in relation to self-reports) source of data on personality (see Greenwald & Banaji, 1995; McClelland et al., 1989; Wegner & Vallacher, 1977; Westen, 1991; Winter, John, Stewart, Klohnen, & Duncan, 1998).

Implicit social cognitions are components of cognitive structure (e.g., implicit motives, justification mechanisms) and cognitive process (e.g., selective attention) that (a) determine individuals' perceptual, emotional, and behavioral adjustments to their environments (see Allport, 1937; Millon, 1990) but (b) are not accessible to individuals through introspection (see Epstein, 1994; Erdelyi, 1992; Greenwald & Banaji, 1995; Kilstrom, 1999; Nisbett & Wilson, 1977; Westen, 1990, 1991; Winter et al., 1998).

We have discussed implicit motives in Chapter 2 and in the preceding subsection on projective techniques. Implicit biases in reasoning are another primary category of implicit social cognitions. Implicit biases in reasoning often take the form of justification mechanisms, which we have defined in previous chapters as unconscious predilections to reason in ways that enhance the rational appeal of motive-based or dispositional behavior. We have described JMs for aggression in Chapter 1 and JMs for achievement/fear of failure in Chapter 2. We have presented general domains of implicit reasoning biases and justification mechanisms in Chapter 3, where we also discussed their effects on reasoning strategies.

Implicitness in social cognitions is believed to be a function of one or more of the following factors (see Baumeister, 1982; Baumeister & Scher, 1988; Brewin, 1989; Fiske & Taylor, 1984, 1991; Greenwald & Banaji, 1995; Kilstrom, 1999; Miller, 1987; Nisbett & Wilson, 1977; Pyszczynski & Greenberg, 1987; Ross, 1977; Schneider, 1991; Taylor, 1991; Westen, 1990, 1991; Winter et al., 1998):

- Basic biological drives that have not reached consciousness
- Developmental or learning experiences that have been lost to memory
- Cognitive processing that was at one time consciously controlled but has become automatic and lost to introspection
- Cognitive processes that unconsciously serve to enhance or to protect self-esteem and subjective well-being

By virtue of their being hidden from introspection, implicit social cognitions cannot be assessed through the use of self-reports (see Greenwald & Banaji, 1995; Nisbett & Wilson, 1977). To study implicit (social) cognitions, Greenwald and Banaji (1995) note, "indirect measurements are theoretically essential" (p. 5). These authors state further that "investigations of implicit cognitions require indirect measures, which neither inform the subject of what is being assessed nor request self-report concerning it" (p. 5). Winter et al. (1998) offer similar views, agreeing with Greenwald and Banaji and asserting that "motives (like other cognitions) may often be *implicit,* that is, not accessible to consciousness and therefore measurable only by indirect means" (p. 232).

Indirect measures "are identifiable chiefly by their lack of the defining feature of direct measures, that is, by their not alerting the subject to the identity of the [variable] being measured" (Greenwald & Banaji, 1995, p. 8). The projective techniques reviewed above are indirect measures. In regard to psychometric development, Greenwald and Banaji (1995) base the following conclusion on a review of the current state of indirect measurement:

Research on latency decomposition, projective tests, and miscellaneous other procedures indicate indirect measurement of individual differences in implicit social cognition is possible. At the same time, such measurement has not yet been achieved in the efficient form needed to make research investigation of individual differences in implicit social cognition a routine undertaking. (p. 20)

They go on to say that when efficient indirect methods are developed and made available, "there should follow the rapid development of a new industry of research on implicit cognitive aspects of personality and social behavior" (p. 20).

It is noteworthy that Greenwald and Banaji (1995) do not believe that projective techniques offer an "efficient" way to measure implicit social cognitions. A measurement system is efficient when it produces a valid assessment with a minimum of effort, expense, and error. It is unlikely that projective techniques will ever be considered "efficient," if for no other reason than the lengthy amount of time required to score their open-ended and subjective responses.

In the next section, we describe a recently introduced attempt to build an efficient, indirect measurement system for implicit social cognitions. This system is efficient in the sense that it has been shown to furnish valid assessments (observed empirical validities are comparatively high) with a minimum of effort/expense (it is based on paper-and-pencil testing, can be administered to large groups of individuals, and is easily scored) and error (it is reliable). The target of measurement is the individual's facility in using and willingness to use implicit reasoning biases—namely, justification mechanisms—when reasoning. Below, we describe a system developed to measure whether individuals have the facility and willingness to use the justification mechanisms for aggression that we described in Chapter 1.

This discussion is illustrative. It builds on prior research in which the system was first used to measure whether people implicitly reason in ways that justify avoiding as opposed to approaching achievement-oriented tasks (James, 1998). In the following section we demonstrate how the system may be generalized to measure implicit reasoning biases associated with other behaviors; in this specific instance, the behavior of interest is aggression.

An Efficient, Indirect System for
Measuring Implicit Reasoning Biases

We begin with a review of material presented in Chapter 1 regarding the implicit reasoning biases (justification mechanisms) associated with aggression. The present treatment is augmented by a more intensive treatment of implicit reasoning biases for aggression.

The conceptual foundation for the indirect measurement system rests on four propositions. The first of these defines the objective of measurement, which, as discussed above, is whether individuals possess the facility and willingness to use justification mechanisms for aggression. The second proposition addresses how individual differences occur in the facility and willingness to use these implicit reasoning biases. The third proposition specifies how individual differences in the facility and willingness to use these implicit reasoning biases can be measured indirectly. The fourth and final proposition defines how scores furnished by the indirect measurement system are to be interpreted. The overview of the measurement system presented below is organized in terms of these four propositions.

- *Proposition 1:* Aggressive individuals often engage in the use of implicit reasoning biases to enhance the rational appeal of their aggressive behavior.

Murray (1938) defines the motive to aggress as a desire to overcome opposition forcefully, to fight, to revenge an injury, to attack another with intent to injure or kill, and to oppose forcefully or punish another. Contemporary work on aggression combines both the implicit and explicit components of this motive (see Winter et al., 1998) with trait-based behavior to describe the "aggressive individual." An aggressive individual (a) chooses to use some form of aggression, including passive aggression, to deal with evocative, especially frustrating, situations; (b) dislikes if not hates the target of aggression; (c) desires to inflict harm on this target; (d) has diminished self-regulatory capacities, which suggests underdeveloped internal prohibitions or standards against aggressing (although sufficient self-regulation may be present to make the aggression indirect and/or passive); and (e) sees limited response options, which denotes that the individual sees aggression as the most efficacious response to frustration and anger (see Bandura, 1973; Baron & Richardson, 1994; Baumeister, Smart, & Boden, 1996; Berkowitz, 1993; Crick & Dodge, 1994; Gay, 1993; Huesmann, 1988; Millon, 1990; O'Leary-Kelly, Griffin, & Glew, 1996).

Aggressive individuals tend to behave in ways that others might describe as antagonistic, belligerent, bellicose, combative, contentious, hostile, malicious, malevolent, offensive, obstreperous, pugnacious, truculent, unfriendly, or "passive-aggressive" (see the reference citations above). But aggressive people want to believe that their behavior is justified. That is, they want such things as fighting with peers, being in-subordinate, withholding effort, and engaging in intentionally harmful criticisms of others to appear as rational and sensible, as opposed to ir-rational or foolish (see Anderson, 1994; Gay, 1993; James, 1998; Tedeschi & Nesler, 1993; Toch, 1993).

Consequently, aggressive individuals often attempt to enhance the rational appeal of their hostile acts by casting them as forms of self-de-fense intended to respond to physical or verbal attacks initiated by their targets (see Anderson, 1994; Averill, 1993; Baron & Richardson, 1994; Baumeister et al., 1996; Berkowitz, 1993; Brehmer, 1976; Crick & Dodge, 1994; Felson & Tedeschi, 1993; Gay, 1993; Huesmann, 1988; James, 1998; Millon, 1990; Tedeschi & Nesler, 1993; Toch, 1993). This attempt to justify aggression as self-defense is often a product of im-plicit biases in the causal attributions made by the aggressor about the behaviors of a target(s).

For example, the aggressor may harbor an unconscious predilection to see or to seek out malevolent purpose or harmful intent as the moti-vation for the behavior of a target (see Crick & Dodge, 1994; Dodge & Coie, 1987). Indeed, this bias may permeate the aggressive person's im-plicit cognitive system such that he or she views the actions of others through a prism that leads him or her to evaluate those actions as stem-ming from hostile or malevolent intent (see Anderson, 1994; Tedeschi & Nesler, 1993; Toch, 1993). With this bias in place, an aggressive person may see even a benign or friendly act by another person, such as an offer to assist on a project, as having a hidden, hostile agenda designed inten-tionally to inflict harm, either now or in the future (e.g., by pretending to assist, the target can sabotage the aggressor's work or make the ag-gressor look incompetent). The implicit proclivity to see or seek out hostile intent as a reasonable cause of the behaviors of others has been designated the Hostile Attribution Bias (see Crick & Dodge, 1994; Dodge & Coie, 1987).

A second implicit reasoning bias that serves to justify aggression is re-ferred to as the Retribution Bias. This bias involves an unconscious ten-dency to confer logical priority to reparation or retaliation over recon-ciliation (see Anderson, 1994; Baumeister et al., 1996; Bradbury & Fincham, 1990; Crick & Dodge, 1994; Dodge, 1986; Laursen & Collins, 1994; Nisbett, 1993). This bias is reflected in an implicit proclivity to de-termine that aggression is a reasonable response if the intent of the be-havior is to restore respect or to exact restitution for a perceived wrong.

The Retribution Bias is especially apparent in reasoning that tacitly indicates that a person would rather retaliate than forgive, be vindicated as opposed to cooperate, or obtain revenge rather than maintain a relationship. This bias underlies classic justifications for aggression based on wounded pride, challenged self-esteem, and perceived disrespect.

Additional justifications for aggression include the Derogation of Target Bias and the Victimization by Powerful Others Bias. The Derogation of Target Bias consists of an unconscious tendency to characterize targets as deserving of aggression because they are evil, immoral, or untrustworthy (see Averill, 1993; Gay, 1993; Toch, 1993). This bias may or may not be accompanied by an inclination to attend selectively to, indeed seek out, what the aggressor regards as acts of inequity, exploitation, injustice, and oppression by powerful others such as supervisors, teachers, employing organizations, and institutions (e.g., the Internal Revenue Service). Selective attention and confirmatory searches both engender and reinforce unconscious inclinations to conclude that one is being victimized by powerful others. Reasoning is thus said to be shaped implicitly by the Victimization by Powerful Others Bias. This reasoning is used to justify acts of aggression toward others as warranted corrections of inequities or legitimate strikes against oppression (see Averill, 1993; Finnegan, 1997; Tedeschi & Nesler, 1993; Toch, 1993).

A particularly compelling example of the implicit nature of justifications for aggression is the Potency Bias (James, 1998). Many aggressive individuals filter interactions with others through a prism that frames these interactions as contests to establish dominance versus submissiveness (see Anderson, 1994; Baron & Richardson, 1994; Crick & Dodge, 1994; Gay, 1993; Hogan & Hogan, 1989; Millon, 1990; Tedeschi & Nesler, 1993; Wright & Mischel, 1987). Such framing is the cornerstone for reasoning that suggests that acting aggressively is a demonstration of strength, bravery, or fearlessness, and that not acting aggressively is a sign of weakness, fearfulness, cowardliness, or impotence. An aggressive person may thus justify aggression by reasoning that (a) aggression is an act of strength or bravery that gains respect from others or (b) to show weakness is to invite powerful others to take advantage of you.

A sixth and final bias is the Social Discounting Bias. This bias involves a tendency to favor socially unorthodox and antisocial reasons as logically probable causes of social events and relationships (see Finnegan, 1997; Gay, 1993; Huesmann, 1988; Loeber & Stouthamer-Loeber, 1998;

Millon, 1990; Toch, 1993). Such reasoning indicates a tendency to have disdain for traditional ideals and conventional beliefs. Framing and analysis further point to a lack of sensitivity, empathy, and concern for social customs, often with an accompanying lack of prohibitions against aggression. Analyses of social events lean toward the cynical and critical, with an intent to belittle and denigrate, and a proclivity to associate positive outcomes with aggression.

In sum, aggressive individuals see themselves as victims of inequitable and hostile treatment by peers (e.g., coworkers) and/or powerful entities such as supervisors and employing organizations. They then use their perception that they are being exploited and abused to justify aggressive behaviors. They do not think of their aggressive actions as unfounded aggression; rather, they view them as the justifiable acts of oppressed persons who are seeking retribution, retaliation, or vindication, or who are even acting in self-defense.

Justification Mechanisms

In Chapter 1, we displayed descriptions of the six implicit reasoning biases that underlie justification of aggression in Table 1.1; for convenience, we reproduce that information here in Table 4.2. These biases were identified or suggested by searches of aggression literatures in psychology and other social sciences, combined with information obtained from the popular press (e.g., Anderson's 1994 account of street gangs in the *Atlantic Monthly*). The objective of the searches was to identify a seminal set of implicit biases that define, shape, and guide the myriad specific instances of framing and implicit hypothesizing that aggressive individuals use to justify aggressive behaviors. James (1998) has suggested the term *justification mechanisms* to refer to these primary biases. In the present context, justification mechanisms are defined as implicit biases whose purpose is to define, shape, and otherwise influence reasoning so as to enhance the rational appeal of behaving aggressively.

- *Proposition 2:*   Reasoning based on JMs for aggression is often not convincing or logically persuasive to nonaggressive individuals.

Nonaggressive individuals lack impulses to engage in dominance contests with their teachers or supervisors, to fight with their peers or

Table 4.2 Justification Mechanisms Used to Develop Conditional Reasoning
Measurement System for Aggression

1. *Hostile Attribution Bias:* A tendency to see malevolent intent in the actions of others. Even benign or friendly acts may be seen as having hidden, hostile agendas designed intentionally to inflict harm. An especially virulent form of this bias occurs when benign or positive acts are attributed to selfish concerns and negative incentives (e.g., an aggressive subordinate interprets a helpful suggestion by a supervisor as an intentional attempt to demean the subordinate's work).

2. *Derogation of Target Bias:* A tendency to attempt to make the target more deserving of aggression. For example, a number of negative characteristics may be ascribed to the target (e.g., corrupt, dishonest, evil, immoral, underhanded, unethical, untrustworthy) or the positive traits of the target may be ignored, undervalued, or depreciated.

3. *Retribution Bias:* A tendency to confer logical priority to reparation or retaliation over reconciliation. Reflected in implicit beliefs that aggression is warranted in order to restore respect or exact restitution for a perceived wrong. Bias is also indicated by whether a person would rather retaliate than forgive, be vindicated as opposed to cooperate, and obtain revenge rather than maintain a relationship. This bias underlies classic rationalizations for aggression based on wounded pride, challenged self-esteem, and disrespect.

4. *Victimization by Powerful Others Bias:* A tendency to frame self as a victim and to see self as being exploited and taken advantage of by the powerful (e.g., government agencies). Sets the stage for arguing that aggression is acting out against injustice, correcting inequities, redressing wrongs, or striking out against oppression.

5. *Potency Bias:* A tendency to frame and reason using the contrast of strength versus weakness. For example, people with a strong Potency Bias tend to frame others on a continuum ranging from strong, assertive, powerful, daring, fearless, or brave to weak, impotent, submissive, timid, sheepish, compliant, conforming, or cowardly. This bias is used to justify aggression via arguments such as (a) aggression (e.g., confrontations with teachers, fights with coworkers) results in one's being perceived as brave or as a leader by others, and (b) weakness/submissiveness invites aggression because it shows that one is willing to submit.

6. *Social Discounting Bias:* A tendency to call on socially unorthodox and frequently antisocial beliefs in interpreting and analyzing social events and relationships. People with this bias are disdainful of traditional ideals and conventional beliefs; they may be insensitive, unempathic, and unfettered by social customs. They are often directly cynical or critical, with few subliminal channels for routing antisocial framing and analysis.

coworkers, or to cause harm to powerful organizations such as their employers by engaging in obstreperous or intentionally disruptive behavior. There is little or no incentive to possess JMs to enhance the rational appeal of aggressive behaviors. Thus reasoning tends not to be shaped by the types of implicit reasoning biases summarized in Table 4.2. Nonaggressive individuals are not disposed to frame others through a lens of dominance-submissiveness, nor is malevolent intent the default option for attributions regarding the causes of others' behavior. Nonaggressive people are not constantly looking for slights or disrespect in the comments of others, and they are not inclined to reason in ways that give preference to retribution over reconciliation. They are also not disposed to see themselves as victims.

Basically, nonaggressive people are not prone to engage in implicit cognitions that enhance the rational appeal of aggression. Moreover, they are likely to reject justifications and rationalizations for aggression as superficial, far-fetched, and inappropriate (see Gay, 1993, chap. 1; Huesmann, 1988). On the other hand, reasoning based on the JMs in Table 4.2 can be subtle and may exploit uncertainties in facts and evidence, which means that (a) the reasoning cannot be rejected outright on logical grounds, and therefore (b) the reasoning must be considered tenable. In conditions of uncertainty, nonaggressive individuals will tend to be skeptical or doubtful of reasoning based on JMs (Crick & Dodge, 1994; Dodge, 1986; Dodge & Coie, 1987; Dodge & Crick, 1990; Gay, 1993; Huesmann, 1988; James, 1998).

To illustrate, nonaggressive individuals are likely to be skeptical of an aggressive individual's assertion that the behavior of another is due to hostile intent. Unless there is clear supporting evidence or logic suggesting otherwise, nonaggressive people are also likely to question that retribution and retaliation are more reasonable responses to social discord than attempts to cooperate and reconcile. And they will tend to grow weary of aggressive individuals' consistent attempts to decipher hidden agendas, designed to victimize and exploit people like them, in the behaviors of powerful others.

The basic suggestion is that (a) even though nonaggressive people may be unable to reject reasoning based on JMs on strictly logical or empirical grounds, (b) they regard such reasoning as improbable, dubious, socially unorthodox, unrealistic, provocative, extreme, nonconstructive, and/or slanted. Thus reasoning based on JMs typically will not be convincing or logically persuasive to nonaggressive individuals.

Nonaggressive individuals *will* be receptive to less extreme, more probable, more realistic, socially orthodox, conventional, prosocial, and nonprovocative reasoning about the justifiability of aggression (see Crick & Dodge, 1994; Gay, 1993; Huesmann, 1988; James, 1998). This would be reasoning that logically counterbalances aggressive individuals' attempts to enhance the rational appeal of behaving aggressively. It is reasoning that appears to nonaggressive individuals to offer sound, sensible, and rational alternatives to aggressive individuals' attempts to justify aggression. For example, in contrast to aggressive individuals' proclivities to reason in terms of JMs, nonaggressive individuals will be inclined to do the following:

- See amicable or benign intent (as opposed to hostile intent) as the default option in seeking explanations for the actions of others
- Build dialectics that include both the positive and the negative characteristics (as opposed to just the negative characteristics) of others
- Be attentive to ways in which they can cooperate and get along
- Reason from the perspective that employees can accept subordinate roles without being exploited, demeaned, or made victims of injustices and inequities
- Analyze social events from the perspective that society benefits from respect for traditional ideals and conventional beliefs as well as from acceptance of social customs

When aggressive individuals rely implicitly on JMs to enhance the logical appeal of aggression, and nonaggressive individuals judge that these attempted justifications lack logical credibility, reasoning is said to be *conditional* on the personalities of the reasoners (James, 1998). More generally, reasoning about aggression is conditional when discretionary judgments about whether aggression is or is not justified covary with whether the reasoner is aggressive or nonaggressive.

We should note that in Chapter 1, we contrasted aggressive individuals with socially adaptive individuals. We suggested that counteracting aggressive individuals' desires to fight, to overcome perceived opposition forcefully, and to attack coworkers or the organization with intent to cause harm are socially adaptive individuals' desires to seek friendships, to cooperate with others, to have trust in the goodwill of others, and to live in a harmonious, peaceful environment. In the present treatment we are using *nonaggressive* as the opposite of *aggressive*. This is because the measurement system we are about to describe is concerned with the extent to which one is prepared to justify aggression. The most direct and efficient means for describing this system is to contrast (a) aggressive people who are prepared to justify aggression with (b) nonaggressive people who are not prepared to justify aggression.

Nonaggressive has the same connotation as the term *socially adaptive,* which is a predilection to be civil, friendly, polite, congenial, cooperative, and courteous. Basically, nonaggressiveness and social adaptiveness indicate a readiness to act in the typical, acceptable, normative, socially orthodox, expected (role-prescribed) ways that characterize most people in most work environments.

Use of Discretionary Judgments of Logical Persuasiveness to Make Inferences About JMs

In measurement terms, we have described how latent variables (i.e., implicit propensities to reason based on JMs) influence manifest indicators of these variables (i.e., discretionary judgments regarding the logical persuasiveness of reasoning based on JMs). Paradigms developed for the measurement of (psychological) latent variables invert this causal process. That is, measurements are taken on what is observable, namely, the manifest indicators (what is and is not logically convincing). These measurements are then used to make inferences about individual differences on the latent variables (propensities to use JMs to reason).

More specifically, we begin with people for whom we wish to assess the propensity to engage JMs in reasoning. We provide these people with reasoning that is known to be based on JMs and contrast it with reasoning based on more conventional, socially adaptive assumptions. We then ask the people to judge which is more logically persuasive, the reasoning based on JMs or the contrasting reasoning. People who see the reasoning based on JMs as logically more persuasive than reasoning based on the more conventional assumptions are inferred to have a moderate to strong propensity to engage JMs in reasoning (James, 1998). We describe the measurement system designed to accomplish these tasks below.

- *Proposition 3:*   The proclivity to see reasoning based on JMs as logically more persuasive than reasoning based on more conventional assumptions can be measured indirectly through a modification of traditional inductive reasoning problems.

A tacit means was designed to offer reasoning based on JMs to respondents. This is followed by use of an indirect procedure to measure respondents' discretionary judgments of whether this reasoning is logically persuasive. The process begins with the respondents' being given premises (e.g., data, events, logical arguments, explanations, assumptions) built around themes known to trigger JMs for aggressive individuals. For example, the following premises are designed around the theme of a powerful other (i.e., American automobile manufactures) taking advantage of and exploiting less powerful victims (i.e., customers):

1. The quality of American cars has gotten better in the past 15 years.
2. American carmakers started to build better cars when they began to lose business to foreign carmakers, especially the Japanese.
3. Many American buyers thought that foreign cars were better made.

Respondents are then given an inductive reasoning task; they in effect are asked to reason "from given premises to a reasonable but logically uncertain conclusion" (see Sternberg, 1982, p. 235). Alternative conclusions are furnished, and respondents are asked to identify which one of the conclusions most reasonably follows from the premises, given that more than one conclusion may appear reasonable.

One such conclusion is that "American carmakers built cars to wear out 15 years ago so they could make a lot of money selling parts." This conclusion offers respondents the opportunity to bestow logical priority to reasoning that is implicitly based on the Hostile Attribution Bias and the Victimization by Powerful Others Bias. It is designed to appeal to aggressive individuals' unconscious proclivity to favor hostile intent and exploitation of victims (over nonmalevolent and nonmanipulative intent) when making attributions about the most reasonable causes of the behaviors of powerful others. A person's selection of this conclusion as the most logically convincing and persuasive of the conclusions offered furnishes a single piece of evidence that the Hostile Attribution Bias and Victimization by Powerful Others Bias are implicitly instrumental in shaping and guiding the individual's reasoning.

It is noteworthy that these are not the only explanations for why some respondents judge this conclusion to be the most reasonable. For example, a respondent may have had negative experiences with an American automobile manufacture that influence his or her reasoning on this problem. One should not, therefore, place undue weight on the responses to a single problem. What is important for measurement is whether a respondent consistently selects reasoning based on the Hostile Attribution Bias/Victimization by Powerful Others Bias, or other JMs, across a set of problems that vary in terms of inductive argument and subject matter.

It is expected that nonaggressive individuals will tend to acknowledge that the conclusion above is plausible and that it cannot be rejected (or accepted) with logical certainty. It is also expected that nonaggressive individuals will not, on the average, find this conclusion to be logically persuasive. This is because it tacitly suggests that American carmakers held a deeply cynical attitude toward customers, that profit by any means overrode other concerns, such as pride in product and attracting repeat customers. Nonaggressive individuals are predicted to consider such reasoning to be improbable, extreme, and unrealistic.

A different conclusion was designed to appeal to nonaggressive individuals' need for an answer that, to them, is more probable and realistic. This conclusion is "The Japanese knew more than Americans about building good cars 15 years ago." This inference follows logically from the premises but lacks the provocativeness and cynicism of the first conclusion. It offers a rational, socially adaptive alternative to the first conclusion. A person's selection of this alternative as the most logically persuasive of the conclusions offered provides a single piece of evidence that the Hostile Attribution Bias and Victimization by Powerful Others Bias are *not* implicitly instrumental in shaping and guiding that person's reasoning.

Aggressive respondents are expected to acknowledge the plausibility of this second conclusion. However, they are expected to determine that the first conclusion shows greater insight into the true intentions of American automobile makers.

Respondents are not alerted to the identity of the implicit cognitions that are the subject of measurement (Greenwald & Benaji, 1995). The premises and alternative conclusions are presented to respondents as inductive reasoning problems, such as those found in standardized tests of critical reasoning skills (e.g., the Watson-Glaser Critical Thinking Appraisal). Respondents are asked to identify which conclusion follows most reasonably from each premise, given that more than one conclusion may seem reasonable. To enhance the face validity of the task, and to protect the indirect nature of measurement, the alternative conclusions are embedded within a set of four conclusions, as shown in Problem 1 in Table 4.3. Two of the conclusions (i.e., alternatives a and b) are meant to be clearly illogical and rejected by respondents (which is usually the case). Alternative d is the conclusion designed to appeal to aggressive respondents; it is referred to as the *AG alternative.* Alternative c,

Table 4.3 Illustrative Conditional Reasoning Items

1. American cars have gotten better in the past 15 years. American carmakers started to build better cars when they began to lose business to the Japanese. Many American buyers thought that foreign cars were better made.

   Which of the following is the most logical conclusion based on the above?
   a. America was the world's largest producer of airplanes 15 years ago.
   b. Swedish carmakers lost business in America 15 years ago.
   c. The Japanese knew more than Americans about building good cars 15 years ago.
   d. American carmakers built cars to wear out 15 years ago so they could make a lot of money selling parts.

2. The old saying "an eye for an eye" means that if someone hurts you, then you should hurt that person back. If you are hit, then you should hit back. If someone burns down your house, then you should burn down that person's house.

   Which of the following is the biggest problem with the "eye for an eye" plan?
   a. It tells people to "turn the other cheek."
   b. It offers no way to settle a conflict in a friendly manner.
   c. It can be used only at certain times of the year.
   d. People have to wait until they are attacked before they can strike.

the conclusion targeted for nonaggressive individuals, is called the *NA alternative.*

The process described above is referred to as the *conditional reasoning measurement system* (James, 1998). Each reasoning problem is referred to as a *conditional reasoning problem,* or *CR problem.* The term *conditional reasoning* connotes that (a) discretionary judgments of the logical persuasiveness of alternative conclusions to the same set of premises are (b) implicitly contingent on the personalities of the reasoners (i.e., whether respondents are aggressive or nonaggressive).

Problem 2 in Table 4.3 further illustrates the conditional reasoning procedure. The themes in this problem are retribution and victimization. Alternatives a and c are clearly illogical. Alternative d offers respondents the opportunity to determine that reasoning implicitly based on the Retribution Bias and the Victimization (by Powerful Others) Bias has logical priority. This inference is designed to appeal to aggressive individuals' favoring of retribution over reconciliation and reasoning that striking first is a justifiable means to avoid being attacked and becoming a victim. A respondent's selection of this conclusion as the most logically persuasive of the conclusions offered provides evidence that the Retribution Bias and Victimization Bias are implicitly instrumental in shaping that person's reasoning.

It is expected that nonaggressive respondents will reject alternative d as extreme and unnecessarily provocative even though it appears to follow logically from the premise. Alternative b is targeted to appeal to nonaggressive individuals' need for a more prosocial alternative to counterbalance the antagonistic and provocative tenor of alternative d. A person's selection of alternative b provides evidence that the Retribution Bias and Victimization Bias are not implicitly instrumental in shaping that individual's reasoning.

Conditional Reasoning Test for Aggression

The Conditional Reasoning Test for Aggression, known as the CRT-A, was developed recently (James & McIntyre, 2000). The CRT-A comprises 22 CR problems, including the two problems in Table 4.2, plus three actual inductive reasoning problems (to further protect the indirect nature of the system). The average Flesch-Kincaid Grade Level score for the 22 CR problems, an indicator of reading level provided by Microsoft Word, is approximately 7.0 (i.e., seventh grade). A test based on a "verbal-visual" version of the CR problems, the VCRT-A, was designed to have a threshold reading level of approximately fifth to sixth grade (Green & James, 1999). In the VCRT-A, bare-bones versions of CR problems are presented both verbally and in written form using a VCR and television. The written component is overlaid on a photograph consistent with the basic theme of the CR problem. The current VCRT-A contains 14 CR problems, 12 of which are shared with the CRT-A. There are no inductive reasoning problems in the VCRT.

The 22 CR problems in the CRT-A evolved over a series of developmental studies, including the eight empirical validity and psychometric studies summarized below. To be considered for retention, a CR problem had to significantly predict behavioral indicators of aggression, preferably in more than one sample. Retained CR problems also had low correlations with potential confounds, namely, intelligence, gender, and race. A significant part-whole correlation (i.e., correlation of problem with the total score described below) was required. Each problem was reviewed by a logician for face validity as an inductive reasoning task. Problems were rewritten or deleted based on this review.

Initially, an attempt was made to have each of the six JMs listed in Table 4.2 represented in the CR problems. Five of these six JMs are represented in 3 or more of the problems that survived to become members of the 22-problem pool. The exception, the Derogation of Target Bias, is represented by only a single problem in this pool. This is largely a result of (a) the difficulty of writing problems to capture this bias and (b) the inability of the problems that were written to survive the empirical tests described above.

Scoring of the 22 CR problems follows a straightforward method proposed by James (1998). Respondents are given a +1 for every AG alternative they select, a zero for every logically incorrect alternative they select (an infrequent event), and a −1 for every NA alternative they select. These scores are summed to furnish a raw composite score. These scores are then transformed, through linear transformation (so as to preserve the distribution of scores), into a standard scale that has a mean of 6.0 and a standard deviation of 1.67.

- *Proposition 4:* A propensity to select alternatives (over multiple CR problems) that are based on implicit cognitive biases that enhance the rational appeal of aggression (i.e., JMs) indicates an "implicit cognitive readiness" to engage in some form of aggression in the future.

The fourth and final proposition specifies how the composite scores on the CRT-A (and earlier CRTs as well as the VCRT-A) are interpreted (see Ozer, 1999). A high score on this scale indicates that a respondent is inclined to accord logical priority to AG alternatives when solving a number of CR problems. These discretionary judgments serve as indirect indicators that JMs are instrumental in guiding and shaping the respondent's reasoning. Moreover, a strong proclivity to reason in ways that tacitly justify aggression suggests that the respondent is implicitly prepared and willing to engage in some form of aggressive behavior in the future (James, 1998). Indeed, it is predicted that he or she has a strong "implicit cognitive readiness to aggress."

A low score on this scale indicates that a respondent tends to accord logical priority to NA alternatives when solving CR problems. These discretionary judgments serve as indirect indicators that JMs are *not* instrumental in guiding and shaping the respondent's reasoning. In contrast to those with high scores, a weak or nonexistent proclivity to reason in ways that tacitly justify aggression suggests that the respondent is not implicitly prepared to engage in aggressive behavior (James, 1998). Indeed, it is predicted that he or she lacks an implicit cognitive readiness to aggress.

Scores ranging between the weak and strong poles on the scale indicate selection of a few but not a large number of AG alternatives (compared with other respondents). JMs appear to be only sporadically instrumental in shaping and guiding reasoning. Implicit cognitive readiness to aggress is therefore likely to be only modest or indeterminate.

In sum, scores on the composite scale are interpreted in terms of individual differences in respondents' implicit cognitive readiness to aggress. Individuals with high scores on the implicit cognitive readiness to aggress scale, or ICR-A scale, are expected to have a significantly greater probability of engaging in aggressive acts than individuals with low or moderate scores. The degree to which scores from the ICR-A scale correlate significantly with aggressive behavior thus becomes a key test of the scale's empirical and construct validity. In the next section, we present the model that guided the tests of empirical/construct validity.

Model for Empirical Validation Analyses

Figure 4.1 presents the paradigm that guided tests of the following hypothesis: The higher the score on the ICR-A scale, the greater the probability of engaging in what for aggressive individuals is an act of aggression. The model begins with the characteristics of aggressive individuals discussed earlier. It proceeds to the implicit social cognitions that these individuals are believed to use to justify aggressive behavior. Individuals for whom JMs are instrumental in shaping reasoning are characterized as having a strong implicit cognitive readiness to aggress.

The final component of the model involves multiple ways in which individuals with a strong readiness to aggress might seek what they see as retribution, retaliation, vindication, or self-defense. The behaviors listed in this component are drawn from recent treatments and discussions of the many ways aggressive individuals may behave aggressively (see Averill, 1993; Baron & Richardson, 1994; Burroughs & Jones, 1995; Buss, 1961; Buss & Perry, 1992; Folger & Baron, 1996; James, 1998; Neuman & Baron, 1998; O'Leary-Kelly et al., 1996; Shepperd, 1993;

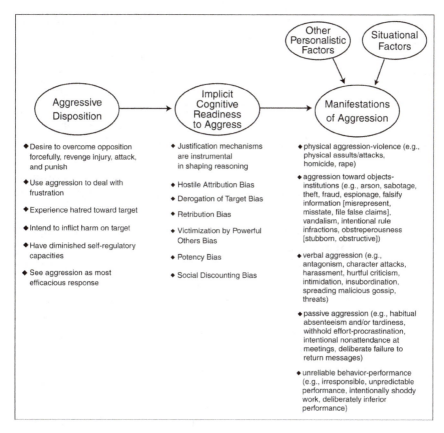

Figure 4.1. Model Relating Implicit Cognitive Readiness to Aggress to Manifestations of Aggression

VandenBos & Bulatao, 1996). For example, aggressive individuals may seek retribution for perceived wrongs by engaging in violent acts meant to be highly injurious to the targets. However, whereas violent acts such as physical assault and homicide are visible and dramatic, they also tend to have low base rates (see Baron & Richardson, 1994; Borum, 1996; Neuman & Baron, 1998).

Most acts of aggression by aggressive individuals involve less visible and dramatic attempts to harm other individuals, groups, or institutions (see Baumeister et al., 1996; Hogan & Hogan, 1989; Neuman & Baron, 1998). Here we have a wide array of options, as indicated in Figure 4.1 (which does not exhaust all possibilities). Aggressive individuals may seek retaliation or vindication by withholding effort in attempts to disrupt organized and planned activities. Passive-aggressive activities such as habitual absences and procrastination are exemplars. Or aggressive individuals may manifest their implicit cognitive readiness to aggress by defending their honor through verbally assaulting others (e.g., harassment, intimidation, threats, spreading malicious gossip, insubordination). As a final illustration, aggressive individuals may engage in what they see as justified retribution against institutions (e.g., employing organizations) by engaging in theft, damaging equipment, committing fraud, misrepresenting information, or purposely doing shoddy work.

Basically, aggressive individuals differ in how they express an implicit cognitive readiness to aggress. How this implicit readiness is channeled into specific types of aggression is thought to be a function of a number of personalistic variables, such as degree of anger, desire for self-preservation, learned means of dealing with anger and frustration, and impulsiveness (see Bandura, 1973; Baron & Richardson, 1994; Baumeister et al., 1996; Crick & Dodge, 1994; Huesmann, 1988; Millon, 1990; Wright & Mischel, 1987). Situational factors are also likely to shape or constrain manifestations of aggression (e.g., feasibility of desired behavior, probability of being caught) as well as to trigger aggressive acts (e.g., receipt of a failing grade, criticism by a supervisor, failure to be promoted; see Berkowitz, 1993; Folger & Baron, 1996; Neuman & Baron, 1998).

Potential direct effects, mediators, and moderators engendered by personal characteristics and situational factors are indicated but not specified in Figure 4.1. This is because it must first be ascertained whether implicit cognitive readiness to aggress can validly predict behavioral indicators of aggression using the most simple and straightforward of models. If the measurement fails here, then there is little to champion moving to more complex models. Thus the link tested in Figure 4.1 simply views the relationship between implicit cognitive readiness to aggress and each of the behaviors in Figure 4.1 as probabilistic. The hypothesis states that people with a strong implicit cognitive readiness to aggress, as indicated by high scores on the ICR-A scale, are more likely than people who lack a strong implicit cognitive readiness to aggress to engage in each of the behaviors in Figure 4.1.

Note that all of the behaviors in Figure 4.1 share the common denominator that they can be employed by aggressive individuals to harm other individuals (causes physical and/or psychological damage) and/or an organizations (e.g., impedes productivity, weakens morale, undermines authority, encourages rebelliousness). Even the passive-aggressive behaviors, such as habitual absences and tardiness, take a toll on productivity, morale, and stability. It follows that the behaviors listed in Figure 4.1 may serve as ways in which aggressive individuals may manifest aggression (see Neuman & Baron, 1998).

Investigators were able to gain access to data on many of the aggressive behaviors listed in Figure 4.1. Limited data were available on the more extreme forms of aggression (e.g., fighting). However, as reported above, these forms of aggression have very low base rates. The less extreme forms of aggression (e.g., habitual absenteeism, disruptive attrition, work unreliability, poor performance appraisals, and falsification of effort) have higher base rates and are much more susceptible to measurement. These latter criteria received the majority of attention. Eight empirical validation studies were conducted on field samples of employees in work organizations or students. Although neither exhaustive nor conclusive, these studies offered an initial if not a fair test of the potential of scores on the ICR-A scale to predict actual aggressive behaviors.

Psychometric Evaluation of the Conditional Reasoning Test for Aggression

In this section, we present the following information:

- Estimates of reliability for scores on the ICR-A scale
- Validities furnished by scores on the ICR-A scale
- Correlations between scores on the ICR-A scale and intelligence, gender, and race
- Correlations between scores on the ICR-A scale and self-report measures of aggression
- Comparative validities for scores from the ICR-A scale and self-report measures of aggression

This information is drawn from the test manual for the CRT-A (James & McIntyre, 2000).

Estimates of Reliability

Three types of reliability were estimated. The set of estimates involved internal consistency estimates (alpha coefficients) for five factors identified in a factor analysis of the 22 CR problems in the CRT-A. The items factored by JM (i.e., each factor represented one of the JMs in Table 4.2, with the exception of the Derogation of Target Bias). This factor analysis was conducted on a sample of 1,603 individuals, approximately half of whom were college students; the remainder were nonacademic employees. Beginning with Factor 1, the alphas were .87, .82, .81, .76, and .74, respectively. These results suggested that the CR problems associated with each factor provided a reliable estimate of the true score on the JM represented by the factor.

The second type of reliability involved internal consistency estimates for the ICR-A scores on the CRT-A and the VCRT. The estimate of reliability for the 22-problem CRT-A was based on the same sample as that used in the factor analysis ($N = 1,603$). A Kuder-Richardson (Formula 20) coefficient (see Gulliksen, 1950, chaps. 16, 21) was .76. This value indicates that the total score on the 22-problem CRT-A is a reliable estimate of the true score that would be obtained if all possible CR problems from a heterogeneous domain of problems labeled *implicit cognitive readiness to aggress* were answered.

The second internal consistency estimate was obtained for the 14-problem VCRT administered to 225 college students. The Kuder-Richardson estimate was .78.

The third and final type of reliability was based on a hybrid alternative forms analysis. Undergraduates in one of the first development samples ($N = 276$) were given an early version of a 25-problem CRT for aggression during the first week of a semester. Two months later they were given a VCRT, which at that time had 12 of the 25 CRT problems translated into the VCRT format. Percentage agreement was computed for each of the 12 problems, and values ranged from 64.9% to 94.6%, with a mean of 81.4%. The estimated correlation between the total score on the 12-problem VCRT and a composite score based on the 12 CRT problems used to construct the VCRT was .82. This correlation, in concert with the estimates of agreement, indicated a reasonable degree of stability in responses to CR problems as well as a reasonable degree of comparability in the scores produced by a CRT format and a VCRT format.

Table 4.4   Uncorrected Validities for ICR-A Scales

Sample and Criterion	Composition	Instrument	Experimental Design	Uncorrected Validity
1. Supervisory rating (overall performance)	140 patrol officers	CRT	concurrent	−.49
2. Absences (lack of class attendance)	188 undergraduates	CRT	predictive	.37
3. Lack of truthfulness about extra credit	60 undergraduates	VCRT	experiment	.49
4. Absences (lack of work attendance)	97 nuclear facility operators	CRT	postdictive	.42
5. Student conduct violations	225 undergraduates	VCRT	postdictive	.55
6. Attrition	135 restaurant employees	CRT	predictive	.32
7. Absences (lack of work attendance)	105 package handlers	CRT	predictive	.34
8. Work unreliability	111 temporary employees	CRT	predictive	.43

NOTE: All correlations are statistically significant ($p < .05$). *Uncorrected* means not corrected for either range restriction or attenuation due to unreliability in either the predictor or the criterion. *Concurrent* means that predictor and criterion data were collected at approximately the same time. *Predictive* denotes that predictor data were collected before criterion data. *Postdictive* refers to the use of archival criterion data to validate a contemporaneous predictor.

In sum, initial indications are that the scores furnished by conditional reasoning instruments for aggression are reliable. The estimates of internal consistency above are comparable to the estimates obtained for a CRT developed to measure achievement motivation (James, 1998).

Results of Eight Empirical Validation Studies

Results of empirical validation studies conducted on eight separate samples are presented in Table 4.4. These results furnished strong support for the hypothesis that the higher the score on the ICR-A Scale, the greater the likelihood of engaging in one of the behavioral manifestations of aggression presented in Figure 4.1. Specifically, individuals whose scores indicated a moderate to strong implicit cognitive readiness to aggress had significantly greater probabilities of engaging in aggressive acts than did individuals whose scores indicated a low implicit cognitive readiness to aggress. For example, students with comparatively higher scores on the ICR-A scale were more likely than students with lower scores to have committed student conduct violations ($r = .55$), to have misrepresented (i.e., been untruthful about) the extra-credit points they deserved for participating in an experiment ($r = .49$), and to have been absent from class ($r = .37$).

Patrol officers with higher ICR-A scores were more likely than patrol officers with lower scores to have poor performance ratings ($r = -.49$). Temporary workers with higher scores were more likely to be unreliable ($r = .43$), whereas nuclear facility operators and package handlers with higher scores were more likely to be absent from work ($rs = .42$ and $.34$, respectively). Finally, new restaurant employees with higher ICR-A scores were more likely to quit within 30 days of being hired ($r = .32$).

Based on absolute values and Fisher z transformations, the average validity across the eight studies in Table 4.4 is .43. If we were to follow current convention and correct the .43 value for such things as unreliability in the criterion and range restriction in the predictor (see Schmidt & Hunter, 1998), then the value could surpass .60, depending on the assumptions used for corrections. However, the observed values in Table 4.4 reflect what can be expected practically in regard to the use of the CRT-A scale in applications such as selection and placement.

The magnitudes of the empirical validities, which were all based on a priori scoring or cross-validation, also deserve brief mention. To put a mean validity of .43 in perspective, consider that uncorrected empirical validities for single predictors against behavioral criteria rarely exceed .40 for aptitude measures and .30 for (primarily self-report) personality measures (see Barrick & Mount, 1991, 1993; Ghiselli, 1966; Hough, 1992; Hough et al., 1990; Hurtz & Donovan, 2000; Mischel, 1968; Salgado, 1997; Schmitt et al., 1984; Tett et al., 1991). The mean of .43 indicates that the ICR-A scale is capable of generating validities of comparatively substantial magnitudes for single psychological predictors.

Correlations Between Scores on the
ICR-A Scale and Critical Intellectual Skills

Correlations between scores on the ICR-A scale and critical intellectual skills are presented in Table 4.5. These statistics were reported for

Table 4.5   Correlations Between Scores on ICR-A Scale and Critical Intellectual Skills

Sample	Intelligence Scale	n	Sample Composition	Correlation
Sample 2	ACT	188	undergraduates	−.06
Sample 3	ACT	60	undergraduates	−.05
Sample 5	ACT	225	undergraduates	−.08

NOTE: All correlations are statistically significant ($p < .05$). ACT = American College Testing.

the three samples from the eight empirical validation samples that involved undergraduates. Measurement of critical intellectual skills was based on scores from tests developed by American College Testing (ACT). Scores were obtained from student records after the students gave their informed consent.

Of initial note is that there is no theoretical reason to expect a correlation between implicit cognitive readiness to aggress and intelligence. If a correlation were observed, then critical intellectual skills might in some way be confounded with responses to the CR problems. For example, NA alternatives might in some rational way, perceptible by intelligent respondents, be "more logical" than the AG alternatives. However, the correlations in Table 4.5 indicate that no such confounding took place. Critical intellectual skills were not significantly correlated with the scores on the ICR-A scale.

Correlations Between Scores on the ICR-A Scale and Gender and Race

Correlations between scores on the ICR-A scale and gender are presented in the top part of Table 4.6, and correlations with race are presented in the bottom part of the table. Statistics involving gender are presented for the six samples from the eight empirical validity studies that included reasonably large proportions of females (.25 or greater). Statistics for race are presented for the three samples from this set for which race data were available and the proportion of respondents in the largest minority group was .05 of the total sample or greater.

Scores on the ICR-A scale did not correlate with gender in four of the six samples, which included both academic and working groups. Small but significant correlations were obtained in two academic samples.

Table 4.6   Relationships Between Scores on ICR-A Scale and Gender and Race

		Correlations With Gender (Male = 0, Female = 1)		
Sample	*Composition*	*Proportion Female*	*Point-Biserial Correlation*	*Biserial Correlation*
Sample 2	188 undergraduates	.34	−.08	−.10
Sample 3	60 undergraduates	.60	−.22*	−.29*
Sample 5	225 undergraduates	.49	−.20*	−.25*
Sample 6	120 restaurant employees	.66	−.06	−.08
Sample 7	105 package handlers	.26	.04	.05
Sample 8	111 temporary employees	.36	.07	.09

		Relationships With Race		
Sample	*Composition*	*Proportion*	*Race*	*Relationship*
Sample 2	188 undergraduates	.90	white (0)	r = .06[a]
		.10	African American (1)	(r = .10)[b]
Sample 7	105 package handlers	.23	white	F = 1.43
		.52	African American	
		.24	Hispanic	
		.01	Asian	
Sample 8	111 temporary employees	.82	white (0)	r = .07
		.18	African American (1)	(r = .10)

a. Point-biserial correlation.
b. Biserial correlation.
*$p < .05$.

These are point-biserial correlations. This estimator was used because gender is a true dichotomy. On the other hand, the biserial correlation is the more accurate estimator when p values depart from .50 (Lord & Novick, 1968). Thus biserial correlations are also reported in Table 4.6. There were no inconsistencies in the statistical inferences based on the two estimators. Both sets of correlations indicated a tendency for young, adult, educationally motivated males to have slightly higher scores than young, adult, educationally motivated females. This tendency was not consistent across all undergraduate samples and did not extend to more intellectually heterogeneous samples. In all, a generally low and nonsignificant correlation between gender and the ICR-A scale is indicated.

Race was uncorrelated with scores on the ICR-A scale. The nonsignificant biserial/point-biserial correlations in Samples 2 and 7 indicated that mean scores on the ICR-A scale did not differ significantly between African Americans and whites. The nonsignificant F test in Sample 8 had similar implications (a t test between whites and African Americans was also nonsignificant). There was thus no indication that members of different races were more or less implicitly prepared to aggress.

Relationships Between Scores on the ICR-A Scale and Self-Report Measures of Aggression

Self-report measures of conscious cognitions have a history of low and often nonsignificant correlations with measures of implicit cognitions (Greenwald & Banaji, 1995; James, 1998; Kilstrom, 1999; McClelland et al., 1989; Winter et al., 1998). It was expected, therefore, that correlations between self-report measures of aggression and scores on the ICR-A scale would be, at best, modest. Results presented in the top part of Table 4.7 for Samples 3 and 5 indicate that this expectation was realized. The implicit cognitions measured by the ICR-A scale shared no more, and typically less than, 7% of their variance with conscious cognitions based on self-ascriptions of aggression from two recognized personality inventories (Dutifulness in Sample 5 was expected to be an indicator of low aggressiveness).

The bottom part of Table 4.7 presents the results of a multiple regression analysis (multiple R, zero-order correlations, and beta weights), which regressed behavioral criteria on the ICR-A scale and the self-report measures (and ACT scores in Study 3), and a dominance analysis (Relative Importance). By way of brief explanation, dominance analysis estimates the "relative importance of the p predictors in a specific model" (Budescu, 1993, p. 549). These relative importance values can be interpreted as the proportion or percentage that a particular variable contributes to the R^2. For example, in Study 3, the proportional contribution of the ICR-A scale to prediction (i.e., to R^2) was approximately 83%. The PRF-based self-report of aggression had approximately an 8% proportional contribution to prediction. Thus, of these two predictors, the ICR-A scale was the more important.

The findings of the dominance analysis denote that the ICR-A scale was relatively more important (i.e., contributed a greater percentage to

Table 4.7 Correlations With Self-Report Measures and Multiple
Regression-Dominance Analysis

Correlations With ICR-A Scale

Sample	Composition	Self-Report Measure	Correlation
3	60 undergraduates	PRF Aggression	.14
		PRF Dominance	.05
		PRF Impulsivity	.11
5	225 undergraduates	NEO-PI-R Angry Hostility	.26*
		NEO-PI-R Dutifulness	−.18*

Multiple Regression-Dominance Analysis

Sample	Criterion	Multiple R	Variable	Zero Order r	Beta Weight	Relative Importance
3	Lack of Truthfulness About Extra Credit	.55*	ICR-Aggression	.49*	.51	82.83%
			ACT	−.07	−.12	2.89%
			PRF Aggression	.16	.17	8.11%
			PRF Impulsiveness	.14	.14	6.05%
			PRF Dominance	.05	.04	.72%
5	Student Conduct Violations	.61*	ICR-Aggression	.55*	.53*	77.60%
			NEO Angry Hostility	.26*	.21	16.00%
			NEO Dutifulness	−.18*	−.13*	6.43%

NOTE: PRF = Personality Research Form (Jackson, 1967); NEO-PI-R = NEO Personality Inventory (Revised)
(Costa & McCrae, 1985, 1992a).
*$p < .05$.

the R^2) than the self-report measures in predicting lack of truthfulness about extra credit in Sample 3 and student conduct violations in Sample 5. The ICR-A scale was also relatively more important than critical intellectual skills (ACT scores) in predicting the truthfulness criterion.

Interestingly, both the ACT scores and self-report personality measures failed to attain significant zero-order validities or beta weights in Sample 3 (to maintain consistency, all correlations in the table are biserials). On the other hand, both of the NEO self-report scales attained significance against the student conduct criterion, and the Angry Hostility scale appeared to make a value-added contribution of 16% to the prediction of student conduct violations. Still, this was far short of the 77.6% proportional contribution made by the ICR-A scale to the R^2.

Conclusions

A fair conclusion would seem to be that the ICR-A scale offers a valid, efficient, and indirect system for measuring propensity to engage in aggression. This suggests that evaluators will be able to supplement ubiquitous self-report items for aggression (e.g., "I often feel angry") with inductive reasoning tasks that, for example, ask whether the primary logical weakness with an "eye for an eye" is (a) not having a means to settle a conflict amicably or (b) having to wait until attacked in order to strike. Problems such as the latter offer an indirect means for gaining insight into the implicit processing of individuals. More important, they provide a means for identifying people with cognitive systems that are primed to promote aggression.

Concluding Comments

Guion and Gottier (1965) and Guion (1965) engendered considerable consternation about personality testing in organizations with their conclusion that there is little predictive validity in personality test scores. A well-thought-of text in psychometrics proclaimed that the major source of variance in self-report measurements of personality is social disability (Nunnally, 1967). The ensuing period of 20 or so years is aptly captured by Goldberg's (1993) statement, "Once upon a time, we had no personalities" (p. 26). Goldberg goes on to say, "Fortunately, times change." The resurgence of interest in personality in organizational research is documented by many recent contributions, including an article by House, Shane, and Herold titled "Rumors of the Death of Dispositional Research Are Vastly Exaggerated" (1996).

Yet it is also true that recent meta-analyses have reported that the average, uncorrected validity between self-descriptions of personality and salient, naturally occurring behavioral (performance) criteria is approximately .12, with a maximum rarely exceeding .30 (see Barrick & Mount, 1991; Schmitt et al., 1984; Tett et al., 1991). (In a recent review, Schmidt & Hunter [1998] declined to report uncorrected coefficients.) Mischel reached this same conclusion in 1968 based on a review of general personality at that time. What has happened in the intervening 30 years to enhance the validity of personality measures? The answer with respect to self-report measures is that instruments such as the revised

CPI, the HPI, and the NEO are improved self-report measures. But they are still self-report measures, and the ceiling on validity has changed little. Thus, in the context of self-reports, we believe that it is fair to ask: Are the factors that got personality research into trouble in the 1960s still in place at the beginning of the 21st century?

We submit that the answer would be yes if new research had not shown us a way to involve self-reports in a more useful and valid measurement paradigm. This system also involves projective techniques. We proceed, therefore, to the next chapter, where we provide an overview of several versions of the new measurement paradigm. Self-reports are included in all versions. The versions vary as a function of what is used as a projective technique—fantasy-based procedures such as the TAT or measures based on conditional reasoning.

5 Three Fertile Domains
for Future Personality
Research in Organizations

It is, of course, impossible to forecast creativity. Nonetheless, it is possible to identify seminal ideas in the study of personality that are likely to have impacts on research in multiple disciplines, including industrial and organizational behavior. An example is interactional psychology. An ancient idea that was given scientific texture and direction in the 1970s (see Chapter 2), interactional psychology is the parent theoretical paradigm for much of the present personality research in industrial and organizational psychology and organizational behavior (Kristof, 1996; Schneider, 1996). It gives substance to the models that guide our research, such as person-environment fit and attraction-selection-attrition (see Chapter 2). In this chapter, we present what we believe are three promising new themes for research on personality in organizations. Although perhaps less basic and of narrower bandwidth than interactional psychology, these three ideas have the potential to effect at least minor paradigm shifts in how we do personality research in organizational settings

The first of the three themes is *integrative models of personality assessment*. This idea is based on models of personality assessment that unite indirect measures of latent motives with self-report measures of traits. We shall describe how these models have provided several instances of significantly enhanced understanding and prediction of behavioral and emotional outcomes. The second theme is *coherence*. We treated this theme briefly in Chapter 2; here we delve into the concept of coherence more fully. Our objective is to show how (a) defining traits as recurring patterns in how people respond to diverse situations (b) changes our approach to investigating cross-situational consistency. The third theme is *differential framing*. We have discussed differential framing in each of the preceding chapters as the means by which individuals with different personalities impute qualitatively different meanings to behaviors, people, environments, and events. In this chapter we shall focus on what the term *qualitative differences* means and how it might be introduced into research on such things as positive- negative affective experiences.

Integrative Models of Personality Assessment

A long history of antagonism and rivalry characterizes interactions between people who rely on projective tests such as the Thematic Apperception Test (TAT) to measure personality and those who rely on self-report instruments such as the California Psychological Inventory (see Winter, John, Stewart, Klohnen, & Duncan, 1998). In part, the rivalry has been engendered by attempts to measure different aspects of personality. As we have discussed in Chapter 4, self-reports typically focus on self-descriptions of traits, which is to say recognized dispositions to behave in characteristic, habitual, or cross-situationally consistent ways. Projective techniques such as the TAT focus on measuring needs, with particular attention given to the latent (unrecognized, nonconscious) aspects of needs.

Self-reports may also be used to measure needs, but the focus is generally limited to self-ascriptions of manifest needs. Correlations between self-reports of manifest needs and either manifest or latent needs measured by projective techniques tend to be low (see Winter et al., 1998). Indeed, measures based on projective techniques tend to correlate only modestly if at all with self-report measures (Greenwald &

Banaji, 1995; James, 1998; Kilstrom, 1999; McClelland, Koestner, & Weinberger, 1989; Winter et al., 1998). This has led to a dialectic in which the different camps of measurement attempt to defend/promote their preferred systems of assessment while discounting alternative measurement systems. Tacit in this continuing debate is the assumption that one method of measurement is superior to others.

A likely resolution to the debate is in sight. Some have realized that pitting projective and self-report measurement systems against each other is counterproductive for everyone. They have also realized that differences in the approaches to measurement—projective versus self-report—are less salient than the fact that two different aspects of personality are involved, namely, latent motives and traits. Of critical importance is the recognition that we must measure both implicit motives and traits if we are to understand personality more fully.

A new spirit of collaboration has evolved in which it is stipulated that the projective and self-report measurement systems assess different but functionally related systems of personality. Projective techniques measure latent or manifest motives (desires, wishes), whereas the traits measured by self-reports focus on consistencies in physical, emotional, and cognitive behavior. The key to collaboration is that we can obtain a much better understanding of why people behave as they do by integrating information about motives (with emphasis on latent motives), as measured by projective techniques, with information about behavioral consistencies gleaned from self-reports.

The theoretical foundation for integrating (latent) motives with traits is the "channeling hypothesis" (Winter et al., 1998), which we describe below. We then discuss the personality-based model for explaining behavior that evolved from the channeling hypothesis as well as empirical tests of this model.

Channeling Hypothesis

To quote Winter et al. (1998), "Motives involve wishes, desires, or goals (often implicit or nonconscious), whereas traits channel or direct the ways in which motives are expressed in particular actions throughout the life course" (p. 231). The basic idea here is that a number of people could have the same latent motive but express that motive in quite different ways because they have different traits. Moreover, the same behavior (trait) might be serving as a channel for different motives for different people. Thus to understand a person's personality, one must assess that individual's latent motives and how those motives are channeled into behavior by characteristic behaviors (traits).

Winter et al. translated the channeling hypothesis into a substantive and testable system by proposing an "integrative model" that begins with a motive and then adds a variation on a trait that should serve as a channel for the motive. Winter et al. used the affiliation motive and the trait of extraversion-introversion for illustrative purposes. They built an integrative model by looking at the confluence between high-low scores on the affiliation motive and whether a person is disposed toward extraversion or introversion. We describe this model below.

Integrative Model

The integrative model for the affiliation motive and extraversion-introversion trait is partially reproduced in Table 5.1. Definitions for key variables correspond to those presented in earlier chapters. To review briefly, a person with a strong affiliation motive has needs to establish and to maintain friendships and associations with others; to experience warm, positive, friendly, or intimate relationships; and to engage in friendly, cooperative acts. Winter et al. (1998) note also that this motive might engender a defensive or "prickly" reaction if a person is threatened or stressed. Extraverts are characteristically talkative, active, outgoing, sociable, gregarious, spirited, expressive, and outspoken. Introverts are typically quiet, reserved, shy, modest, withdrawn, inhibited, and retiring.

The confluence between extraversion and a high need for affiliation is presented in the upper-right quadrant of Table 5.1. Winter et al. suggest that individuals in this cell would pursue a wide range of relationships without conflict because of the congruity between the latent affiliation motive and characteristic interactive style. Congruity between motive and trait is also in evidence for the confluence of a low need to affiliate and introversion (lower-left quadrant). Members of this cell were described as caring little for what others think and working effectively, indeed contentedly, by themselves.

The remaining two cells are predicated on incongruities between latent motives and traits. The upper-left quadrant consists of affiliation-motivated introverts, who Winter et al. describe as individuals desirous of affection and friendship but uncomfortable in many interpersonal

Table 5.1 Hypotheses About the Interactions of the Affiliation Motive and Extraversion-Introversion

	In Combination With	
Motive	*Introversion*	*Extraversion*
High affiliation	Wants affection and friendship, but ill at ease in many interpersonal situations	Unconflicted in pursuit of wide-ranging interpersonal relationships
Low affiliation	Comfortable and most effective when working alone; not concerned about what others think	Well regarded and adept at interpersonal relations, but not dependent on them

situations. Not only do we suspect that this description strikes a chord with many readers, but we believe that these same individuals will empathize with Winter et al.'s characterization of these individuals as desiring a few warm and deep relationships as opposed to a large number of friendships. More troubling, however, is Winter et al.'s prediction that those who fall within this cell are likely to experience conflict in these close relationships when they become withdrawn and introspective, as introverts are prone to do.

An extravert with a low need for affiliation seems a bit far-fetched until we imagine some politicians who, although charismatic, popular, and interpersonally adept, are not reliant on interpersonal relations with others for emotional sustenance. Indeed, the driving force for these individuals may be the power motive. Thus the manifest extraversion displayed by these individuals is not driven by the affiliation motive, but serves (i.e., channels) instead their need to impress and to influence people. This point underscores a caveat emphasized by Winter et al., that a two-variable model leaves much to be explained about even narrow behavioral domains. Nevertheless, even though incomplete and in rudimentary form, we believe that Winter et al.'s integrative model indicates a creative paradigm shift for personality research.

Test of the Integrative Model

Winter et al. tested the integrative model presented in Table 5.1 on two samples of college women. The first sample was composed of 51 women from Mills College; the second was made up of 89 women from

Radcliffe College. While students, the women in both samples were given the Thematic Apperception Test to measure their affiliation motive and the California Psychological Inventory (CPI) to measure their extraversion-introversion (we have described these instruments in Chapter 4). Approximately 25 years later, when the women were generally in their 40s, data were obtained from the samples on specific life outcomes. We shall focus here on one group of illustrative outcomes from this set: (a) marriage and family by age 28, followed by divorce (Mills sample); (b) number of marriages and divorces (Radcliffe sample); (c) self-rated dissatisfaction with intimate relationships (Mills sample); and (d) self-described problems with intimacy (Radcliffe sample).

Results of attempts to predict these four outcomes based on the integrative model are presented graphically in Figures 5.1 and 5.2. These figures denote that the joint relationship of the affiliation motive and the extraversion-introversion trait takes the form of an interaction in this case (a different form of relationship is presented later). To be specific, the direction and magnitude of the regression slope linking behavioral outcomes (marriage and divorce; Figure 5.1) and attitudinal outcomes (dissatisfaction in intimate relationships; Figure 5.2) to the affiliation motive are dependent on whether the subjects are introverts or extraverts. All interactions reached significance at acceptable levels.

Perhaps the most direct method for interpreting Figures 5.1 and 5.2 is to view them in terms of motive-trait congruence and incongruence, much as we just did with Table 5.1. The Mills sample in Figure 5.2 provides a good exemplar for all of the graphs. If we look only at the slope for introverts, we find that relationship dissatisfaction increases as the affiliation motive increases (i.e., the slope is positive). These results suggest that when introverts have a low motive to affiliate (congruence), they are likely to be satisfied with intimate relationships (or at least not dissatisfied). In concert with Table 5.1, Winter et al. interpreted these data to indicate that intimate relationships are not particularly salient for women with low needs to affiliate.

However, when introverts have a high need to affiliate (incongruence), they are likely to experience dissatisfaction with intimate relationships (and to experience a greater frequency of divorces—see Figure 5.1). As discussed in relation to the integrative model, affiliation-motivated introverts desire a few intimate relationships, but then have trouble sustaining them. Winter et al. (1998) suggest that

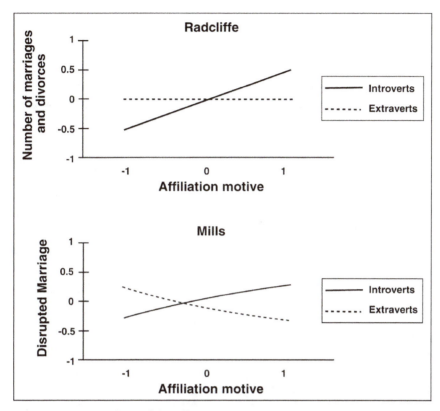

Figure 5.1. Joint Effects of the Affiliation Motive and Extraversion on Marriage and Divorce Across the Radcliffe and Mills Samples

affiliation-motivated introverts, with their more inward focus and preferences for privacy and solitude, should find such relationships overarousing, troublesome, conflicted, and even at times aversive.... To a partner they may seem remote and even withholding. If they are lucky, they may find an understanding partner, with whom they develop a deep, intense relationship—perhaps after one or two false starts. On the average and over time [, however], they may tend to *establish intimate relationships that become problematic and fail.* (p. 240)

Let us turn now to the regression slope for extraverts in Figure 5.2 for the Mills sample. This slope is negative, which means that dissatisfaction with intimate relationships begins high when the affiliation motive

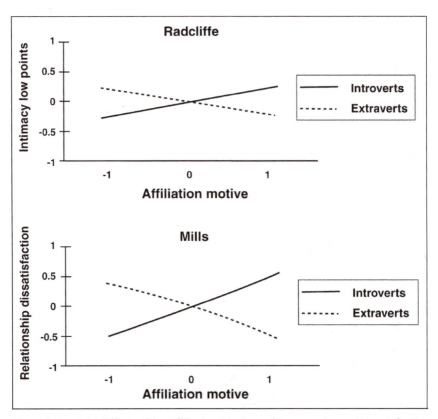

Figure 5.2.   Joint Effects of the Affiliation Motive and Extraversion on Dissatisfaction in Intimate Relationships Replicated Across the Radcliffe and Mills Samples

is low and progressively decreases (i.e., becomes more positive or less negative) as the need to affiliate increases. This suggests that in congruent situations in which extraverts have a high affiliation motive, we tend to find people who are happy (not dissatisfied) and nonconflicted with intimate relationships (and have fewer divorces in the Mills sample— see Figure 5.1). However, in incongruent situations characterized by extraverts with a low need to affiliate, we tend to find more disrupted marriages (in the Mills sample only) and dissatisfaction with intimate relationships (both samples). Winter et al. attribute the latter results to people who simply did not care for close relationships and thus failed to derive satisfaction from them. In fact, such relationships may be framed as constraining or time-consuming. A similar set of interpretations would ensue for the Radcliffe sample in Figure 5.2, and reference was made above to key aspects of the data in Figure 5.1.

As a general statement, we agree with Winter et al.'s (1998) conclusion that "traits channel the ways in which motives are expressed in behavior and life outcomes" (p. 243). Introverts and extraverts express a strong need for affiliation in different ways, behaviorally and emotionally. Moreover, the ease and comfort with which an individual expresses a motive appears to be related to whether or not it is congruent with that person's characteristic ways of adapting to his or her environment. Extraverts appear to have a comfortable and nonconflicted path for expressing a strong motive to affiliate. The path for affiliation-motivated introverts appears to be rocky and strewn with psychological hazards. On the other hand, introverts appear to adapt to a low need to affiliate better than do extraverts. We pursue this issue of congruence between motives and traits below.

Integrative Models Based on
Self-Reports and Conditional Reasoning

The Achilles' heel of the integrative models presented by Winter et al. (1998) is their reliance on the TAT projective technique to measure latent motives. The psychometric properties of the TAT and other free-response, fantasy-based projective tests have been considered suspect by the psychometric community for some time. As we noted in Chapter 4:

> Interrater reliabilities and construct validity of the scoring systems designed to score the free-response, fantasy-based projective tests have long been, and continue to be, of concern to psychometricians (Aiken, 1994; Anastasi, 1982; Cohen, Montague, Nathenson, & Swerdlik, 1988; Groth-Marnat, 1984; Kaplan, 1982). A particularly disquieting feature is that scores on the TAT rely on subjective content analyses of completely unstructured responses to evocative pictures. Not only may a respondent be inconsistent in his or her fantasies on different occasions, but also the highly subjective scoring of a particular respondent may be a function of who does the scoring or whether responses are in oral or written form (see Dana, 1982).

Simply stated, we need measures of latent motives that are less limited psychometrically than free-response, fantasy-based projective tests such as the TAT.

The recently introduced conditional reasoning techniques provide some candidates to fill this gap. The possible contribution of conditional reasoning techniques to integrative models has recently been tested in research (see Bing, Burroughs, Whanger, Green, & James, 2000; James, 1999); we describe these tests below.

As noted above, self-reports of personality focus on how individuals perceive their own traits (e.g., characteristic behaviors, emotions, and preferences). Various forms of self-presentation biases (e.g., social desirability) may be present in self-reports. Nonetheless, the developers of conditional reasoning agreed with Hogan (1986) and Hogan, Hogan, and Roberts (1996) that even with these biases, self-perceptions of traits are salient considerations in the measurement of personality. It is simply important to know how individuals view themselves, even though the lenses through which they do the viewing may be a bit rosy.

In Chapter 4, we described the Conditional Reasoning Test for Aggression (CRT-A), which measures whether people possess an implicit cognitive readiness to aggress. An implicit readiness to aggress is indicated when a person's reasoning is unconsciously shaped by certain types of biases. The purpose of these biases is to justify aggression. They do so by unconsciously guiding the framing of the events surrounding aggression and the inferences made about the causes and effects of aggressive behavior in ways that enhance the rational appeal of behaving aggressively. Because these implicit biases serve to justify aggression, they are referred to as justification mechanisms, or JMs.

Basically, people who rely strongly on JMs to reason about aggression score highly on the implicit cognitive readiness to aggress (ICR-A) scale. For our purposes here, we may think of scores on the ICR-A scale as representing the strength of the latent or implicit motive to aggress. Aggression was included in Murray's (1938) compendium of basic human needs (see Table 3.1), and an implicit cognitive readiness to aggress indicates latent motivation.

Like Winter et al. (1998), James and colleagues were especially intrigued with the question of personality makeup when traits, as measured by self-reports, are congruent or incongruent with latent motives, such as measured by the ICR-A scale. To address this question, an integrative model was constructed based on measurements of aggression from self-reports and measurements of aggression from the CRT-A. This model, designated the *integrative model of assessment for aggres-*

sion, is presented below. A summary of a recently completed empirical test of the model accompanies this presentation.

Integrative Model of Assessment for Aggression

This integrative model is presented in Table 5.2. Illustrative items used in well-accepted personality surveys (e.g., CPI, HPI, NEO; see Chapter 4) to measure self-perceptions of anger, hostility, and aggression are shown at the top of the model. The justification mechanisms used in the ICR-A scale to measure the latent aggression motive are presented on the upper-left side of the model. The lower-left side of the model presents contrasting reasoning proclivities of nonaggressive individuals (see Chapters 1 and 4). The cells of the model reflect "personality types" derived from attempts to integrate these two sources of information. The four cells in the model are based on pure types or prototypes. In truth, a continuum exists for both the ICR-A scale and self-ascribed aggression. Crossing these two continua generates a large number of cells representing degrees of variation from the prototypes presented in the cells of Table 5.2.

The upper-right cell consists of persons who view themselves as aggressive and who possess the corresponding JMs to enhance the logical appeal of aggressive behaviors. Members of this cell were designated *Manifest Aggressives* to denote that latent motives revealed by reasoning proclivities and self-perceptions of trait (characteristic) behaviors are congruent, and all point to seeing oneself as justifiably aggressive. Manifest Aggressives are aware of their aggressiveness. They also possess the cognitive fingerprint for aggression. That is, they are prone to reason that it is possible to commit aggressive acts without being malicious or combative. Manifest Aggressives view their aggressive behaviors as the justifiable acts of oppressed persons who are seeking retribution, retaliation, or vindication, or who are even acting in self-defense.

The lower-left cell of Table 5.2 contains individuals who view themselves as nonaggressive and who, congruently, tend to reason implicitly in ways that promote nonaggressiveness. Their reasoning logically counterbalances aggressive individuals' attempts to enhance the rational appeal of behaving aggressively. Members of this cell are prototypically socially adaptive or prosocial individuals; to maintain consistency with the greater psychological community (see Buss & Finn, 1987;

Table 5.2 Integrative Model of Personality Assessment for Aggression

	Low Self-Reported Aggression	High Self-Reported Aggression
Conditional reasoning test	"I am quite soft-spoken." "It takes a lot to get me mad." "I seldom feel like hitting anyone."	"I often get angry at the way people treat me." "Life is a matter of 'push or be shoved.'"
	Latent Aggressives	*Manifest Aggressives*
	Do not see themselves as aggressive Engage in subtle acts of aggression (e.g., passive-aggressive acts, which are misrepresented as nonaggressive)	Perceive themselves as aggressive Have well-developed cognitive structure to justify aggressive behavior Engage in overt and covert acts of aggression
JMs for Aggression		
Hostile Attribution Bias		
Derogation of Target Bias		
Retribution Bias		
Victimization by Powerful Others Bias		
Potency Bias		
Social Discounting Bias		
	Prosocials	*Overcompensating Prosocials*
	Perceive themselves as prosocial Are reliable, friendly, and nonaggressive Attribute acts of others to helpful and cooperative motives	Perceive themselves as aggressive, which stimulates desire to inhibit aggression Are overly self-monitoring, self-critical, and rigid in behavior
Nonaggressive Contrasts to JMs		
Impartial attributions		
Constructive framing		
Implicit helpful intent		
Relationship oriented		
Conventional values		

Wright & Mischel, 1987), the researchers designated these persons *Prosocials*. Prosocials have internalized societal ideals and lack the aggressive tendencies that trigger proclivities to frame and to analyze behaviors toward others in ways that justify acting aggressively. Prosocials harbor no implicit bias to see malevolent intentions in the actions of others, they favor cooperation and harmony over vengeance and retribution, and their perceptions of others do not pass through a prism of potency that evaluates each person as dominant or submissive in relation to themselves. Prosocials are thus prone not only to discern and refute reasoning based on JMs for aggression, but also to offer reasoning engendered implicitly by impartial, constructive, and prosocial proclivities.

The upper-left cell contains individuals who see themselves as non-aggressive but have JMs in place to enhance the rational appeal of aggression. This incongruous pattern suggests that persons in this cell do not behave overtly in a manner that they could characterize as being aggressive (e.g., physically or verbally abuse someone, steal from a disliked employer). They are, consequently, able to maintain perceptions of themselves as nonaggressive. The latent motive to aggress expresses itself in ways that these individuals do not frame as being aggressive, which means that the behaviors must be subtle and subject to misrepresentation. A key role for JMs here appears to be to protect the facade that what is truly aggressive expression is not really aggression. To illustrate: The Hostile Attribution Bias may help to foster in a husband the illusion that his wife intentionally and malevolently intended to hurt his feelings through some action. This in turn might trigger his ignoring his wife for a period of time. The husband does not see omitting his wife from his cognizance as the act of passive aggression that it is, but as recovery time to mend his own feelings.

Individuals in this cell are referred to as *Latent Aggressives* to indicate that they are unaware of their latent desire (readiness) to aggress and tend to experience the illusion that their aggressive behavior is not really aggressive. Whereas this illusion could encompass the framing of aggressive acts as self-defense, we suspect that latent aggressiveness is more likely to be expressed in ways that can be misrepresented as nonaggressive. Passive-aggressive acts appear to be prime candidates for such misrepresentation (e.g., giving someone the silent treatment, failing to return phone calls, leaving a room when someone else enters it, refusing to attend meetings when a particular person is present).

Finally, the reasoning of individuals in the lower-right cell of Table 5.2 tends to be unconsciously shaped by nonaggressive assumptions even though these same individuals consciously perceive themselves as hostile and aggressive. Conditional reasoning in this incongruity is believed to find expression as inhibitory mechanisms intended to dampen self-ascribed aggressive tendencies. To illustrate, individuals in this cell are likely to be self-monitors, to be highly self-critical, and to be distrustful of their own basic instincts and motives (which they see consciously as aggressive). Behavior is likely to have a strong sense of self-control and lack of spontaneity, perhaps to the point of being rigid. These individuals are thus referred to as *Overcompensating Prosocials*.

Test of the Integrative Model for Aggression

An initial test of the integrative model described above was based on data from a study on college undergraduates regarding truthfulness about extra-credit points (Green & James, 1999). To describe this study briefly, 60 student volunteers consented to complete a CRT for aggression and the Jackson Personality Research Form (PRF). The students were told beforehand that they would have 1 hour to complete these tasks. When they reported to a classroom at 1:00 p.m. to participate in the experiment, they were kept waiting 10 minutes for latecomers to arrive. The CRT was then administered, which took 15 minutes. This was followed by the 300-item PRF, which could be finished in the allotted time if respondents worked diligently. During the next half hour, the students were repeatedly reminded that they had to leave by 2:00. A few minutes before 2:00 p.m., the students were asked to stop and fill in a slip for extra-credit points. The experimenter had presigned the slip, and the students were asked to drop their completed slips in a box on the way out.

To fill in their slips, students had to indicate how many extra-credit points they deserved. Departmental rules, well advertised and well-known by students, granted 5 points for participation in an experiment lasting 1 hour or less (the case here) and 10 points for participation in an experiment lasting more than 1 hour. The initial hypothesis for the study (i.e., prior to the development of an integrative model) was that students with higher ICR-A scores would be more likely to misrepresent the extra credit they deserved.

Of initial note is that the students in general were unhappy with the overall extra-credit system because it was overloaded. This was in part a problem that stemmed from students' waiting until the end of a semester to chase what extra-credit points were then available (this study was purposely conducted late in the semester). The students' being kept waiting for 10 minutes and being consistently reminded to work quickly were intentional actions by the experimenter designed to trigger further anger and resentment (e.g., hostile attributions, victimization, antisocial reactions) on the part of aggressive individuals toward the dominant figure and departmental representative (namely, the experimenter). This in turn was thought to stimulate their propensity to "fight back," perhaps even to seek some retribution, by misrepresenting extra credit.

The initial hypothesis was supported; scores on the ICR-A scale had a biserial correlation of −.49 with whether a student truthfully represented or misrepresented the extra-credit points he or she deserved. Of the 60 students, 9 misrepresented their points.

The next step in the process consisted of a reanalysis of these data based on hypotheses engendered by the integrative model for aggression presented in Table 5.2. Whereas not all students finished the PRF, all responded to all or almost all of the self-report items in the Aggression scale of that instrument. Scores on this scale were included with those from the ICR-A scale in a hierarchical regression analysis designed to predict truthfulness. (This is the same statistical approach that Winter et al. [1998] used to test their integrative model.) The last or unrestricted equation in this analysis included the interaction between the self-report measure of trait-based aggression and the CRT measure of motive-based aggression. An interaction was tested because the integrative model of assessment for aggression (hereafter referred to as the *integrative model*) theoretically predicted that implicit cognitive readiness to aggress would moderate relationships between self-descriptions of aggressiveness and truthfulness. (Self-reports could also be made the moderator inasmuch as interactions are symmetrical.)

Specifically, Latent Aggressives were expected to be truthful because lying is the type of obviously antisocial/aggressive behavior that they see themselves as wishing to avoid. By contrast, Manifest Aggressives were expected to lie as a means of expressing their unhappiness and frustration with the experiment and the extra-credit program in general. These predictions suggested that the slope relating truthfulness

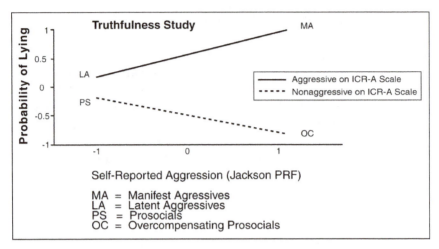

Figure 5.3.   Empirical Test of the Integrative Model for Aggression

about extra credit to self-reports of aggressiveness would be positive for students with comparatively higher scores on the ICR-A scale. Inspection of the slope for students labeled Aggressives in Figure 5.3 supported this prediction. (This slope is based on students who had scores on the ICR-A scale equal to plus one standard deviation from the mean of this scale; see Stolzenberg, 1980, for statistical procedures. This is the same statistical technique that Winter et al. [1998] used to generate Figures 5.1 and 5.2. However, in contrast to Winter et al., James and colleagues used the latent motive as the moderator rather than the predictor.)

In contrast, Prosocials were, on the average, expected to be truthful about the extra credit they deserved. Overcompensating Prosocials were expected to be, if possible, even more truthful, a product of a high degree of self-monitoring and rigid control of behavior to avoid any semblance of impropriety. These predictions suggested that the slope relating truthfulness about extra credit to aggressiveness would be flat (no Prosocials lied) or negative (a few Prosocials lied) for students with lower scores on the ICR-A scale. The slope for nonaggressive students, as measured on the ICR-A scale in Figure 5.3, supported this prediction. This slope is slightly negative. (This slope is based on students who scored minus one standard deviation from the mean on the ICR-A scale, which indicates latent nonaggressive motives.) The statistical analysis underlying Figure 5.3 is based on a highly significant interaction between the self-reports and conditional reasoning measures in predicting truthfulness.

Winter et al. (1998) emphasize the desirability of attempting to replicate interactions. Accordingly, an attempt was made to replicate the results of the study described above. The replication study, conducted by Bing et al. (2000), was based on data obtained from 176 employees who represented most occupations in a large hospital (e.g., accounting, food service, laboratory technicians, management, nurses, physical therapists, a few physicians). Part of the performance evaluation package included ratings from an average of five peers on the 28-item Deviant Behavior Description Checklist (Robinson & Bennett, 1995). A factor-analytically derived subscale on this checklist included behaviors classified as "actively aggressive" (e.g., took property from work, purposely littered work environment). Bing et al. refer to the average of five peer ratings on this subscale as "mean active deviance."

The Jackson PRF and the CRT-A were administered to employees while they were at work. Predictions regarding integration of self-reports with conditional reasoning followed the same pattern hypothesized for truthfulness about extra credit. That is, Latent Aggressives were expected to have low mean active deviance, Manifest Aggressives were expected to have the highest mean active deviance of the individuals studied, Prosocials were expected to have low mean active deviance, and Overcompensating Prosocials were expected to have very low mean active deviance. These hypotheses produced the same basic slope predictions as those proposed for the study of truthfulness.

Results of the test of the hypothesized interaction are displayed in Figure 5.4. As above, the interaction is highly significant. What is most striking, however, is the similarity in the patterns of slope differences when Figure 5.4 is compared to Figure 5.3. (This similarity in patterns is not unlike the similarities found in Figures 5.1 and 5.2.) Not only are the slopes in Figure 5.4 consistent with the theoretical predictions produced by the integrative model, but these slopes are also consistent with those in Figure 5.3.

In sum, a laboratory test and a field test of the integrative model for aggression were concordant in their support of the theoretical position that it is the joint product of self-reports and latent motives, as assessed by conditional reasoning, that is most efficacious in predicting aggressive behaviors. These results thus extend the work of Winter et al.

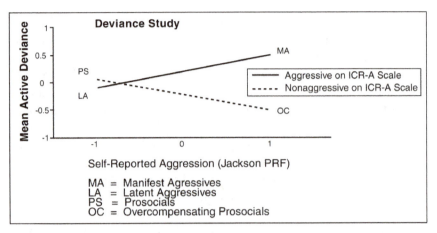

Figure 5.4.   Empirical Test of the Integrative Model for Aggression

(1998) into a new domain of personality, with the use of a more psycho-metrically sound measure of latent motives. However, a potential haz-ard with new models is that they often become crystallized before they have been fully tested. Our initial concern in this regard is that *integra-tive* not become synonymous with *interactional*. In other words, inte-grative models may take many forms, only some of which involve inter-actions and moderators. We present an example of an integrative model that does not involve interactions below.

Integrative Model of Assessment for Achievement Motivation

The approach described above to test an integrative model for ag-gression was extended to construct and test a second integrative model. This model was based on self-reports of achievement motivation and a conditional reasoning measure of achievement motivation. This model was designated the *integrative model of assessment for achievement motivation.*

The integrative model is presented in Table 5.3 (James, McIntyre, & LeBreton, 2000). Illustrative items used in well-accepted personality in-ventories to measure self-perceptions of achievement motivation (and fear of failure) are shown at the top of the model. The justification mechanisms (JMs) for people whose relative motive strength (RMS) fa-vors achievement motivation (i.e., AMs—see Chapter 2 and the discus-sion below) as well as the JMs for those whose RMS favors fear of failure

Table 5.3 Integrative Model of Personality Assessment for Achievement Motivation

	Self-Reported Fear of Failure	Self-Reported Achievement Motivation
	"I am easygoing."	"I am driven to get ahead."
	"I get anxious in testing situations."	"I strive to achieve all I can."
	"I am not obsessive about work."	"I am something of a workaholic."
Conditional reasoning test	"I move to another task if a problem is too difficult."	"I have a strong desire to be a success."

	Hesitant AMs	*Congruent AMs*
	Have conscious concerns about stress and avoiding obsessions	Approach achievement-oriented tasks
	Have an underlying enthusiasm for plunging into achievement-oriented tasks	Are ambitious, aspiring, and industrious
	Experience many approach-avoidance conflicts	

JMs for Achievement Motivation		*AM Pretenders*
Personal Responsibility Bias		Perceive themselves as high achievers, but are disposed to reason based on FF JMs
Opportunity Bias		
Positive Connotation of Achievement Striving Bias		Experience conscious pressure to approach achievement-oriented tasks, but actually approach those tasks on which they can deflect responsibility for failure
Malleability of Skills Bias		
Identification With Achievers Bias		

	Congruent FFs	
	Avoid achievement-oriented tasks	
	Are fearful, nervous, and anxious	

JMs for Fear of Failure
Negative Connotation of Achievement Striving Bias
External Attribution Bias
Liability/Threat Bias
Fixed Skills Bias
Indirect Compensation Bias
Identification With Failures Bias

(i.e., FFs) are presented along the left-hand side of the model. Presented within the model is a typology based on attempts to integrate these two sources of information. As with aggression, the four cells in the model are based on pure types (e.g., a clear AM versus a clear FF crossed with high versus low self-ascribed achievement motivation). In reality, a continuum exists for both relative motive strength and self-ascribed achievement motivation. Crossing these two continua generates a large number of cells representing degrees of variation from the prototypes presented in Table 5.3.

The upper-right cell consists of persons who view themselves as achievement motivated and who possess the corresponding JMs to enhance the logical appeal of achievement behaviors. Members of this cell were designated *Congruent AMs* to denote that motives revealed by reasoning proclivities and self-reports of traits are compatible. Congruent AMs are ambitious, aspiring, and industrious. These behaviors are supported by JMs that encourage the framing of demanding objectives as opportunities worth commitment and sacrifice, where enthusiasm and perseverance will eventually produce success.

The lower-left cell contains individuals who (a) view themselves as low or at least below average in achievement motivation and somewhat anxious in high-demand situations and (b) reason on the basis of FF JMs, which furnish safety mechanisms designed to protect FF individuals from high-demand, potentially stressful activities that could cause them psychological damage (e.g., being subjected to humiliation and disappointment, experiencing a sense of incompetence). Basically, self-perceptions that suggest fear of failure are protected by FF JMs, which serve to dampen enthusiasm for achievement and to justify avoidance of achievement activities or withdrawal from such activities when success becomes uncertain or failure becomes likely. Individuals in this cell were designated *Congruent FFs*.

The upper-left cell comprises individuals who see themselves as non-achievers but who, incongruously, reason in ways that enhance the rational appeal of achievement. These appear to be individuals with conscious concerns for the stress and obsessiveness that can characterize some high achievers. These conscious concerns may serve to dampen if not inhibit a strong latent disposition (indicated by AM JMs) to plunge into achievement-oriented tasks. The accompanying proclivity to reason in ways that justify approaching demanding tasks is likely to engender strong approach-avoidance conflicts with the self-perception of being cautious and stress avoidant. When reason wins out, approach of achievement-oriented tasks will occur, but it will likely be a careful, deliberate approach subject to being arrested if stress is indicated. These individuals were consequently labeled *Hesitant AMs.*

Finally, the lower-right cell of Table 5.3 contains individuals who see themselves as high achievers but who, incongruously, have FF JMs in place. These individuals are, like Congruent FFs, fearful, nervous, and anxious when faced with achievement-oriented tasks. However, unlike Congruent FFs, these individuals' perceptions of themselves as achievers check most attempts to engage openly in avoidance/withdrawal behaviors. Instead, to remain consistent with their self-perceptions, these individuals experience conscious pressure to approach achievement-oriented tasks. The extant FF JMs likely play a protective, albeit subtle, role here. One means by which the FF JMs can subtly protect these individuals from the uncertainties and potential aversive consequences of achievement striving is to shield them from responsibility for failure, should failure occur.

For example, individuals in this cell may attempt only those achievement-oriented tasks for which an excuse of nonaccountability is available (e.g., failure, if it occurs, is due to uncontrollable external forces). A second example consists of what we have described in Chapter 2 as "unnecessary diffusion of responsibility." Unnecessary diffusion occurs when, in an attempt to avoid complete responsibility for important decisions, an executive disperses decision-making responsibility to others, such as subordinates, committees, or teams. Such dispersion is unnecessary, even counterproductive, but the executive justifies it as a form of participative management or empowerment. The designation *AM Pretenders* was used to describe the individuals in this cell because they are really FFs who want to be viewed by themselves and others as AMs.

We will describe the test of the integrative model presented in Table 5.3 shortly. First, however, we want to summarize a conditional reasoning system that was developed to assess the relative strengths of the latent motives to achieve and to avoid failure.

Measurement of Relative Motive
Strength Through Conditional Reasoning

Justification mechanisms are typically used unknowingly by both AMs and FFs. Specifically, reasoning biases imperceptibly shape the reasoning space and define the nature and parameters of what both AMs and FFs take to be rational behavior. The difference between AMs and FFs is that these personality types employ different JMs (see Tables 2.1 and 2.2 in Chapter 2), and thus they arrive at different, and often opposing, judgments about what is and what is not a justifiable decision about whether to approach or avoid challenging tasks.

James (1998) used these differences in (conditional) reasoning to design a new measurement system to assess the dispositional component of resultant achievement motivation (Atkinson, 1957, 1978; McClelland, 1985b). This component consists of the strength of the latent motive to achieve in relation to the strength of the latent motive to avoid failure. James refers to the difference in the relative strengths of these two latent motives as *relative motive strength*. A conditional reasoning test (CRT) was designed to assess relative motive strength; this test is referred to as the CRT-RMS.

The basic premise of the CRT-RMS is that (a) it is possible to infer whether the motive to achieve is dominant or subordinate to the motive to avoid failure by (b) assessing what a person judges to be the more logical—reasoning based on JMs for approach to achievement-oriented objectives or reasoning based on JMs for avoidance of achievement-oriented objectives. If a person consistently sees reason in arguments that advance the logical appeal of approach over avoidance, then it is inferred that this person's relative motive strength favors the need to achieve. Conversely, if a person consistently attributes greater reasonableness to arguments that favor avoidance over approach, then it is inferred that this person's relative motive strength favors the need to avoid failure. A category also exists for cases in which neither type of reasoning or motive has a mandate.

A set of conditional reasoning (CR) problems was designed to measure what a person considers more logical, reasoning based on JMs for AMs or reasoning based on JMs for FFs. An illustrative CR problem is as follows (the discussion that follows is drawn largely from James, 1998):

Studies of the stress-related causes of heart attacks led to the identification of the Type A personality. Type A persons are motivated to achieve, involved in their jobs, competitive to the point of being aggressive, and eager, wanting things completed quickly. Interestingly, these same characteristics are often used to describe the successful person in this country. It would appear that people who wish to strive to be successful should consider that they will be increasing their risk for heart attack.

Which one of the following would most *weaken* the prediction that striving for success increases the likelihood of having a heart attack?

    a. Recent research has shown that it is aggressiveness and impatience, rather than achievement motivation and job involvement, that are the primary causes of high stress and heart attacks.

    b. Studies of the Type A personality are usually based on information obtained from interviews and questionnaires.

    c. Studies have shown that some people fear being successful.

    d. A number of nonambitious people have heart attacks.

This problem requires analysis of the question, Does striving to achieve cause stress-related illnesses such as an increased risk of cardiovascular disease? The stem to the problem advocates an answer of yes. That is, it is asserted that people who strive to achieve have Type A personalities and therefore are increasing their risk of heart attack. The reasoning task is to find a weakness in this assertion.

Alternatives b and c are not reasonable answers to this problem. Discarding the two incorrect alternatives leaves alternatives a and d as possible answers. One of these alternatives is based on a JM for achievement motivation, and one is based on a JM for fear of failure. Which one of these two answers a person judges to be more reasonable is determined by whether his or her reasoning is more strongly influenced by AM or FF implicit reasoning biases or JMs.

The AM alternative.   Let us consider first the alternative based on a JM for achievement motivation. AMs will disagree strongly with the assertion in the stem that people who strive to achieve are increasing their risk for cardiovascular disease. Indeed, a number of AMs (e.g., highly motivated scholars, authors, physicians, executives, and lawyers) were interviewed in the process of problem development. Their analyses of the stem typically included reasoning such as the following:

> It is indeed probable that overload produces stress, and that some people are so obsessed with achievement that they overload themselves and create potentially injurious strains. However, this is an extreme state of affairs and does not apply to ordinary conditions. Simply because a few individuals exercise poor judgment does not imply that strong desires to achieve, to be enthused about one's job, to enjoy competing with peers for promotions,

and to want to progress quickly up career ladders will necessarily evolve into stress and cardiovascular disease. Indeed, motivation, involvement, initiative, competitiveness, and ambition are not stressors. They are forerunners to productivity, attainment of rewards, and a sense of overall (positive) well-being.

This kind of reasoning is indicative of the JM called the Positive Connotation of Achievement Striving Bias. For example, we see AMs' proclivity to frame attempts to achieve as expressions of dedication and commitment that produce productivity, attainment of rewards, and positive affect. In keeping with a positive orientation, we may infer a proclivity to discount associations between achievement striving/job involvement and negative dispositions such as hostility and impatience. Alternative a was designed to draw out this implicit proclivity. That is to say, alternative a is based on the Positive Connotation of Achievement Striving JM. This alternative, if one believes it to be reasonable, identifies a serious logical weakness in the assertion that achievement striving enhances the risk of cardiovascular disease. It stipulates that aggressiveness and impatience, but not achievement motivation and job involvement, are the true causes of increased risk of heart attacks.

Note that in selecting this alternative, a respondent endorses the implicit argument that there is no or very little association between achievement striving and both impatience and hostility. We expected this to be so for AMs, who, given their positive framing of achievement, would *not* be disposed to characterize their need to achieve as an inducement for impatience or hostility.

The FF alternative.   The assertion in the stem—that striving to achieve increases stress and enhances the likelihood of having a heart attack—furnishes reasonable justification to some respondents for avoiding achievement-oriented tasks. These asserted causal links are actually based on two FF JMs. The first such JM is the Negative Connotation of Achievement Striving Bias. This justification denotes a predilection to assume that achievement striving causes stress. The second JM is the Leveling Bias, which in the present context involves associating the stress from striving to achieve with an increased risk of cardiovascular disease.

Interviews with recognized FFs (based on demonstrated behavior) in the process of problem development supported the hypothesis that people high in fear of failure would agree that achievement striving increases stress and the risk of cardiovascular disease. Although they were aware of at least some of the counterarguments, such as that many successful people do not experience cardiovascular disease, recognized FFs were particularly sympathetic to the inference that striving to succeed increases the *risk* of heart attack.

FFs were also inclined to support this assertion with corroborating assumptions, inferences, and theories. They assumed that evidence can be garnered to support the assertion—business executives, for example, have an abnormally high rate of heart attacks. They inferred that it is possible to explain how an achievement orientation spawns stress—people striving to succeed tend to be obsessive, to overload themselves, to be intolerant of normal delays, and to become angry and hostile if their strivings are frustrated. FFs also believed implicitly that the obverse corroborates the assertion—people who take a more relaxed approach to work are less likely to demonstrate symptoms of stress such as exhaustion, illness, burnout, and chronic anxiety about how one's career is progressing.

FFs' penchant to agree with the assertion suggests that they will be less than enthusiastic about weakening the argument that achievement striving engenders stress and cardiovascular disease. Yet the reasoning problem asks for a logical weakness. The reasoning offered by the AM alternative (alternative a) does not fill this role for FFs because FFs are inclined to associate achievement striving with hostility and impatience.

To deal with occasions in which respondents are asked to weaken an assertion with which they agree, the "wounding response" was developed (James, 1998). As the name suggests, the logical solution only "wounds" the favored argument in the stem. It is thus possible to satisfy the requirement for logical weakening but in truth cause only minor logical damage to it. Alternative d represents the wounding response. The fact that a number of nonambitious people have heart attacks weakens the argument that striving to succeed is the only or even a strong cause of cardiovascular disease. However, it leaves open the logical possibility that, for ambitious people, striving to succeed does induce stress and increases the risk of cardiovascular disease.

Relative motive strength. Multiple CR problems have been developed, each of which offers a choice between AM and FF solutions. Respondents are given a score of +1 for every AM alternative they select, a zero for every logically incorrect alternative they select (an infrequent event), and a −1 for every FF alternative they select. These scores are then summed to furnish a composite score on the RMS scale.

The objective of measurement is to determine whether an individual *consistently* prefers AM alternatives or FF alternatives. Respondents who consistently select AM alternatives are believed to possess a motive structure in which the motive to achieve dominates the motive to avoid failure. These respondents have strongly positive scores on the RMS scale and are considered to be AMs. Conversely, consistent selection of FF alternatives is indicative of a motive structure in which the motive to avoid failing dominates the motive to achieve (i.e., the respondents scored as FFs on the RMS scale because they have strongly negative scores). Lack of a consistent pattern of favoritism suggests that neither type of motive dominates, and relative motive strength is regarded as "indeterminate."

We return now to the test of the integrative model presented in Table 5.3.

Tests of the Integrative Model
of Achievement Motivation

The integrative model for achievement motivation was tested on a sample of 263 middle-level managers who participated in an assessment center. The criterion consisted of scores on an in-basket exercise. High scores on this exercise were obtained by managers who were willing to assume personal responsibility for the outcomes of their business decisions. A correlation (empirical validity) of .39 was obtained between scores on the RMS scale and performance on the in-basket exercise. Scores from this scale correlated .32 with scores on Achievement via Independence from the CPI. The CPI is the self-report measure used in this study; like the CRT-RMS, it was given to the managers during the assessment center. The self-ascriptions of achievement motivation furnished by the CPI correlated .38 with in-basket performance.

A prediction based on the integrative model was that Congruent AMs would score the highest of all types in Table 5.3 on the in-basket exercise. Hesitant AMs were also predicted to score highly, although their cautious approach to achievement-oriented tasks indicated that they probably would not score as highly as Congruent AMs. These predic-

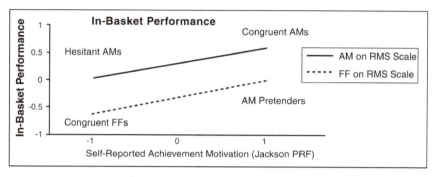

Figure 5.5. Empirical Test of the Integrative Model for Achievement Motivation

tions implied a modestly positive slope for the regression of in-basket performance on self-ascribed achievement motivation for individuals identified as AMs by the RMS scale. The results presented in Figure 5.5 support this prediction. (Statistical procedures employed to generate the slopes in this figure are analogous to those used to generate Figures 5.3 and 5.4. The illustrative slope for AMs is based on scores plus one standard deviation above the mean on the RMS scale.)

The anxiety of being evaluated in an evocative, high-demand situation should inhibit the performance of Congruent FFs. That is, the anticipation of failure and its accompanying embarrassment should produce "test anxiety" (see Sarason, 1978), which in turn should interfere with performance (i.e., "choking under pressure"). The behavioral result was predicted to be the lowest scores of any of the four subgroups of managers on the in-basket exercise. AM Pretenders were also expected to experience a sense of pressure. However, conscious efforts to achieve may have a salutary effect on AM Pretenders' concentration and thus their performance. Consequently, their performance was predicted to be higher than that of Congruent FFs. On the other hand, anxiety over possible failure should have interfered at least partially with performance on a high-stress event such as an in-basket exercise. The predicted result was comparatively lower scores for AM Pretenders than for Congruent AMs.

No prediction was offered regarding differences in performance between AM Pretenders and Hesitant AMs, which precluded making predictions regarding differences in regression slopes between AMs and FFs.

The hypotheses offered above for FFs suggested (a) a positive slope for the regression of in-basket performance on self-reported achievement motivation, and (b) a difference in intercepts between the regression slopes for AMs and FFs. The results, presented in Figure 5.5, confirmed these predictions. Moreover, the slope for FFs was weakly, in terms of significance ($p < .07$), more positive than the slope for AMs. This difference denoted that the variance in in-basket performance between Congruent FFs and AM Pretenders was slightly greater than the difference between Hesitant AMs and Congruent AMs.

The key to Figure 5.5, however, is a highly significant difference ($p < .001$) in the intercepts. These results, combined with the weak indication of an interaction, argued for the use of an additive model on which to base integration of conditional reasoning and self-reported motivation. Congruent AMs had the highest in-basket scores of all subgroups because they were high on both self-ascribed achievement motivation and relative motive strength. Congruent FFs had the lowest performance of all subgroups because they were low on both self-ascribed achievement motivation and relative motive strength. In-basket performances of Hesitant AMs and AM Pretenders fell between those of the two congruent subgroups—Hesitant AMs because their conscious apprehension dampened their latent enthusiasm, and AM Pretenders because their conscious desire to achieve was dampened by their latent apprehension.

An opportunity to replicate the test of the integrative model for achievement motivation was provided by a study of 267 college undergraduates. Overall grade point average (GPA) served as the criterion. Data were available both on the RMS scale from a CRT-RMS and on the Achievement Striving facet of the Conscientiousness factor of the NEO-PI-R. Scores on the RMS scale correlated .00 with scores on self-reported Achievement Striving.

Predictions were based on the additive interpretation of the integrative model. Congruent AMs were predicted to have the highest performance scores (GPAs) of all subgroups because they were high on both self-ascribed achievement motivation and relative motive strength. These are individuals who see themselves as achievement oriented and who have the JMs in place to justify huge expenditures of effort to achieve. Congruent FFs were predicted to have the lowest GPAs of all subgroups because these are individuals who do not see themselves as high in achievement motivation and are prepared to justify avoidance

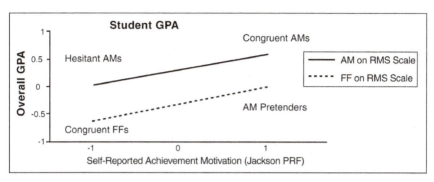

Figure 5.6. Empirical Test of the Integrative Model for Achievement Motivation

of high-demand situations (or to rationalize failure, should it occur). The GPAs of Hesitant AMs and AM Pretenders were hypothesized to fall between those of the two congruent subgroups.

These predictions produced two primary statistical hypotheses. First, the regression slopes relating GPA to self-reported achievement motivation for the AMs and the FFs were both predicted to be positive. Second, the two slopes were predicted to be roughly parallel in slope and significantly varied in intercept.

Graphic results of the statistical analyses are presented in Figure 5.6. Both hypotheses were confirmed. An additive model fit the data. This means that the conditional reasoning measure combined with the self-report measure to enhance prediction significantly over either of the personality measures taken separately. Moreover, the intercepts for the AM and FF regression slopes varied significantly, whereas the slopes did not. Most striking is the similarity in the patterns of slopes when Figure 5.5 is compared with Figure 5.6. The results displayed in Figure 5.6 appear to replicate those presented in Figure 5.5. Thus two field tests, one based on middle-level managers and one based on students, coincided in their support of an additive integrative model for achievement motivation.

General Comments Regarding Integrative Models

Results of four tests of integrative models, involving two different personality domains and two replications, indicate that Winter et al. (1998) are correct in their assumption that traits channel the ways in which latent motives are expressed in cognitive, emotional, and physical behaviors. For example, individuals with strong motives to aggress may, depending on different characteristic ways of behaving, engage in active forms of aggression, such as verbal or physical attack (Manifest Aggressives), or in passive forms of aggression, such as withholding effort (Latent Aggressives). Or individuals with strong motives to achieve may commit themselves completely and intensely to the pursuit of excellence and mastery (Congruent AMs), or they may approach achievement-oriented tasks with hesitation resulting from conflict over whether to approach a challenging task or to avoid a possible psychological hazard (Hesitant AMs).

If research continues to indicate that the same motive is channeled and expressed in different ways by individuals with different traits, then personality research is in for some serious changes. Theoretically, models of the form presented in Tables 5.1, 5.2, and 5.3 will need to be considered. In fact, these rather simple integrative models are likely to give way to more complex models that consider multiple motives and traits simultaneously. Statistically, the days when chi-square and bivariate correlation were the workhorses for personality research will be over. Researchers will need a serious dose of mathematical sophistication to keep current, not to mention to contribute, to the field. A similar statement applies to psychometric sophistication, where the problem-plagued free-response, fantasy-based projective tests will give way to more sophisticated techniques, such as conditional reasoning.

Earlier, we noted our agreement with Winter et al. (1998) that the ease and comfort with which a latent motive is expressed appears to be related to whether or not it is congruent with an individual's characteristic ways of adapting to his or her environment. The research on aggression and achievement motivation also indicates that congruence between latent motive and trait is less likely to engender conflict than is lack of congruence. However, the motive to avoid failure and a characteristic pattern of avoidance behavior are also congruent. Yet the JMs for fear of failure suggest that FFs are consistently engaged in a conflict between motive-driven avoidance and culturally valent achievement. So things may get a bit more complex than the simple hypothesis of congruence indicates.

Finally, the statistical form taken by the integrative relation between latent motive and trait appears to depend on the personality variables under examination. Both additive and nonadditive models have been replicated. Future research may identify still other patterns (e.g., curvilinear relations with or without additivity), and multivariate models are likely when multiple motives and/or traits are considered simultaneously. This again underscores the need for researchers to undertake training in sophisticated statistical techniques.

In sum, integrative models represent the cutting edge in personality research. Organizational researchers conducted some of the initial studies in this area. The way is open for additional organizational researchers to continue this trend.

Coherence

We have defined a trait as a disposition to behave in a relatively consistent manner over time and across different situations. We noted in Chapter 2 that the qualifier *across different situations* has proven to be slippery and a source of confusion and controversy (see Buss, 1989; Epstein & O'Brien, 1985; Funder & Colvin, 1991; Kenrick & Funder, 1988; Pervin, 1990; Wright & Mischel, 1987). To illustrate a fundamental source of concern: Suppose that an individual is designated a Congruent AM based on the integrative model for achievement motivation. We know that this person has a strong latent motive to achieve and is disposed to behave in a manner considered indicative of the trait of achievement motivation. Does the phrase *across different situations* suggest that he or she will select demanding goals and devote intense and persistent effort to accomplishing these goals in divergent areas, such as business, science, music, and athletics? Or, thinking within the confines of organizational research, does being designated a Congruent AM suggest that an individual will devote intense and persistent effort to accomplishing demanding goals in each aspect of a job or vocation? For example, do all Congruent AM college professors seek to excel in research, teaching, committee work, student counseling, mentoring, community service, professional activities, informal leadership with peers, and faculty governance?

The answer to both questions is no. We proceeded in Chapter 2 to describe how a fragile understanding has developed about what is meant by consistency of behavior over diverse situations. This understanding is based on two premises. The first is that people are "situationally discriminative" (see Mischel, 1990; Mischel & Peake, 1982; Mischel &

Shoda, 1999). In reference to the current example, Congruent AMs may express their desire and behavioral disposition to achieve in many different ways. For example, manifest achievement motivation could be expressed behaviorally through striving to become a successful entrepreneur, or a successful author, or a successful scientist, or a successful teacher, or a successful boxer, or a successful thief. Values have a strong influence on the specific path that each person pursues in his or her quest to behave in a manner that satisfies a desire and willingness to achieve (see Locke, 1991; McClelland et al. 1989). Moreover, people develop senses regarding the types of situations in which they are likely to succeed. A not insignificant component of this sense of "self-efficacy" is expectancy based on judgments of whether one has the skills, or is capable of developing the skills, to succeed (see Gist & Mitchell, 1992).

The second premise, that of "coherence," builds on the situational discriminativeness premise to argue that behavior is organized even though it may not appear to be. That is, as a result of value-based, situationally discriminative choices of areas in which to excel, behavior appears to be situationally specific at a molecular level. However, at a molar level, a replicable pattern is seen in how a person behaves (i.e., does or does not attempt to excel) among diverse situations (see Grote & James, 1991). Over time and replications of the same or similar situations, a pattern will emerge that indicates an enduring tendency to call forth achievement behaviors in some situations (e.g., to excel in research) and to hold back attempts to achieve in other situations (e.g., faculty governance). This pattern of engagement-nonengagement is referred to as a *cross-situational profile*. When replicable, it indicates a lawfulness and consistency to behavior (see Magnusson, 1976). The term *coherence* is used to indicate the stability or replicability of cross-situational profiles (see Grote & James, 1991; Mischel, 1984).

Situational Discriminativeness in Organizational Research

The situational discriminativeness premise is implicitly accepted in many domains of organizational research. An exemplar is the idea of person-environment (P-E) fit described in Chapter 2. When options are available, people typically prefer to decide which types of vocations and work environments are best for them. Research has shown that these decisions are based on the congruence or fit between an individual's (a) values, interests, and skills and (b) perceived attributes of a vocation and/or a work environment, as reflected by such things as the skill requirements and challenge of a job, pay levels and benefits, supportiveness of leadership, opportunities for promotion, and organizational norms regarding loyalty and compliance (see Bretz & Judge, 1994; Cable & Judge, 1994, 1996, 1997; Chatman, 1989, 1991; Chatman & Barsade, 1995; Edwards & Harrison, 1993; Gustafson & Mumford, 1995; Hogan & Blake, 1996; Hogan et al., 1996; Judge & Ferris, 1992; Kristof, 1996; O'Reilly, Chatman, & Caldwell, 1991; Rynes, Bretz, & Gerhart, 1991; Schaubroeck, Ganster, & Jones, 1998; Schneider, Goldstein, & Smith, 1995; Schneider, Smith, & Goldstein, 2000; Schneider, Smith, Taylor, & Fleenor, 1998; Turban & Keon, 1993).

To illustrate, values in the P-E fit research generally concern conscious interests, desires, goals, preferred modes of conduct, preferred rewards and incentives, expectations, and plans (see Chapter 2). In applications regarding vocational choice, values are often framed in terms of vocational interests and measured using instruments such as the Strong-Campbell Interest Inventory (see Campbell, 1974), which in its 1994 revised form is the Strong Interest Inventory (SII). This instrument and many others like it are based on Holland's (1973, 1985a) taxonomy of occupational interests. Reviewed recently by Hogan and Blake (1996), this taxonomy of interests generates the following six occupational types:

- *Realistic:* practical, hands-on, real-world individuals who prefer action-oriented vocations
- *Investigative:* people with abstract, analytic, theory-oriented interests
- *Artistic:* imaginative and impractical individuals who try to entertain, amuse, and fascinate others
- *Social:* people who are interested in helping, serving, and assisting others
- *Enterprising:* people who attempt to manipulate, persuade, and outperform others
- *Conventional:* people with interests in counting, regulating, and organizing people and things

A Congruent AM who expresses interests consistent with the Enterprising type is likely to direct his or her achievement motivation toward succeeding in business occupations. (This presumes a belief on the part of the individual that he or she possesses, or can develop, the requisite skills to be successful in business.) Conversely, a Congruent AM who is interested in artistic endeavors is likely to devote intense and persistent effort to becoming a successful musician (or actor, artist, dancer, and so on). Additional examples are easily imagined. In each example, we would see what in effect is an extension of the channeling hypothesis (Winter et al., 1998). That is, traits channel the expression of motives, and values/self-efficacy channel the vocations in which the traits are expressed.

Values and efficacy are also likely to channel the type of organization in which an individual manifests his or her traits. For example, our enterprising, Congruent AM is likely to seek out a "nonrestrictive" type of organizational climate. As described in Chapter 2, nonrestrictive climates are characterized by managers who place confidence in employees, who value and emphasize independent accomplishment, and who encourage employees to develop their full potentials to perform (see James, Demaree, Mulaik, & Ladd, 1992). These "systems values" define an organizational climate and culture that is characterized by decentralization of overall authority structures, minimal formalization of communications and standardization of job requirements, reward and incentive systems based on individual merit, and a penchant to adopt innovative ideas for solving problems.

On the other hand, our artistically inclined Congruent AM is likely to gravitate toward organizational settings that encourage or at least tolerate emotional, expressive, impulsive, nonconforming, and entertaining behavior. Organizations of interest to such individuals include theater companies, art communities, orchestras, and academic settings.

Based on the discussion above, one might surmise that organizational researchers have the situational discriminativeness concept well in hand. Although this is true in such areas as vocational interests and P-E fit, it is much less true in other domains of organizational research. Furthermore, the concept of coherence has yet to be abused through overuse in organizational studies. This is unfortunate because it suggests that the rebirth of personality research in organizations is incomplete if not somewhat rudimentary, having missed one of the key concepts in personality. Perhaps of even more concern is that in its present state, organizational research appears to have been misinterpreting some of its research data. We address these points below.

In Search of Coherence

We have discussed how traits channel motives and how values/self-efficacy channel vocational choice and organizational selection. Now that we have the individual in a vocation and an organization in which to ply that vocation, let's consider behavior on different organizational tasks. To add a bit of drama to this discussion, we shall assume that neither employers nor organizational researchers have knowledge of the personality makeup of the subjects. Indeed, the objective of the research is to ascertain the level of "motivation" of each subject.

We could use a number of different approaches to this problem, and all would essentially provide the same inferences. Our illustrative vehicle will be assessment centers for managers, because this is where we have traits such as motivation (and leadership, agreeableness, interpersonal skills) measured on multiple exercises (a surrogate for multiple tasks or situations). This also appears to be an area that could benefit from the introduction of the concept of coherence.

Let us begin with a brief introduction to assessment centers. Organizations needed a means to assess organization members' potential to become successful managers. They also needed a way to circumvent the problems indigenous to collecting accurate performance data in natural settings (e.g., random shocks in economy; see Austin & Villanova, 1992; Feldman, 1981). These two needs combined to stimulate the development of procedures to measure performance on new tasks under controlled observational conditions. Exercises were constructed that ostensibly enabled researchers to control for a variety of factors and yet presented examinees with tasks or experiences that were representative of those they had yet to face in real life. In the context of personnel selection, these exercises were referred to as *situational tests.*

Situational testing became popular during and following World War II. The tests were initially used to assess individuals' suitability for military, especially intelligence, endeavors. The basic approach was to place examinees in situations that closely resembled or simulated real performance situations. For example, the U.S. Office of Strategic Services (OSS) used a variety of situational tests to assess tolerance of stress. The selection of candidates for intelligence officers was based on examinees' performance on these tests.

The OSS's assessment program for selecting intelligence officers served as the prototype for what we refer to today as *assessment centers.*

The effectiveness of assessment centers for management selection was demonstrated by Bray and his colleagues (see Bray, 1984; Bray, Campbell, & Grant, 1974; Bray & Grant, 1966; Howard & Bray, 1988). The formats of assessment centers vary widely, and centers may last from a few hours to a few days. The basic idea is to assemble a set of situational tests on which each examinee is evaluated. We shall focus here on the types of situational tests used often to assess managerial potential.

An illustrative situational test, or "exercise," found often in assessment centers for managers is the *leaderless group discussion* (LGD) (see Bass, 1954). A typical LGD asks a group of candidates to discuss a work-related problem, such as how to terminate a disruptive employee or how to restructure the organization to enhance employee morale. The strategy for discussion is purposely left unstructured, and no leader is designated. Moreover, participants usually do not know each other. The objective of the exercise is to determine which participant(s) is sufficiently motivated and skilled to take over the group and lead it in a productive discussion (Bass, 1960).

Additional examples of tests include role-playing and in-basket exercises. In the former kinds of exercises, one examinee might be assigned the role of manager while another examinee is assigned the role of union representative, with the two given the task of negotiating a new labor contract. Each examinee is evaluated on how he or she behaves interpersonally to solve the problem. In in-basket exercises, examinees are often given information and data and then are asked to complete a task, such as developing an effective strategy for marketing or deciding who should be hired for a job (see Brannick, Michaels, & Baker, 1989). Examinees are evaluated on the quality of their strategies/decisions and their willingness to take responsibility for their choices.

After examinees are assessed on each exercise by one or more assessors (who typically differ for each exercise), the assessors collate information and attempt to rate each examinee on his or her potential to become an effective manager. (Particular centers might add a test of intellectual aptitude and/or a self-report personality survey and/or an interview to the mix.) Validities of these assessments of managerial potential in relation to such things as promotion rate tend to be of modest but useful magnitude (see Gaugler, Rosenthal, Thornton, & Bentson, 1987; Goffin, Rothstein, & Johnston, 1996; Klimoski & Brickner, 1987; McEvoy & Beatty, 1989; Russell & Domm, 1995).

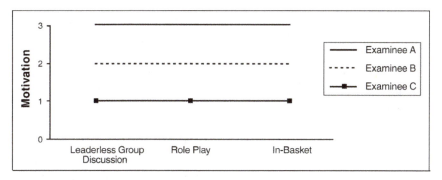

Figure 5.7. Cross-Situational Profiles for Absolute Cross-Situational Consistency

We focus here on assessment centers because they furnish one of the few occasions in organizational research in which the same individuals are assessed on the same traits over multiple situations (exercises). Assessment centers thus provide a unique opportunity to test key concepts in personality, such as cross-situational consistency and coherence. Organizational researchers have been partially aware of this unique opportunity and have used assessment center data to examine whether behavior (i.e., performance) on different exercises is "cross-situationally consistent," which would indicate the presence of a trait, or "situationally specific," which would indicate that behavior varies as a function of the exercise or situation (see Brannick et al., 1989; Bycio, Alvares, & Hahn, 1987; Coovert, Craiger, & Teachout, 1997; Sackett & Dreher, 1982; Schneider & Schmitt, 1992; Shore, Shore, & Thornton, 1992).

An advanced statistical technique known as confirmatory factor analysis is often used to contrast cross-situational consistency with situational specificity. This statistic is beyond our scope here, but the basic issues that concern us can be dealt with by simple models that extend to more elaborate statistical processes. Let us return, therefore, to the objective, which is to use an assessment center to ascertain the level of "motivation" of each of a set of examinees. A salient question in this assessment process is whether the data indicate the presence of a trait of motivation.

Figure 5.7 displays results for three examinees, each of whom has participated in each of three assessment center exercises (i.e., a leaderless group discussion, a role-playing exercise, and an in-basket exercise).

The "motivation" of each examinee has been assessed in each exercise or "situation" (by different assessors in each exercise). The "cross-situational (exercise) profile" for each examinee is shown in Figure 5.7. Each of these cross-situational profiles reflects "absolute cross-situational consistency." This is because each examinee demonstrates the same basic *level* of motivation in each situation (exercise).

Given that situations are truly diverse, the results in Figure 5.7 provide a strong case for the "trait" of motivation. Each examinee continues to behave in the same way even though the situations vary. Our assessors would have considerable confidence in concluding that Examinee A is highly motivated, Examinee B is moderately motivated, and Examinee C has low motivation.

There is general agreement among most personality researchers that absolute cross-situational consistency occurs with about the same frequency as legitimate sightings of leprechauns. Thus no one can, or does, require absolute cross-situational consistency to infer that a trait exists. Although Figure 5.7 presents an enviable scenario, it is not a realistic one.

The cross-situational profiles presented in Figure 5.8 reflect "relative cross-situational consistency." The average (over examinees) level of motivation per situation varies systematically over situations. This denotes that situations account for variance in motivation. Specifically, leaderless group discussions engender very high motivation, role-playing exercises engender moderate to high motivation, and in-basket exercises trigger moderate motivation. However, differences in situations do not account for all of the variance in motivation. Examinees still vary significantly *within* each situation. Moreover, the *relative* standing of examinees, or the rank ordering of examinees, is consistent over situations. This is what is meant by *relative* cross-situational consistency.

There is further agreement among most personality researchers that relative cross-situational consistency provides reasonably strong evidence for a trait. Note that situations have effects, which suggests that, on the average, situations set bounds on potency of motivation (or some situations are generally evocative and some are not). It is the relative consistency of rank ordering that is important from a trait or individual difference perspective. The interpretation of the trait is that Examinee A is more motivated than either Examinee B or Examinee C across diverse situations. Examinee B is comparatively in the middle of

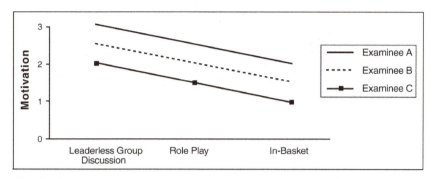

Figure 5.8. Cross-Situational Profiles for Relative Cross-Situational Consistency

the pack in motivation, whereas Examinee C is consistently the least motivated of the group.

Tests of relative cross-situational consistency are the objectives of research on assessment centers. Results of these tests generally indicate that differences in situations (exercises) account for variance in performance. This is not surprising and does not contraindicate the presence of traits. The similarities of rank orderings on the same trait over situations, determined by correlations, tend to be modest for each of the traits included in research. The case for traits can thus be said to be modest, perhaps even equivocal. Or can it?

An illustration of a generally equivocal set of relationships is provided in Figure 5.9. The rank ordering within the LGD exercise is correlated .50 with the rank orderings within both the role-playing and in-basket exercises, whereas the rank ordering within the role-playing exercise is correlated −.50 with the rank ordering within the in-basket exercise. The absolute level of motivation also varies by situation. According to current standards for interpreting such data in organizational research, investigators would likely suggest a situational (exercise) effect and a weak or equivocal case for traits. It would be difficult to make general statements about the motivation of each examinee from either an absolute or a relative perspective.

Unfortunately, this approach fails to consider coherence. Suppose we have the same three examinees repeat the assessment center. Suppose further that we obtain the cross-situational profiles shown in Figure 5.10. At first blush, it may appear that an equivocal case has again been obtained for traits. That is, it is equivocal until we notice that the

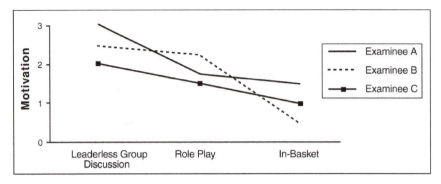

Figure 5.9. Cross-Situational Profiles for Equivocal Case of Relative Cross-Situational Consistency

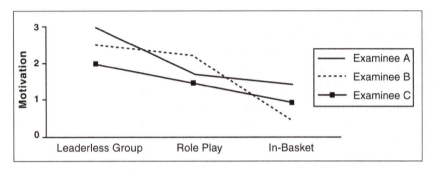

Figure 5.10. Cross-Situational Profiles for Coherence

cross-situational profiles in Figure 5.10 are identical to those in Figure 5.9. Each examinee behaves as he or she behaved before in each situation. *Coherence* is the term used to describe this consistency or replicability in patterns of behavioral responses to diverse situations. And, as we have stressed, coherence is indicative of the presence of a trait.

Basically, there is a lawfulness to behavior that goes unnoticed if we focus only on consistency of rank orders. This lawfulness is revealed only if we examine cross-situational profiles for replicability, which is to say coherence. Inasmuch as repeated measurements are a very rare event in organizational research, replicability is almost never investigated. But then, with rare exceptions (see Grote & James, 1991),

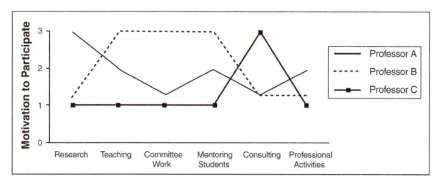

Figure 5.11. Cross-Situational Profiles for Three College Professors

cross-situational profiles are not considered either. A possible if not likely result of this failure to consider cross-situational profiles and the coherence of such profiles is misinterpretation of data. Data such as those shown in Figure 5.9 could be, and quite possibly have been, (mis)interpreted as indicative of equivocal support of traits.

That is the bad news. The good news is that we in organizational research are awakening to the problems of disregarding cross-situational profiles and coherence. Additional good news is that coherence is an area that provides a vast array of research opportunities. And it is an obvious next step as we move forward to tests of channeling hypotheses and integrative models. An important first task for coherence research is the development of procedures for interpreting cross-situational profiles. One approach that researchers have used on student samples is to cluster cross-situational profiles to create "types" based on similarity of response patterns to situations (Grote & James, 1991).

In closing this treatment of coherence, we shall return to a prior illustration. The scenario was that of a college professor and situational discriminativeness. Inasmuch as many of the readers of this text are college professos or aspire to be such, we assume this scenario is relevant. In Figure 5.11 we present the cross-situational profiles of three illustrative college professors. We ask the readers to be the judges of whether these profiles indicate (a) lack of relative cross-situational consistency and therefore no indication of a trait or (b) cross-situational profiles that are likely to replicate and thus indicate a trait, or more likely the constellation of several traits.

Differential Framing

Psychology has been increasingly fascinated with biases in how people see and think about the world. Accumulating evidence suggests that these biases are driven by implicit (latent, unconscious) motives (see Aspinwall & Taylor, 1997; Brewin, 1989; Crocker & Major, 1989; Dweck & Leggett, 1988; Einhorn & Hogarth, 1978; Feldman, 1981; Fiske & Taylor, 1984, 1991; Funder, 1987; Greenwald & Banaji, 1995; Jussim, 1991; Nisbett & Wilson, 1977; Pyszczynski & Greenberg, 1987; Rothman & Salovey, 1997; Taylor, 1991; Taylor & Brown, 1988; Taylor & Lobel, 1989; Taylor, Pham, Rivkin, Armor, 1998; Thompson, Armstrong, & Thomas, 1998; Westen, 1991; Wood, 1989). Biases engendered by latent motives are often mapped into consciousness and made public by the *adjectives* that individuals use to describe evocative behaviors, people, situations, or events. Thus much of the research cited above has focused on *framing*, which is the name given to the cognitive process of associating interpretative adjectives with behaviors, people, situations, or events. In our discussion of implicit social cognition in Chapter 3, we defined framing as the valuation of attributes and events in terms of their "meaning" (substance, intent, psychological significance) to the individual.

We also described differential framing in Chapter 3. Differential framing occurs when people with different latent motives frame behaviors, persons, environments, and events in qualitatively disparate ways (James, 1998). Some examples:

> AMs are prone to frame a change in school curriculum in terms of its effects on brighter students (e.g., Will the change make these students more or less attractive to good colleges?), whereas FFs are prone to frame the same change in terms of its effects on less bright students (e.g., As a result of the change, will these students be singled out or stigmatized as intellectually inferior?).

> On meeting a new person, aggressive individuals are prone to pass the person through a prism of potency, the purpose of which is to evaluate his or her strength versus weakness, probability of becoming a rival, and likelihood of being dominant or submissive in a relationship. Nonaggressive individuals are more likely to pass the person through a prism of friendship, the goal of which is to evaluate the likelihood of the development of a warm and trusting relationship with this person.

Emotionally unstable, neurotic individuals are predisposed to frame work situations in terms of stress, threat, constraints, and aversive outcomes, which engenders negative affect and dissatisfaction (e.g., anxiety, uneasiness, apprehension, dread). Emotionally stable people are predisposed to frame the same work situations in terms of commitment, motivation, opportunity, and rewards, thereby engendering positive affect and satisfaction (attraction, happiness, engagement, contentment).

Agreeable individuals are disposed to frame authority figures as leaders, defenders, protectors, and possible mentors. Disagreeable individuals are more likely to frame these same individuals as exploiters, tyrants, oppressors, and adversaries.

We noted in Chapter 3 that the impetus for differential framing is the fact that everyone wants to believe that his or her own behavior is justified, which is to say rational and sensible as opposed to irrational and foolish. In attempts to justify behavior, people develop unrecognized biases, referred to as justification mechanisms, the purpose of which is to enhance the rational appeal of motive-based behavior. Inasmuch as people with different motives behave differently, they develop different, generally qualitatively different, JMs. When these qualitatively different JMs are mapped onto perceptions of the same behaviors, people, environments, or events with the implicit purpose of justifying different behaviors, we have differential framing.

More specifically, psychological significance or meaning in the context of differential framing denotes that a behavior, person, environment, or event is interpreted in such a way as to serve an underlying motive. That is, framing implicitly enhances the logical appeal of motive-based behavior. From the perspective of a perceiver engaged in differential framing (which does not encompass all perception), the psychological significance of a behavior, person, environment, or event is determined by the role of that behavior, person, environment, or event in justifying motive-based behavior. The psychological significance of the behavior, person, environment, or event will increase to the extent that it can be framed in such as way as to enhance its contribution to the rational appeal of motive-based behavior.

In sum, people with different motives engage in different behaviors, and they develop different JMs to justify these behaviors. Different JMs indicate (a) different implicit assumptions about what constitutes rational behavior and (b) different schemata or beliefs for imputing psychological significance or meaning to behavior and the people, contexts, and events that surround behavior. Inasmuch as JMs vary qualitatively, the (differential) framing that derives from them also tends to vary qualitatively.

The illustrations above support these points. In the first example, AMs frame changes in school curriculum from the perspective of high performers, which is a product of a bias (JM) to identify and empathize with those like themselves who succeed in demanding situations (see Table 2.1). FFs frame these same changes from the perspective of poor performers, which reflects a bias to identify and empathize with those like themselves, who (usually) have not done well in demanding situations (see Table 2.2). AMs' selective focus on high performers is *qualitatively* different from FFs' selective focus on poor performers. We suggest that this qualitative disparity in focus is indicative of a qualitative disparity in what is psychologically significant to AMs and FFs. And this we believe is of paramount importance to our understanding of the psychological makeup of AMs and FFs.

Consider next the qualitative disparity in the ways that aggressive and nonaggressive individuals frame new acquaintances. What is psychologically significant to aggressive individuals is whether the acquaintance is (a) strong, assertive, powerful, daring, fearless, or brave versus (b) weak, impotent, submissive, timid, sheepish, compliant, or cowardly. How the new acquaintance fares on these perceptions will determine how the aggressive individual behaves toward him or her. Nonaggressive individuals have a qualitatively different focus. What is psychologically significant to them is whether the acquaintance conveys a sense of (a) warmth, friendship, affection, or camaraderie versus a sense of (b) distance, coolness, restraint, or indifference. Here again, perception determines behavior.

In a similar vein, what is psychologically significant to emotionally unstable and negative-affect-disposed individuals about job environments is the perceived amount of stress, threat, constraints, and aversive outcomes in these environments. Their goal is to find environments with minimal levels of these attributes, presumably to avoid or to obtain relief from negative affective experiences such as anxiety, uneasiness, apprehension, dread, and dissatisfaction.

Psychologically stable, positive-affect-prone individuals (differentially) frame job environments from the perspectives of commitment, motivation, opportunity, and rewards. These interpretative schemata derive their psychological significance from their roles in engendering positive affective experiences such as attraction, happiness, engagement, contentment, and satisfaction. Emotionally stable individuals are also likely to seek out environments that offer them occasions to work intensely, to commit themselves to something important, to better themselves, and to obtain rewards. They may also leave organizations that fail to offer such opportunities.

Finally, the psychological significance of authority figures to agreeable individuals resides in how these individuals function as leaders, defenders, protectors, and mentors. Accordingly, agreeable people tend to (differentially) frame the actions of authority figures from the perspectives of leadership, guardianship, protection, and mentoring. Authority figures who fail to score high in these domains are not likely to receive support from agreeable individuals.

To disagreeable individuals who perhaps have a tendency toward aggressiveness, authority figures have meaning as exploiters, tyrants, oppressors, and adversaries. Such disagreeable individuals thus see the actions of authority figures through an interpretative lens that is sensitive to exploitation, tyranny, oppression, and adversity. To them, authority figures represent a contest for dominance.

In sum, differential framing focuses on qualitative disparities in what people with different motives and different JMs consider psychologically significant about behavior, people, environments, and events. The respective framing is important because it influences motive-relevant behavior. The conditional reasoning systems described in Chapter 4 and earlier in this chapter rely strongly on the fact that how a respondent (differentially) frames a reasoning problem determines the type of logical appeal to which he or she will be most responsive. In other words, differential framing is the first step in conditional reasoning.

Our objective here, however, is not to rehash conditional reasoning. Rather, we shall concentrate on how researchers might harness the concept of differential framing to contribute to other domains of organizational research. For illustrative purposes, we suggest how differential framing might contribute to dispositional research on job satisfaction.

Does Job Satisfaction Have Dispositional Components?

For years it was assumed that situational antecedents determine an individual's satisfaction with a job. Indeed, the facets of overall job satisfaction were (and are) generally defined by situational variables such as satisfaction with pay, satisfaction with coworkers, satisfaction with leaders, and satisfaction with the work itself. Research initiated by Staw and Ross (1985), with contributions by a host of others (e.g., Arvey, Bouchard, Segal, & Abraham, 1989; Gerhart, 1987; Judge & Locke, 1993; Levin & Stokes, 1989; Newton & Keenan, 1991; Staw, Bell, & Clausen, 1986; Steel & Rentsch, 1997), questioned the basic assumption that job satisfaction is exclusively determined by situational conditions and events.

Staw and colleagues proposed an individual differences component to job satisfaction such that some people are disposed to be satisfied with their jobs and other people are disposed to be dissatisfied. This hypothesis was supported by evidence collected on repeated measurements of job satisfaction, which demonstrated that job satisfaction is temporally stable. That is, repeated measurements on job satisfaction show that individual differences in who is and who is not satisfied are significantly and often moderately correlated over time. This is a necessary but not sufficient condition for a dispositional tendency (see Chapter 2).

The most recent research by Steel and Rentsch (1997) suggests that the correlation between repeated measurements on job satisfaction, taken 10 years apart, is in the .40 range. This relationship is higher for people performing the same work at both times of measurement (the correlation reflects temporal stability) than it is for people performing different types of work at each time of measurement (the correlation reflects cross-situational consistency with a time lag). Steel and Rentsch conclude that job satisfaction has both dispositional and situational antecedents.

Based on their recent broad review of subjective well-being in a multitude of social environments, Diener, Suh, Lucas, and Smith (1999) reach a similar conclusion. Consistent with Staw and Ross (1985), these researchers found that general satisfaction has a dispositional component. Also consistent with Staw and Ross (and Arvey et al., 1989) is their hypothesis that a possibly biologically based personality trait that leads one to see positive or negative content in one's life explains the disposition to be satisfied or dissatisfied with one's job.

Recent research has shown that a propensity to see positive or negative affect in one's life is related significantly to the disposition to be satisfied or dissatisfied with one's job (see Cropanzano, James, & Kovonovsky, 1993; Duffy, Ganster, & Shaw, 1998; Judge, 1992; Judge & Locke, 1993; Judge, Locke, Durham, & Kluger, 1998; Levin & Stokes, 1989; Staw et al., 1986). In a typical study, self-report measures of positive-negative affectivity are correlated with self-reports of job satisfaction. For example, positive-negative affectivity might be measured by the PANAS (Watson, Clark, & Tellegen, 1988). Illustrative items are as follows: "Generally (on the average) I feel: interested, enthusiastic, strong, distressed, scared, nervous, etc." (each emotion is measured on a scale varying from 1 = *strongly disagree* to 5 = *strongly agree*). Job satisfaction might be assessed by any number of measures, almost all of which measure satisfaction with one's work, coworkers, supervisor, pay, opportunities for promotion, and the like.

Studies such as those described above are a good first step in testing the hypothesis that people who frame the world in positive terms, and thereby experience positive emotions, are predisposed to experience more positive job satisfaction than are people who are predisposed to frame the world in negative terms, thereby engendering the experience of negative emotions. Unfortunately, these studies contain no measure of how people frame the world. We simply have a measure of two emotional tendencies, one pertaining to general affectivity and one pertaining to an attitude in a specific type of situation (i.e., jobs). Without measurement and testing of the key causal mechanism, differential framing, explanation of the general to specific emotion correlation is speculative and open to alternative interpretations.

One such alternative explanation is that the emotion-satisfaction correlation is spurious due to a common method of measurement and redundancy in the constructs being correlated (see Williams, Gavin, & Williams, 1996). Another alternative explanation is that unmeasured situational factors engender similar affect and satisfaction at two points in time (Davis-Blake & Pfeffer, 1989).

Assessing the Effects of Positive and Negative Affectivity on Job Satisfaction Through Differential Framing

To reiterate briefly, emotionally unstable people frame evocative situations, which include work situations, through a lens that places psychological significance on stress, threat, constraints, and aversive outcomes. These are neurotic individuals with a proclivity to experience negative affect (e.g., anxiety, uneasiness, apprehension, dread) in general and dissatisfaction with their jobs (see Chapter 3; see also George, 1996; Tellegen, 1982, 1985). In contrast, emotionally stable people frame evocative situations through interpretative prisms that affix psychological significance to commitment, motivation, opportunity, and rewards. These are self-reliant individuals with a penchant to experience positive affect (e.g., attachment, happiness, engagement, and contentment) in general and satisfaction with their jobs. (It is noteworthy that our treatment of positive and negative affect is based on recent research indicating that positive and negative affectivity are bipolar; see Barrett & Russell, 1998; Russell & Carroll, 1999.)

Based on the above, the hypotheses we believe should be tested are as follows:

1. Emotionally unstable people will tend to frame work and other evocative environments in terms of stress, threat, constraints, and aversive outcomes. Compared with emotionally stable individuals, they will be more likely to experience negative affect in these environments. In regard to work environments specifically, they will tend to be dissatisfied.

2. Emotionally stable people will frame work and other salient environments in terms of commitment, motivation, opportunity, and rewards. Compared with emotionally unstable individuals, they will be more likely to experience positive affect in these environments. In regard to work environments specifically, they will tend to be satisfied.

To test these hypotheses, we must be able to identify emotionally stable and emotionally unstable individuals. One of the personality inventories described in Chapter 4 may be used for this purpose. We also need to be able to assess general affective tendencies and specific job satisfaction. A plethora of methods will suffice here (see the works cited above); examples would be the PANAS, described above, for general affective tendencies and the Job Descriptive Index (Smith, Kendall, & Hulin, 1969) for job satisfaction.

Unfortunately, no means currently exist to measure the key intervening causal mechanism that ties emotional stability to general affect and then to satisfaction. We need a way to access the type of lens used by each individual to impute psychological significance to environments. We need to know if this lens interprets incoming stimuli in terms of (a) stress, threat, constraints, and aversive outcomes or (b) commitment, motivation, opportunity, and rewards.

The general "framing" literatures that exist in decision theory and experimental cognition are of little help here. These literatures (a) place essentially no emphasis on individual differences and (b) employ experimental procedures that would be very difficult to effect in the field (e.g., signal detection). Field studies of framing tend to lean toward the same type of self-report techniques that are used to measure the other variables in our study. For example, we might simply design a set of items that ask individuals to rate the degree to which each of our key adjectives (stress, threat, commitment, rewards, and so on) is associated with work environments. Or we might get a bit more sophisticated and design a forced-choice system in which a respondent must choose between negative and positive adjectives. For example:

Work: stressful or rewarding (choose one)

We are not enthused about these options because they are subject to the self-report method variance problem that plagues the other measures in this study. As an alternative, James and McIntyre (1996) have suggested an indirect measurement procedure for differential framing that could be adapted to the present problem. The suggested process involves a test for synonyms. It is not a self-report measure, and it is expressly designed to capture qualitative differences in framing.

Respondents are presented with a stimulus word and are asked to identify a synonym from one of three alternatives. The rationale is to use a stimulus word and alternatives that implicitly trigger (a) emotionally unstable individuals' proclivities to frame in terms of negative psychological attributes and (b) emotionally stable individuals' propensities to frame in terms of positive psychological attributes. The answers to each problem provide opportunities for emotionally unstable people and emotionally stable people to exercise their respective framing proclivities. The basic idea is that emotionally unstable and emotionally stable individuals will reveal their latent framing propensities through the alternatives they select as the correct answers to the problems.

To illustrate, individuals could be asked to select the most reasonable synonym for each of the 10 stimulus words listed in Table 5.4. It is expected that emotionally unstable respondents will tend to select the synonyms in the first column of the table as the correct answers to the problems. (In a real test, the answers to the various stimulus words

Table 5.4   Illustrative Measure of Differential Framing for Positive-Negative
Affectivity

Pick the word that is most like the stimulus word in meaning:

Stimulus Words	Possible Synonyms		
Responsible	blamable	accountable	opportune
Difficult	intractable	strenuous	relentless
Critique	criticize	analyze	exaggerate
Novel	untried	different	candid
Committed	bound	devoted	stipulated
Sensitive	excitable	perceptive	virtuous
Cautious	fearful	careful	spiteful
Composed	dispassionate	calm	gratuitous
Risky	dangerous	unpredictable	ruthless
Absorbed	obsessed	focused	pardoned

would be randomized.) Selection of these synonyms indicates a propensity to frame the world through a lens that ascribes a negative tone to
behaviors, people, environments, and events. In contrast, emotionally
stable people would be expected to select the synonyms in the second
column as the correct answers to the problems. Selection of these synonyms indicates a propensity to frame the world using a lens that im-
parts a positive tone to behaviors, people, environments, and events.
The words in the third column of Table 5.4 are not synonyms for the
stimulus word. They are included to mask the true intent of the measurement system, which is to obtain an indirect assessment of propensity to frame differentially in terms of negative or positive tones.

   If this system proves to be valid, then the selection of synonyms
should be significantly predictable by emotional stability. Differential
framing should in turn predict general affective disposition. It should
also have a healthy indirect effect on dispositional tendencies to be satisfied or dissatisfied with one's job. We would thus have tested and confirmed a key link in the theory that explains the dispositional component of job satisfaction. We would have even greater faith in our results
if we have first controlled for differences in situational attributes before
conducting our "dispositional" analysis.

Conclusion

Individual differences in framing are rapidly becoming one of the prominent research topics in psychology. We suspect that the popularity of this area will grow because differential framing opens the door to a much more powerful measurement system, namely, one based on qualitative differences among individuals. Qualitative differences in framing provide a stronger basis for differentiating among individuals than do the typical quantitative systems in use today. The latter systems attempt to measure psychological meaning using common scales for all respondents. For example, a quantitative scale might ask all individuals to rate how much they agree with the statement "My job is challenging." A qualitative approach would first be concerned with whether an individual even thinks of his or her job in terms of how "challenging" it is (compared, say, with "stressful" or "threatening"). We progress in terms of both explanation and predictive power by being able to assess the distinct perspectives and interpretative adjectives that different people use to impute meaning to the same behaviors, environments, and events.

Studies of differential framing are beginning to be seen in the organizational literature. Included here are Pinkley's (1990) study of differential interpretations of conflict; Thompson and Loewenstein's (1992) examination of differential interpretations of interpersonal conflict; Silver, Mitchell, and Gist's (1995) study of attributions for performance; and Franke, Crown, and Spake's (1997) study of gender differences in the ethics of business practices. We expect the frequency of studies such as these to increase substantially.

Finally, the synonyms test illustrates only one of many measurement systems that might be developed to measure differential framing. Areas such as policy capturing and multidimensional scaling appear to be worthwhile candidates for exploring how to capture differences in framing. The opportunity to adapt old approaches or to create new ones to assess differential framing is yet another source for creative endeavor in an area with high probability for scientific contribution.

Closing Comments

We have presented three seminal ideas that we believe will have impacts on personality research in industrial and organizational behavior.

We have suggested how each idea might enhance the quality of current research. We have also noted that each idea requires at least a minor paradigm shift in how personality research is conducted in organizational settings. Integrative models of personality assessment require the procurement of data on implicit motives. Coherence requires the acquisition of repeated measurements on behavior in each of multiple, diverse situations. Differential framing requires the development of techniques to measure qualitative differences in perception. We believe that advances in theory, combined when possible with results of early empirical tests, indicate that a willingness to engage in these new efforts will be rewarded with enhanced understanding and prediction.

We make no claim to having exhausted all possible creative endeavors in personality. In fact, we considered treating subjects such as dysfunctional behavior, the attraction-selection-attrition model, integrity testing, and ability-personality interactions in this chapter. We decided to focus on integrative models, coherence, and differential framing because these are truly novel paradigms that are in the very early stages of development. It is here that enterprising researchers have considerable latitude and opportunity to determine the trajectories that research will take in the near future.

References

Ackerman, P. L., & Heggestad, E. D. (1997). Intelligence, personality, and interests: Evidence for overlapping traits. *Psychological Bulletin, 121,* 219-245.

Aiken, L. R. (1994). *Psychological testing and assessment* (8th ed.). Needham Heights, MA: Allyn & Bacon.

Allport, G. W. (1937). *Personality: A psychological interpretation.* New York: Holt.

Allport, G. W. (1961). *Pattern and growth in personality.* New York: Holt, Rinehart & Winston.

Allport, G. W., & Allport, F. H. (1928). *The A-S Reaction Study.* Boston: Houghton Mifflin.

Allport, G. W., & Odbert, H. S. (1936). Trait-names: A psycho-lexical study. *Psychological Monographs, 47* (Serial No. 211).

American Educational Research Association. (1999). *Standards for educational and psychological testing.* Washington, DC: Author.

Anastasi, A. (1982). *Psychological testing* (5th ed.). New York: Macmillan.

Anderson, E. (1994, May). The code of the streets. *Atlantic Monthly,* pp. 81-94.

Arvey, R. D., Bouchard, T. J., Segal, N. L., & Abraham, L. M. (1989). Job satisfaction: Environmental and genetic components. *Journal of Applied Psychology, 74,* 187-192.

Aspinwall, L. G., & Taylor, S. E. (1997). A stitch in time: Self-regulation and proactive coping. *Psychological Bulletin, 121,* 417-436.

Atkinson, J. W. (1957). Motivational determinants of risk-taking behavior. *Psychological Review, 64,* 359-372.

Atkinson, J. W. (Ed.). (1958). *Motives in fantasy, action, and society.* Princeton, NJ: Van Nostrand.

Atkinson, J. W. (1978). The mainsprings of achievement-oriented activity. In J. W. Atkinson & J. O. Raynor (Eds.), *Personality, motivation, and achievement* (pp. 11-39). Washington, DC: Hemisphere.

Atkinson, J. W. (1981). Studying personality in the context of an advanced motivational psychology. *American Psychologist, 36,* 117-128.

Atkinson, J. W., & McClelland, D. C. (1948). The projective expression of needs: II. The effect of different intensities of the hunger drive on thematic apperception. *Journal of Experimental Psychology, 38,* 643-658.

Austin, J. T., & Villanova, P. (1992). The criterion problem: 1917-1992. *Journal of Applied Psychology, 77,* 836-874.

Averill, J. R. (1993). Illusions of anger. In R. B. Felson & J. T. Tedeschi (Eds.), *Aggression and violence: Social interactionist perspectives* (pp. 171-192). Washington, DC: American Psychological Association.

Bandura, A. (1973). *Aggression: A social learning analysis.* Englewood Cliffs, NJ: Prentice Hall.

Bandura, A. (1977). Self-efficacy: Toward a unifying theory of behavioral change. *Psychological Review, 84,* 191-215.

Bandura, A. (1978). The self system in reciprocal determinism. *American Psychologist, 33,* 344-358.

Bandura, A. (1986). *Social foundations of thought and action: A social cognitive theory.* Englewood Cliffs, NJ: Prentice Hall.

Bandura, A. (1991). Social cognitive theory of self-regulation. *Organizational Behavior and Human Decision Processes, 50,* 248-287.

Banks, C. (1948). Primary personality factors in women: A reanalysis, 1948. *British Journal of Psychology–Statistical Section, 1,* 204-218.

Baron, R. A., & Richardson, D. R. (1994). *Human aggression* (2nd ed.). New York: Plenum.

Barrett, L. F., & Russell, J. A. (1998). Independence and bipolarity in the structure of current affect. *Journal of Personality and Social Psychology, 74,* 967-984.

Barrick, M. R., & Mount, M. K. (1991). The Big Five personality dimensions and job performance: A meta-analysis. *Personnel Psychology, 44,* 1-26.

Barrick, M. R., & Mount, M. K. (1993). Autonomy as a moderator of the relationship between the Big Five personality dimensions and job performance. *Journal of Applied Psychology, 78,* 111-118.

Barrick, M. R., & Mount, M. K. (1996). Effects of impression management and self-deception on the predictive validity of personality constructs. *Journal of Applied Psychology, 81,* 261-272.

Barrick, M. R., Stewart, G. L., Neubert, M. J., & Mount, M. K. (1998). Relating member ability and personality to work-team processes and team effectiveness. *Journal of Applied Psychology, 83,* 377-391.

Barry, B., & Stewart, G. L. (1997). Composition, process, and performance in self-managed groups: The role of personality. *Journal of Applied Psychology, 82,* 62-78.

Bass, B. M. (1954). The leaderless group discussion. *Psychological Bulletin, 51,* 465-492.

Bass, B. M. (1960). *Leadership, psychology and organizational behavior.* New York: Harper & Row.

Baumeister, R. F. (1982). A self-presentational view of social phenomena. *Psychological Bulletin, 91,* 3-26.

Baumeister, R. F., & Scher, S. J. (1988). Self-defeating behavior patterns among normal individuals: Review and analysis of common self-destructive tendencies. *Psychological Bulletin, 104,* 3-22.

Baumeister, R. F., Smart, L., & Boden, J. M. (1996). Relation of threatened egotism to violence and aggression: The dark side of high self-esteem. *Psychological Review, 103,* 5-33.

Becker, T. E., & Colquitt, A. L. (1992). Potential versus actual faking of a biodata form: An analysis along several dimensions of item type. *Personnel Psychology, 45,* 389-406.

Bellack, J., Parsquarelli, B. A., & Branerman, S. (1949). The use of the Thematic Apperception Test in psychotherapy. *Journal of Nervous and Mental Disease, 110,* 51-65.

Bellak, L. (1986). *The TAT, CAT, and SAT in clinical use* (4th ed.). New York: Grune & Stratton.

Berkowitz, L. (1993). *Aggression: Its causes, consequences, and control.* New York: McGraw-Hill.

Bing, M. N., Burroughs, S. M., Whanger, J. C., Green, P. D., & James, L. R. (2000). The integrative model of personality assessment for aggression: Implications for personnel selection and predicting deviant workplace behavior. In J. M. LeBreton & J. F. Binning (Chairs), *Recent issues and innovations in personality assessment.* Symposium conducted at the annual meeting of the Society for Industrial and Organizational Psychology, New Orleans.

Birney, R. C. (1968). Research on the achievement motive. In E. F. Borgatta & W. W. Lambert (Eds.), *Handbook of personality theory and research.* Chicago: Rand McNally.

Block, J. (1995). A contrarian view of the five-factor approach to personality description. *Psychological Bulletin, 117,* 187-215.

Bolton, B. (1992). Review of the California Psychological Inventory, revised edition. In J. J. Kramer & J. C. Conoley (Eds.), *The eleventh mental measurements yearbook* (pp. 138-139). Lincoln, NE: Buros Institute of Mental Measurements.

Borgatta, E. F. (1964). The structure of personality characteristics. *Behavioral Science, 12,* 8-17.

Borkenau, P., & Ostendorf, F. (1990). Comparing exploratory and confirmatory factor analysis: A study on the five-factor model of personality. *Personality and Individual Differences, 11,* 515-524.

Borum, R. (1996). Improving the clinical practice of violence risk assessment: Technology, guidelines, and training. *American Psychologist, 51,* 945-956.

Bouchard, T. J., Jr. (1969). Personality, problem-solving procedure, and performance in small groups. *Journal of Applied Psychology, 53*(1, pt. 2), 1-29.

Bowers, K. S. (1973). Situationism in psychology: An analysis and critique. *Psychological Review, 80,* 307-336.

Bradbury, T. N., & Fincham, F. D. (1990). Attributions in marriage: Review and critique. *Psychological Bulletin, 107,* 3-33.

Brand, C. R. (1984). Personality dimensions: An overview of modern trait psychology. In J. Nicholson & H. Beloff (Eds.), *Psychology survey 5.* Leicester, England: British Psychological Society.

Brannick, M. T., Michaels, C. E., & Baker, D. P. (1989). Construct validity of in-basket scores. *Journal of Applied Psychology, 74,* 957-963.

Bray, D. W. (1984, August). *Assessment centers for research and application.* Psi Chi Distinguished Lecture presented at the annual meeting of the American Psychological Association, Toronto.

Bray, D. W., Campbell, R. J., & Grant, D. L. (1974). *Formative years in business: A long term AT&T study of managerial lives.* New York: John Wiley.

Bray, D. W., & Grant, D. L. (1966). The assessment center in the measurement of potential for business management. *Psychological Monographs, 80.*

Brehmer, B. (1976). Social judgment theory and the analysis of interpersonal conflict. *Psychological Bulletin, 83,* 985-1003.

Bretz, R. D., & Judge, T. A. (1994). Person-organization fit and the theory of work adjustment: Implications for satisfaction, tenure, and career success. *Journal of Vocational Behavior, 44,* 32-54.

Brewin, C. R. (1989). Cognitive change processes in psychotherapy. *Psychological Review, 96,* 379-394.

Briggs, S. R. (1989). The optimal level of measurement for personality constructs. In D. M. Buss & M. C. Cantor (Eds.), *Personality psychology: Recent trends and emerging directions* (pp. 201-209). New York: Springer-Verlag.

Briggs, S. R. (1992). Assessing the five-factor model of personality description. *Journal of Personality, 60,* 253-293.

Budescu, D. V. (1993). Dominance analysis: A new approach to the problem of relative importance of predictors in multiple regression. *Psychological Bulletin, 114,* 542-551.

Burroughs, S. M., & Jones, J. J. (1995, March/April). Managing violence: Looking out for trouble. *OHS Canada,* pp. 34-37.

Buss, A. H. (1961). *The psychology of aggression.* New York: John Wiley.

Buss, A. H. (1989). Personality as traits. *American Psychologist, 44,* 1378-1388.

Buss, A. H., & Finn, S. E. (1987). Classification of personality traits. *Journal of Personality and Social Psychology, 52,* 432-444.

Buss, A. H., & Perry, M. (1992). The aggression questionnaire. *Journal of Personality and Social Psychology, 63,* 452-459.

Buss, A. H., & Plomin, R. (1984). *A temperament theory of personality development* (Rev. ed.). New York: John Wiley

Buss, D. M., & Craik, K. H. (1983). The act frequency approach to personality. *Psychological Review, 90,* 105-126.

Bycio, P., Alvares, K. M., & Hahn, J. (1987). Situational specificity in assessment center ratings: A confirmatory factor analysis. *Journal of Applied Psychology, 72,* 463-474.

Cable, D. M., & Judge, T. A. (1994). Pay preferences and job search decisions: A person-organization fit perspective. *Personnel Psychology, 47,* 317-348.

Cable, D. M., & Judge, T. A. (1996). Person-organization fit, job choice decisions, and organizational entry. *Organizational Behavior and Human Decision Processes, 67,* 294-311.

Cable, D. M., & Judge, T. A. (1997). Interviewers' perceptions of person-organization fit and organization selection decisions. *Journal of Applied Psychology, 82,* 546-561.

Campbell, D. P. (1974). *Manual for the SVIB-SCII Strong Campbell Interest Inventory* (2nd ed.). Stanford, CA: Stanford University Press.

Campbell, D. P., & Van Velsor, E. (1985). The use of personality measures in a management development program. In H. J. Bernardin & D. A. Bownas (Eds.), *Personality assessment in organizations.* New York: Praeger.

Cascio, W. G. (1989). *Managing human resources: Productivity, quality of work life, profiles* (2nd ed.). New York: McGraw-Hill.

Cattell, R. B. (1947). Confirmation and classification of primary personality factors. *Psychometrika, 12,* 197-220.

Cattell, R. B. (1950). *Personality: A systematic, theoretical and factual study.* New York: McGraw-Hill.

Cattell, R. B. (1957). *Personality and motivation structure and measurement.* New York: World Book.

Cattell, R. B. (1965). *The scientific analysis of personality.* London: Penguin.

Cellar, D. F., Miller, M. L., Doverspike, D. D., & Klawsky, J. D. (1996). Comparison of factor structures and criterion-related validity coefficients for two measures of personality based on the five factor model. *Journal of Applied Psychology, 81,* 694-704.

Cervone, D. (1991). The two disciplines of personality psychology. *Psychological Science, 2,* 371-372.

Chatman, J. A. (1989). Improving interactional organizational research: A model of person-organizational fit. *Academy of Management Review, 14,* 333-349.

Chatman, J. A. (1991). Matching people and organizations: Selection and socialization in public accounting firms. *Administrative Science Quarterly, 36,* 459-484.

Chatman, J. A., & Barsade, S. G. (1995). Personality, organizational culture, and cooperation: Evidence from a business simulation. *Administrative Science Quarterly, 40,* 423-443.

Church, A. T., & Katigbak, M. S. (1989). Internal, external, and self-report structure of personality in a non-Western culture: An investigation of cross-language and cross-cultural generalizability. *Journal of Personality and Social Psychology, 57,* 857-872.

Cohen, R. J., Montague, P., Nathenson, L. S., & Swerdlik, M. E. (1988). *Psychological testing: An introduction to tests and measurement.* Mountain View, CA: Mayfield.

Cooper, W. H. (1981). Ubiquitous halo. *Psychological Bulletin, 90,* 218-244.

Coovert, M. D., Craiger, J. P., & Teachout, M. S. (1997). Effectiveness of the direct product versus confirmatory factor model for reflecting the structure of multimethod-multirater job performance data. *Journal of Applied Psychology, 82,* 271-280.

Cortina, J. M., Doherty, M. L., Schmitt, N., Kaufman, G., & Smith, R. G. (1992). The "Big Five" personality factors in the IPI and MMPI: Predictors of police performance. *Personnel Psychology, 45,* 119-140.

Costa, P. T., Jr., & McCrae, R. R. (1985). *The NEO Personality Inventory manual.* Odessa, FL: Psychological Assessment Resources.

Costa, P. T., Jr., & McCrae, R. R. (1988). Personality in adulthood: A six-year longitudinal study of self-reports and spouse ratings on the NEO Personality Inventory. *Journal of Personality and Social Psychology, 54,* 853-863.

Costa, P. T., Jr., & McCrae, R. R. (1992a). *Revised NEO Personality Inventory (NEO-PI-R) and NEO Five-Factor Inventory (NEO-FFI) professional manual.* Odessa, FL: Psychological Assessment Resources.

Costa, P. T., Jr., & McCrae, R. R. (1992b). Trait psychology comes of age. In T. B. Sonderegger (Ed.), *Nebraska Symposium on Motivation: Vol. 39. Psychology and aging* (pp. 169-204). Lincoln: University of Nebraska Press.

Costa, P. T., Jr., McCrae, R. R., & Holland, J. L. (1984). Personality and vocational interests in an adult sample. *Journal of Applied Psychology, 69,* 390-400.

Costa, P. T., Jr., & Widiger, T. A. (Eds.). (1994). *Personality disorders and the five-factor model of personality.* Washington, DC: American Psychological Association.

Cramer, P. (2000). Defense mechanisms in psychology today: Further processes for adaptation. *American Psychologist, 55,* 637-646.

Cramer, P., & Blatt, S. J. (1990). Use of the TAT to measure change in defense mechanisms following intensive psychotherapy. *Journal of Personality Assessment, 54,* 236-251.

Crick, N. R., & Dodge, K. A. (1994). A review and reformulation of social information-processing mechanisms in children's social adjustment. *Psychological Bulletin, 115,* 74-101.

Crites, J. O., Bechtold, H. P., Goodstein, L. D., & Heilbrun, A. B., Jr. (1961). A factor analysis of the California Psychological Inventory. *Journal of Applied Psychology, 45,* 408-414.

Crocker, J. (1981). Judgment of covariation by social perceivers. *Psychological Bulletin, 90,* 272-292.

Crocker, J., & Major, B. (1989). Social stigma and self-esteem: The self-protective properties of stigma. *Psychological Review, 96,* 608-630.

Cronbach, L. J. (1951). Coefficient alpha and the internal structure of tests. *Psychometrika, 16,* 297-334.

Cropanzano, R., James, K., & Kovonovsky, M. A. (1993). Dispositional affectivity as a predictor of work attitudes and job performance. *Journal of Organizational Behavior, 14,* 595-606.

Crowne, D. P. (1979). *The experimental study of personality.* Hillsdale, NJ: Lawrence Erlbaum.

Crowne, D. P., & Marlowe, D. (1960). A new scale of social desirability independent of psychopathology. *Journal of Consulting Psychology, 24,* 349-354.

Crowne, D. P., & Marlowe, D. (1964). *The approval motive.* New York: John Wiley.

Dahlstrom, W. G. (1969). Recurrent issues in the development of the MMPI. In J. N. Butcher (Ed.), *MMPI: Research developments and clinical applications.* New York: McGraw-Hill.

Dana, R. H. (1982). *A human science model for personality assessment with projective techniques.* Springfield, IL: Charles C Thomas.

Davis-Blake, A., & Pfeffer, J. (1989). Just a mirage: The search for dispositional effects in organizational research. *Academy of Management Review, 14,* 385-400.

Diener, E., Suh, E. M., Lucas, R. E., & Smith, H. L. (1999). Subjective well-being: Three decades of progress. *Psychological Bulletin, 125,* 276-302.

Digman, J. M. (1988, August). *Classical theories of trait organization and the Big Five factors of personality.* Paper presented at the annual meeting of the American Psychological Association, Atlanta, GA.

Digman, J. M. (1990). Personality structure: Emergence of the five-factor model. *Annual Review of Psychology, 41,* 417-440.

Digman, J. M., & Takemoto-Chock, N. K. (1981). Factors in the natural language of personality: Re-analysis, comparison, and interpretation of six major studies. *Multivariate Behavioral Research, 16,* 149-170.

Dodge, K. A. (1986). A social information processing model of social competence in children. In M. Perlmutter (Ed.), *Minnesota Symposia on Child Psychology: Vol. 18. Cognitive perspectives on children's social and behavioral development* (pp. 77-125). Hillsdale, NJ: Lawrence Erlbaum.

Dodge, K. A., & Coie, J. D. (1987). Social-information-processing factors in reactive and proactive aggression in children's peer groups. *Journal of Personality and Social Psychology, 53,* 1146-1158.

Dodge, K. A., & Crick, N. R. (1990). Social information-processing bases of aggressive behavior in children. *Personality and Social Psychology Bulletin, 16,* 8-22.

Douglas, E. F., McDaniel, M. A., & Snell, A. F. (1996, August). *The validity of non-cognitive measures decays when applicants fake.* Paper presented at the annual meeting of the Academy of Management, Cincinnati, OH.

Duffy, M. K., Ganster, D. C., & Shaw, J. D. (1998). Positive affectivity and negative outcomes: The role of tenure and job satisfaction. *Journal of Applied Psychology, 83,* 950-959.

Dweck, C. S., & Leggett, E. L. (1988). A social-cognitive approach to motivation and personality. *Psychological Review, 95,* 256-273.

Edwards, A. L. (1957a). *The social desirability variable in personality assessment and research.* New York: Dryden.

Edwards, A. L. (1957b). *Techniques of attitude scale construction.* New York: Appleton-Century-Crofts.

Edwards, J. R., & Harrison, R. V. (1993). Job demands and worker health: Three-dimensional reexamination of the relationship between P-E fit and strain. *Journal of Applied Psychology, 78,* 628-648.

Einhorn, H. J., & Hogarth, R. M. (1978). Confidence in judgment: Persistence of the illusion of validity. *Psychological Review, 85,* 395-416.

Emler, N. P. (1990). A social psychology of reputation. *European Review of Social Psychology, 1,* 173-193.

Endler, N. S. (1975). The case for person-situation interactions. *Canadian Psychological Review, 16,* 12-21.

Endler, N. S., & Magnusson, D. (1976). Toward an interactional psychology of personality. *Psychological Bulletin, 83,* 956-974.

Englehard, G., Jr. (1992). Review of the California Psychological Inventory, revised edition. In J. J. Kramer & J. C. Conoley (Eds.), *The eleventh mental measurements yearbook* (pp. 139-141). Lincoln, NE: Buros Institute of Mental Measurements.

Epstein, S. (1979). The stability of behavior: I. On predicting most of the people much of the time. *Journal of Personality and Social Psychology, 37,* 1097-1126.

Epstein, S. (1983). The stability of confusion: A reply to Mischel and Peake. *Psychological Review, 90,* 179-184.

Epstein, S. (1994). Integration of the cognitive and the psychodynamic unconscious. *American Psychologist, 49,* 709-724.

Epstein, S., & O'Brien, E. J. (1985). The person-situation debate in historical and current perspective. *Psychological Bulletin, 98,* 513-537.

Erdelyi, M. H. (1992). Psychodynamics and the unconscious. *American Psychologist, 47,* 784-787.

Eysenck, H. J. (1952). *The scientific study of personality.* London: Routledge & Kegan Paul.

Eysenck, H. J. (1965). The effects of psychotherapy. *International Journal of Psychiatry, 1,* 97-178.

Eysenck, H. J. (1970). *The structure of human personality* (3rd ed.). London: Methuen.

Eysenck, H. J. (Ed.). (1981). *A model for personality.* New York: Springer-Verlag.

Feldman, J. M. (1981). Beyond attribution theory: Cognitive processes in performance appraisal. *Journal of Applied Psychology, 66,* 127-148.

Feldman, J. M., & Lindell, M. K. (1989). On rationality. In I. Horowitz (Ed.), *Organization and decision theory* (pp. 83-164). Boston: Kluwer Academic.

Felson, R. B., & Tedeschi, J. T. (Eds.). (1993). *Aggression and violence: Social interactionist perspectives.* Washington, DC: American Psychological Association.

Finnegan, W. (1997, December 1). The unwanted. *New Yorker,* pp. 61-78.

Fisher, G. (1967). Normative and reliability data for the standard and the cross-validated Marlowe-Crowne Social Desirability Scale. *Psychological Reports, 20,* 174.

Fiske, D. W. (1949). Consistency of the factorial structures of personality ratings from different sources. *Journal of Abnormal Social Psychology, 44,* 329-344.

Fiske, S. T., & Taylor, S. E. (1984). *Social cognition.* Reading, MA: Addison-Wesley.

Fiske, S. T., & Taylor, S. E. (1991). *Social cognition* (2nd ed.). New York: McGraw-Hill.

Folger, R., & Baron, R. A. (1996). Violence and hostility at work: A model of reactions to perceived injustice. In G. R. VandenBos & E. Q. Bulatao (Eds.), *Violence on the job: Identifying risks and developing solutions* (pp. 51-85). Washington, DC: American Psychological Association.

Franke, G. R., Crown, D. F., & Spake, D. F. (1997). Gender differences in ethical perceptions of business practices: A social role theory perspective. *Journal of Applied Psychology, 82,* 920-934.

Funder, D. C. (1987). Errors and mistakes: Evaluating the accuracy of social judgment. *Psychological Bulletin, 101,* 75-90.

Funder, D. C., & Colvin, C. R. (1991). Explorations in behavioral consistency: Properties of persons, situations, and behaviors. *Journal of Personality and Social Psychology, 60,* 773-794.

Furnham, A. (1992). *Personality at work: The role of individual differences in the workplace.* New York: Routledge.

Gandy, J. A., Dye, D. A., & MacLane, C. N. (1994). Federal government selection: The individual achievement record. In G. S. Stokes, M. D. Mumford, & W. Owens (Eds.), *Biodata handbook: Theory, research, and use of biographical information in selection and performance prediction* (pp. 275-309). Palo Alto, CA: Consulting Psychologists Press.

Gaugler, B. B., Rosenthal, D. B., Thornton, G. C., III, & Bentson, C. (1987). Meta-analysis of assessment center validity. *Journal of Applied Psychology, 72*, 493-511.

Gay, P. (1993). *The cultivation of hatred.* New York: W. W. Norton.

George, J. M. (1996). Trait and state affect. In K. Murphy (Ed.), *Individual differences and behavior in organizations* (pp. 145-171). San Francisco: Jossey-Bass.

George, J. M., & Brief, A. P. (1992). Feeling good—doing good: A conceptual analysis of the mood at work-organizational spontaneity relationship. *Psychological Bulletin, 112*, 310-329.

Gerhart, B. (1987). How important are dispositional factors as determinants of job satisfaction? Implications for job design and other personnel programs. *Journal of Applied Psychology, 72*, 366-373.

Ghiselli, E. E. (1966). *The validity of occupational aptitude tests.* New York: John Wiley.

Gist, M. E., & Mitchell, T. R. (1992). Self-efficacy: A theoretical analysis of its determinants and malleability. *Academy of Management Review, 17*, 183-211.

Goffin, R. D., Rothstein, M. G., & Johnston, N. G. (1996). Personality testing and the assessment center: Incremental validity for managerial selection. *Journal of Applied Psychology, 81*, 746-756.

Goldberg, L. R. (1971). A historical survey of personality scales and inventories. In P. McReynolds (Ed.), *Advances in psychological assessment* (Vol. 2, pp. 293-336). Palo Alto, CA: Science & Behavior.

Goldberg, L. R. (1981). Language and individual differences: The search for universals in personality lexicons. In L. Wheeler (Ed.), *Review of personality and social psychology* (Vol. 2, pp. 141-165). Beverly Hills, CA: Sage.

Goldberg, L. R. (1990). An alternative "description of personality": The Big Five factor structure. *Journal of Personality and Social Psychology, 59*, 1216-1229.

Goldberg, L. R. (1993). The structure of phenotypic personality traits. *American Psychologist, 48*, 26-34.

Goldberg, L. R., & Saucier, G. (1995). So what do you propose we use instead? A reply to Block. *Psychological Bulletin, 117*, 221-225.

Gough, H. G. (1957). *California Psychological Inventory manual.* Palo Alto, CA: Consulting Psychologists Press.

Gough, H. G. (1969). *California Psychological Inventory, revised manual.* Palo Alto, CA: Consulting Psychologists Press.

Gough, H. G. (1987). *California Psychological Inventory: Administrator's guide.* Palo Alto, CA: Consulting Psychologists Press.

Gowan, J. C. (1958). Intercorrelations and factor analysis of tests given to teaching candidates. *Journal of Experimental Education, 27*, 1-22.

Green, P. D., & James, L. R. (1999, May). The use of conditional reasoning to predict deceptive behavior. In L. J. Williams & S. M. Burroughs (Chairs), *New developments using conditional reasoning to measure employee reliability.* Symposium presented at the annual meeting of the Society for Industrial and Organizational Psychology, Atlanta, GA.

Green, S. G., & Mitchell, R. R. (1979). Attributional processes of leaders in leader-member interactions. *Organizational Behavior and Human Performance, 23,* 429-458.

Greenwald, A. G., & Banaji, M. R. (1995). Implicit social cognition: Attitudes, self-esteem, and stereotypes. *Psychological Review, 102,* 4-27.

Grote, G. F., & James, L. R. (1991). Testing behavioral consistency and coherence with the situation-response measure of achievement motivation. *Multivariate Behavioral Research, 26,* 655-691.

Groth-Marnat, G. (1984). *Handbook of psychological assessment.* New York: Van Nostrand Reinhold.

Groth-Marnat, G. (1990). *Handbook of psychological assessment* (2nd ed.). New York: John Wiley.

Guilford, J. P. (1940). *An inventory of factors.* Beverly Hills, CA: Sheridan Supply.

Guilford, J. P., & Martin, H. G. (1943). *The Guilford-Martin Inventory of Factors: GAMIN: Manual of directions and norms.* Beverly Hills, CA: Sheridan Supply.

Guilford, J. P., & Zimmerman, W. S. (1956). Fourteen dimensions of temperament. *Psychological Monographs, 70*(10).

Guion, R. M. (1965). *Personality testing.* New York: McGraw-Hill.

Guion, R. M., & Gottier, R. F. (1965). Validity of personality measures in personnel selection. *Personnel Psychology, 18,* 135-164.

Gulliksen, H. (1950). *Theory of mental tests.* New York: John Wiley.

Gustafson, S. B., & Mumford, M. D. (1995). Personal style and person-environment fit: A pattern approach. *Journal of Vocational Behavior, 46,* 163-188.

Hall, D. T. (1971). A theoretical model of career subidentity development in organizational settings. *Organizational Behavior and Human Performance, 6,* 50-76.

Hargrave, G. E., & Hiatt, D. (1980). Use of the California Psychological Inventory in law enforcement officer selection. *Journal of Personality Assessment, 53,* 267-277.

Hess, A. K. (1992). Review of the NEO Personality Inventory. In J. J. Kramer & J. C. Conoley (Eds.), *The eleventh mental measurements yearbook* (pp. 603-605). Lincoln, NE: Buros Institute of Mental Measurements.

Hinshaw, S. P. (1992). Externalizing behavior problems and academic underachievement in childhood and adolescence: Causal relationships and underlying mechanisms. *Psychological Bulletin, 111,* 127-155.

Hogan, J., & Hogan, R. (1986). *Hogan Personnel Selection Series manual.* Minneapolis: National Computer Systems.

Hogan, J., & Hogan, R. (1989). How to measure employee reliability. *Journal of Applied Psychology, 74,* 273-279.

Hogan, R. (1983). A socioanalytic theory of personality. In M. M. Page (Ed.), *Nebraska Symposium on Motivation, 1982: Personality—current theory and research* (pp. 55-89). Lincoln: University of Nebraska Press.

Hogan, R. (1986). *Hogan Personality Inventory.* Minneapolis: National Computer Systems.

Hogan, R. (1991). Personality and personality measurement. In M. D. Dunnette & L. M. Hough (Eds.), *Handbook of industrial and organizational psychology* (Vol. 2, pp. 873-919). Palo Alto, CA: Consulting Psychologists Press.

Hogan, R., & Blake, R. J. (1996). Vocational interests: Matching self-concept and the work environment. In K. R. Murphy (Ed.), *Individual differences and behavior in organizations* (pp. 89-144). San Francisco: Jossey-Bass.

Hogan, R., & Hogan, J. (1992). *Hogan Personality Inventory manual.* Tulsa, OK: Hogan Assessment Systems.

Hogan, R., & Hogan, J. (1995). *Hogan Personality Inventory manual* (2nd ed.). Tulsa, OK: Hogan Assessment Systems.

Hogan, R., Hogan, J., & Busch, C. (1984). How to measure service orientation. *Journal of Applied Psychology, 91,* 289-295.

Hogan, R., Hogan, J., & Roberts, B. W. (1996). Personality measurement and employment decisions. *American Psychologist, 51,* 469-477.

Hogan, R., & Roberts, B. W. (2000). Socioanalytic perspective on person-environment interaction. In W. B. Walsh, K. H. Craik, & R. H. Price (Eds.), *Person-environment psychology: New directions and perspectives* (2nd ed., pp. 1-23). Mahwah, NJ: Lawrence Erlbaum.

Hogarth, R. M. (1987). *Judgement and choice* (2nd ed.). Chichester, England: John Wiley.

Holland, J. L. (1973). *Making vocational choices: A theory of careers.* Englewood Cliffs, NJ: Prentice Hall.

Holland, J. L. (1985a). *Making vocational choices: A theory of vocational personalities and work environments* (2nd ed.). Englewood Cliffs, NJ: Prentice Hall.

Holland, J. L. (1985b). *Self-directed search.* Odessa, FL: Psychological Assessment Resources.

Holland, J. L., Johnston, J. A., Hughey, K. F., & Asama, N. F. (1991). Some explorations of a theory of careers: VII. A replication and some possible extensions. *Journal of Career Development, 18,* 91-100.

Holmes, D. S. (1978). Projection as a defense mechanism. *Psychological Bulletin, 85,* 677-688.

Holmes, D. S. (1981). Existence of classical projection and the stress-reducing function of attributive projection: A reply to Sherwood. *Psychological Bulletin, 90,* 460-466.

Hough, L. M. (1992). The "Big Five" personality variables—Construct confusions: Description versus prediction. *Human Performance, 5,* 139-155.

Hough, L. M., Eaton, N. K., Dunnette, M. D., Kamp, J. D., & McCloy, R. A. (1990). Criterion-related validities of personality constructs and the effect of response distortion on those validities. *Journal of Applied Psychology, 75,* 581-595.

Hough, L. M., & Schneider, R. J. (1996). Personality traits, taxonomies, and applications in organizations. In K. Murphy (Ed.), *Individual differences and behavior in organizations* (pp. 31-88). San Francisco: Jossey-Bass.

House, R. J., Shane, S. A., & Herold, D. M. (1996). Rumors of the death of dispositional research are vastly exaggerated. *Academy of Management Review, 21,* 203-224.

Howard, A., & Bray, D. W. (1988). *Managerial lines in transition.* New York: Guilford.

Huesmann, L. R. (1988). An information processing model for the development of aggression. *Aggressive Behavior, 14,* 13-24.

Hurtz, G. M., & Donovan, J. J. (2000). Personality and job performance: The Big Five revisited. *Journal of Applied Psychology, 85,* 869-879.

Ilgen, D. R., Barnes-Farrell, J. L., & McKellin, D. B. (1993). Performance appraisal process research in the 1980s: What has it contributed to appraisals in use? *Organization Behavior and Human Decision Processes, 54,* 321-368.

Jackson, D. N. (1967). *Personality Research Form manual.* Goshen, NY: Research Psychologists Press.

James, L. R. (1998). Measurement of personality via conditional reasoning. *Organizational Research Methods, 1,* 131-163.

James, L. R. (1999, May). *Use of conditional reasoning to measure employee reliability.* Paper presented at the annual meeting of the Society for Industrial and Organizational Psychology, Atlanta, GA.

James, L. R., Demaree, R. G., Mulaik, S. A., & Ladd, R. T. (1992). Validity generalization in the context of situational models. *Journal of Applied Psychology, 77,* 3-14.

James, L. R., Hater, J. J., Gent, M. J., & Bruni, J. R. (1978). Psychological climate: Implications from cognitive social learning theory and interactional psychology. *Personnel Psychology, 31,* 783-813.

James, L. R., & McIntyre, M. D. (1996). Perceptions of organizational climate. In K. Murphy (Ed.), *Individual differences and behavior in organizations* (pp. 416-450). San Francisco: Jossey-Bass.

James, L. R., & McIntyre, M. D. (2000). *Conditional Reasoning Test of Aggression test manual.* Knoxville, TN: Innovative Assessment Technology.

James, L. R., McIntyre, M. D., & LeBreton, J. M. (2000, April). *Innovations in selection: Use of conditional reasoning to identify reliable and achievement-motivated employees.* Workshop presented at the annual meeting of the Society for Industrial and Organizational Psychology, New Orleans.

John, O. P. (1989). Towards a taxonomy of personality descriptors. In D. Buss & N. Cantor (Eds.), *Personality psychology: Recent trends and emerging directions* (pp. 261-271). New York: Springer-Verlag.

John, O. P. (1990). The "Big Five" factor taxonomy: Dimensions of personality in the natural language and in questionnaires. In L. A. Pervin (Ed.), *Handbook of personality: Theory and research* (pp. 66-100). New York: Guilford.

Jones, A. P. (1973, August). Functioning of organizational units related to differences in perceived climate and habitability. In *Organizational analysis: Models, methods, and criteria.* Symposium conducted at the annual meeting of the American Psychological Association, Montreal.

Judge, T. A. (1992). The dispositional perspective in human resources research. In G. R. Ferris & K. M. Rowland (Eds.), *Research in personnel and human resources management* (Vol. 10, pp. 31-72). Greenwich, CT: JAI.

Judge, T. A., & Ferris, G. R. (1992). The elusive criterion of fit in human resource staffing decisions. *Human Resource Planning, 15,* 47-67.

Judge, T. A., & Locke, E. A. (1993). Effect of dysfunctional thought processes on subjective well-being and job satisfaction. *Journal of Applied Psychology, 78,* 475-490.

Judge, T. A., Locke, E. A., Durham, C. C., & Kluger, A. N. (1998). Dispositional effects on job and life satisfaction: The role of core evaluations. *Journal of Applied Psychology, 83,* 17-34.

Judge, T. A., Martocchio, J. J., & Thoresen, C. J. (1997). Five-factor model of personality structure and employee absence. *Journal of Applied Psychology, 82,* 745-755.

Jussim, L. (1991). Social perception and social reality: A reflection-construction model. *Psychological Review, 98,* 54-73.

Kagan, J. (1988). The meanings of personality predicates. *American Psychologist, 43,* 614-620.

Kahneman, D., & Tversky, A. (1973). On the psychology of prediction. *Psychological Review, 80,* 237-251.

Kahneman, D., & Tversky, A. (1984). Choices, values, and frames. *American Psychologist, 39,* 341-350.

Kanfer, R., & Kanfer, F. H. (1991). Goals and self-regulation: Applications of theory to work settings. *Advances in Motivation and Achievement, 7,* 287-326.

Kaplan, R. M. (1982). *Psychological testing.* Belmont, CA: Brooks/Cole.

Karni, E., & Levin, J. (1972). The use of smallest space analysis in studying scale structure: An application to the California Psychological Inventory. *Journal of Applied Psychology, 56,* 341-346.

Keiser, R. E., & Prather, E. N. (1990). What is the TAT? A review of ten years of research. *Journal of Personality Assessment, 55,* 800-803.

Kenrick, D. T., & Funder, D. C. (1988). Profiting from controversy: Lessons from the person-situation debate. *American Psychologist, 43,* 23-34.

Kilstrom, J. F. (1999). The psychological unconscious. In L. A. Pervin & O. P. John (Eds.), *Handbook of personality: Theory and research* (2nd ed., pp. 424-442). New York: Guilford.

Klayman, J., & Ha, Y. (1987). Confirmation, disconfirmation, and information in hypothesis testing. *Psychological Review, 94,* 211-228.

Klimoski, R., & Brickner, M. (1987). Why do assessment centers work? The puzzle of assessment center validity. *Personnel Psychology, 40,* 243-260.

Kluger, A. N., Reilly, R. R., & Russell, C. J. (1991). Faking biodata tests: Are option-keyed instruments more resistant? *Journal of Applied Psychology, 76,* 889-896.

Kramer, J. J., & Conoley, J. C. (Eds.). (1992). *The eleventh mental measurements yearbook.* Lincoln, NE: Buros Institute of Mental Measurements.

Kristof, A. L. (1996). Person-organization fit: An integrative review of its conceptualizations, measurement, and implications. *Personnel Psychology, 49,* 1-49.

Kruglanski, A. W. (1989). The psychology of being "right": The problem of accuracy in social perception and cognition. *Psychological Bulletin, 106,* 395-409.

Kruglanski, A. W., & Ajzen, I. (1983). Bias and error in human judgment. *European Journal of Social Psychology, 19,* 448-468.

Kruglanski, A. W., & Klar, Y. (1987). A view from a bridge: Synthesizing the consistency and attribution paradigms from a lay epistemic perspective. *European Journal of Social Psychology, 17,* 211-241.

Kuhl, J. J. (1978). Standard setting and risk preference: An elaboration of the theory of achievement motivation and an empirical test. *Psychological Review, 85,* 239-248.

Kunda, Z. (1990). The case for motivated reasoning. *Psychological Bulletin, 108,* 480-498.

Lam, S. S. K., Hui, C., & Law, K. S. (1999). Organizational citizenship behavior: Comparing perspectives of supervisors and subordinates across four international samples. *Journal of Applied Psychology, 84,* 594-601.

Landy, F. J., & Farr, J. L. (1980). Performance ratings. *Psychological Bulletin, 87,* 72-107.

Latham, G. P., & Locke, E. A. (1991). Self-regulation through goal setting. *Organizational Behavior and Human Decision Processes, 50,* 212-247.

Laursen, B., & Collins, W. A. (1994). Interpersonal conflict during adolescence. *Psychological Bulletin, 115,* 197-209.

Levin, I., & Stokes, J. P. (1989). Dispositional approach to job satisfaction: Role of negative affectivity. *Journal of Applied Psychology, 74,* 752-758.

Lillibridge, J. R., & Williams, K. J. (1992). Another look at personality and managerial potential: Application of the five-factor model. In K. Kelley (Ed.), *Issues, theory, and research in industrial/organizational psychology.* New York: Elsevier Science.

Locke, E. A. (1991). The motivation sequence, the motivation hub, and the motivation core. *Organizational Behavior and Human Decision Processes, 50,* 288-299.

Loeber, R., & Stouthamer-Loeber, M. (1998). Development of juvenile aggression and violence: Some misconceptions and controversies. *American Psychologist, 53,* 242-259.

Lord, F. M., & Novick, M. R. (1968). *Statistical theories of mental tests.* Reading, MA: Addison-Wesley.

Lord, R. G., Foti, R. J., & DeVader, C. L. (1984). A test of leadership of categorization theory: Internal structure, information processing, and leadership perceptions. *Organizational Behavior and Human Performance, 34,* 343-387.

Lord, R. G., Foti, R. J., & Phillips, J. S. (1982). A theory of leadership categorization. In J. G. Hunt, U. Sekaran, & C. Schriesheim (Eds.), *Leadership: Beyond establishment views* (pp. 104-121). Carbondale: Southern Illinois University Press.

Magnusson, D. (1976). The person and the situation in an interactional model of behavior. *Scandinavian Journal of Psychology, 17,* 253-271.

Magnusson, D. (1990). Personality development from an interactional perspective. In L. A. Pervin (Ed.), *Handbook of personality: Theory and research* (pp. 193-224). New York: Guilford.

Matthews, G., & Stanton, N. (1994). Item and scale factor analyses of the Occupational Personality Questionnaire. *Personality and Individual Differences, 16,* 733-743.

McAdams, D. P. (1992). The five-factor model in personality: A critical appraisal. *Journal of Personality, 60,* 329-361.

McClelland, D. C. (1985a). How motives, skills, and values determine what people do. *American Psychologist, 40,* 812-825.

McClelland, D. C. (1985b). *Human motivation.* Glenview, IL: Scott, Foresman.

McClelland, D. C., Atkinson, J. W., Clark, R. A., & Lowell, E. L. (1976). *The achievement motive.* New York: Irvington. (Original work published 1953)

McClelland, D. C., & Boyatzis, R. E. (1982). Leadership motive pattern and long-term success in management. *Journal of Applied Psychology, 67,* 737-743.

McClelland, D. C., Koestner, R., & Weinberger, J. (1989). How do self-attributed and implicit motives differ? *Psychological Review, 96,* 690-702.

McCrae, R. R., & Costa, P. T., Jr. (1987). Validation of the five-factor model of personality across instruments and observers. *Journal of Personality and Social Psychology, 52,* 81-90.

McCrae, R. R., & Costa, P. T., Jr. (1989). Rotation to maximize the construct validity of the factors in the NEO Personality Inventory. *Multivariate Behavioral Research, 24,* 107-124.

McCrae, R. R., & Costa, P. T., Jr. (1990). *Personality in adulthood.* New York: Guilford.

McCrae, R. R., & Costa, P. T., Jr. (1994). *Trait explanations in personality psychology.* Unpublished manuscript, National Institutes of Health, National Institute on Aging, Gerontology Research Center, Baltimore.

McCrae, R. R., Costa, P. T., Jr., & Busch, C. M. (1986). Evaluating comprehensiveness in personality systems: The California Q-set and the five-factor model. *Journal of Personality, 54,* 430-446.

McCrae, R. R., Costa, P. T., Jr., & Piedmont, R. L. (1993). Folk concepts, natural language, and psychological constructs: The California Psychological Inventory and the five-factor model. *Journal of Personality, 61,* 1-26.

McEvoy, G. M., & Beatty, R. W. (1989). Assessment centers and subordinate appraisals of managers: A seven-year examination of predictive validity. *Personnel Psychology, 42,* 37-52.

McHenry, J. J., Hough, L. M., Toquam, J. L., Hanson, M. A., & Ashworth, S. (1990). Project A validity result: The relationship between predictor and criterion domains. *Personnel Psychology, 43,* 335-354.

McNeely, B. L., & Meglino, B. M. (1994). The role of dispositional and situational antecedents in prosocial organizational behavior: An examination of the intended beneficiaries of prosocial behavior. *Journal of Applied Psychology, 79,* 836-844.

Messick, S. (1988). The once and future issues of validity: Assessing the meaning and consequences of measurement. In H. Wainer & H. I. Braun (Eds.), *Test validity* (pp. 33-48). Hillsdale, NJ: Lawrence Erlbaum.

Miller, S. M. (1987). Monitoring and blunting: Validation of a questionnaire to assess styles of information seeking under threat. *Journal of Personality and Social Psychology, 52,* 345-353.

Millham, J., & Jacobson, L. I. (1978). The need for approval. In H. London & J. E. Exner (Eds.), *Dimensions of personality* (pp. 365-390). New York: John Wiley.

Millon, T. (1990). The disorders of personality. In L. A. Pervin (Ed.), *Handbook of personality: Theory and research* (pp. 339-370). New York: Guilford.

Mischel, W. (1968). *Personality and assessment.* New York: John Wiley.

Mischel, W. (1973). Toward a cognitive social learning reconceptualization of personality. *Psychological Review, 80,* 252-283.

Mischel, W. (1984). Convergences and challenges in the search for consistency. *American Psychologist, 39,* 351-364.

Mischel, W. (1990). Personality dispositions revisited and revised: A view after three decades. In L. A. Pervin (Ed.), *Handbook of personality: Theory and research* (pp. 111-134). New York: Guilford.

Mischel, W., & Peake, P. K. (1982). Beyond déjà vu in the search for cross-situational consistency. *Psychological Review, 89,* 730-735.

Mischel, W., & Shoda, Y. (1999). Integrating dispositions and processing dynamics within a unified theory of personality: The cognitive-affective personality system. In L. A. Pervin & O. P. John (Eds.), *Handbook of personality: Theory and research* (2nd ed., pp. 197-218). New York: Guilford.

Mitchell, J. V., Jr., & Pierce-Jones, J. (1960). A factor analysis of Gough's California Psychological Inventory. *Journal of Consulting Psychology, 24,* 453-456.

Mount, M. K., Barrick, M. R., & Stewart, G. L. (1998). Five-factor model of personality and performance in jobs involving interpersonal interaction. *Human Performance, 11,* 145-165.

Murphy, K. R., & Anhalt, R. L. (1992). Is halo error a property of the rater, ratees, or the specific behaviors observed? *Journal of Applied Psychology, 77,* 494-500.

Murray, H. A. (1938). *Explorations in personality.* New York: Oxford University Press.

Murray, H. A. (1943). *Thematic Apperception Test.* Cambridge, MA: Harvard University Press.

Nelson, D. L., & Sutton, C. (1990). Chronic work stress and coping: A longitudinal study and suggested new directions. *Academy of Management Journal, 33,* 165-186.

Neuman, J. H., & Baron, R. A. (1998). Workplace violence and workplace aggression: Evidence concerning specific forms, potential causes, and preferred targets. *Journal of Management, 24,* 391-419.

Newton, T., & Keenan, T. (1991). Further analyses of the dispositional argument in organizational behavior. *Journal of Applied Psychology, 76,* 781-787.

Nicholls, J. C. (1984). Achievement motivation: Conceptions of ability, subjective experience, task choice, and performance. *Psychological Review, 91,* 328-346.

Nicholson, N. (1996). Toward a new agenda for work and personality: Traits, self-identity, "strong" interactionism, and change. *Applied Psychology: An International Review, 45*(3), 189-205.

Nisbett, R. E. (1993). Violence and U.S. regional culture. *American Psychologist, 48,* 441-449.

Nisbett, R. E., & Ross, L. (1980). *Human inference: Strategies and shortcomings of social judgment.* Englewood Cliffs, NJ: Prentice Hall.

Nisbett, R. E., & Wilson, T. D. (1977). Telling more than we can know: Verbal reports on mental processes. *Psychological Review, 84,* 231-259.

Norman, W. T. (1963). Toward an adequate taxonomy of personality attributes: Replicated factor structure in peer nomination personality ratings. *Journal of Abnormal Social Psychology, 66,* 574-583.

Nunnally, J. C. (1967). *Psychometric theory.* New York: McGraw-Hill.

Nunnally, J. C. (1978). *Psychometric theory* (2nd ed.). New York: McGraw-Hill.

Nunnally, J. C., & Bernstein, I. H. (1994). *Psychometric theory* (3rd ed.). New York: McGraw-Hill.

O'Leary-Kelly, A. M., Griffin, R. W., & Glew, D. J. (1996). Organization-motivated aggression: A research framework. *Academy of Management Review, 21,* 225-253.

Ones, D. S., Viswesvaran, C., & Reiss, R. D. (1996). Role of social desirability in personality testing for personnel selection: The red herring. *Journal of Applied Psychology, 81,* 660-679.

O'Reilly, C. A., Chatman, J., & Caldwell, D. F. (1991). People and organizational culture: A profile comparison approach to assessing person-organization fit. *Academy of Management Journal, 34,* 487-516.

Organ, D. W. (1988). *Organizational citizenship behavior: The good soldier syndrome.* Lexington, MA: Lexington.

Ozer, D. J. (1999). Four principles of personality assessment. In L. A. Pervin & O. P. John (Eds.), *Handbook of personality: Theory and research* (2nd ed., pp. 671-688). New York: Guilford.

Paulhus, D. L., Bruce, M. N., & Trapnell, P. D. (1995). Effects of self-presentation strategies on personality profiles and their structure. *Personality and Social Psychology Bulletin, 21,* 100-108.

Peabody, D., & Goldberg, L. R. (1989). Some determinants of factor structures from personality-trait descriptors. *Journal of Personality and Social Psychology, 57,* 552-567.

Pervin, L. A. (1985). Personality: Current controversies, issues, and directions. *Annual Review of Psychology, 36,* 83-114.

Pervin, L. A. (1990). A brief history of modern personality theory. In L. A. Pervin (Ed.), *Handbook of personality: Theory and research* (pp. 3-20). New York: Guilford.

Pervin, L. A. (1994). A critical analysis of current trait theory. *Psychological Inquiry, 5,* 105-113.

Phillips, J. M., Hollenbeck, J. R., & Ilgen, D. R. (1996). Prevalence and prediction of positive discrepancy creation: Examining a discrepancy between two self-regulation theories. *Journal of Applied Psychology, 81,* 498-511.

Piedmont, R. I., & Weinstein, H. P. (1994). Predicting supervisor ratings of job performance using the NEO Personality Inventory. *Journal of Psychology, 128,* 255-265.

Pinkley, R. L. (1990). Dimensions of conflict frame: Disputant interpretations of conflict. *Journal of Applied Psychology, 75,* 117-126.

Piotrowski, C., & Heller, J. W. (1989). Psychological testing in outpatient mental health facilities: A national study. *Professional Psychology: Research and Practice, 20,* 423-425.

Piotrowski, C., & Lubin, B. (1990). Assessment practices of health psychologists: Survey of APA Division 39 clinicians. *Professional Psychology: Research and Practice, 21,* 99-106.

Podsakoff, P. M., Ahearne, M., & MacKenzie, S. B. (1997). Organizational citizenship behavior and the quantity and quality of work-group performance. *Journal of Applied Psychology, 82,* 262-270.

Polyson, J., Norris, D., & Ott, E. (1985). The recent decline in TAT research. *Professional Psychology: Research and Practice, 16,* 26-28.

Pyszczynski, T., & Greenberg, J. (1987). Toward an integration of cognitive and motivational perspectives on social inference: A biased hypothesis-testing model. In L. Berkowitz (Ed.), *Advances in experimental social psychology* (Vol. 20, pp. 297-339). New York: Academic Press.

Raynor, J. O. (1978). Motivation and career striving. In J. W. Atkinson & J. O. Raynor (Eds.), *Personality, motivation, and achievement* (pp. 199-242). Washington, DC: Hemisphere.

Revelle, W., & Michaels, E. J. (1976). The theory of achievement motivation revisited: The implications of inertial tendencies. *Psychological Review, 83*, 394-404.

Roberts, K. H., Hulin, C. L., & Rousseau, D. M. (1978). *Developing an interdisciplinary science of organizations.* San Francisco: Jossey-Bass.

Robinson, S., & Bennett, R. (1995). A typology of deviant workplace behaviors: A multidimensional scaling study. *Academy of Management Journal, 38*, 555-572.

Ross, L. (1977). The intuitive psychologist and his shortcomings: Distortion in the attribution process. In L. Berkowitz (Ed.), *Advances in experimental social psychology* (Vol. 10, pp. 87-116). New York: Academic Press.

Rosse, J. G., Stecher, M. D., Miller, J. L., & Levin, R. A. (1998). The impact of response distortion on preemployment personality testing and hiring decisions. *Journal of Applied Psychology, 83*, 634-644.

Rothbaum, F., Weisz, J. R., & Snyder, S. S. (1982). Changing the world and changing the self: A two-process model of perceived control. *Journal of Personality and Social Psychology, 42*, 5-37.

Rothman, A. J., & Salovey, P. (1997). Shaping perceptions to motivate healthy behavior: The role of message framing. *Psychological Bulletin, 121*, 3-19.

Rotter, J. B. (1946). Thematic Apperception Test: Suggestions for administration and interpretation. *Journal of Personality, 15*, 70-92.

Rush, M. C., Thomas, J. C., & Lord, R. G. (1977). Implicit leadership theory: A potential threat to the internal validity of leader behavior questionnaires. *Organizational Behavior and Human Performance, 20*, 93-110.

Russell, C. J., & Domm, D. R. (1995). Two field tests of assessment center validity. *Journal of Occupational Psychology, 68*, 25-47.

Russell, J. A., & Carroll, J. M. (1999). On the bipolarity of positive and negative affect. *Psychological Bulletin, 125*, 3-30.

Ryan, A. M., & Sackett, P. R. (1987). Pre-employment honesty testing: Fakability, reactions of test takers, and company image. *Journal of Business and Psychology, 1*, 248-256.

Rynes, S. L., Bretz, R. D., & Gerhart, B. (1991). The importance of recruitment in job choice: A different way of looking. *Personnel Psychology, 44*, 487-521.

Sackett, P. R., & Dreher, G. F. (1982). Constructs and assessment center dimensions: Some troubling empirical findings. *Journal of Applied Psychology, 67*, 401-410.

Salgado, J. F. (1997). The five factor model of personality and job performance in the European community. *Journal of Applied Psychology, 82*, 30-43.

Sarason, I. G. (1978). Test anxiety: Concept and measurement. In I. G. Sarason & C. D. Spielberger (Eds.), *Stress and anxiety.* New York: John Wiley.

Saville, P., Nyfield, G., Sik, G., & Hackston, J. (1991, August). *Enhancing the person-job match through personality assessment.* Paper presented at the annual meeting of the American Psychological Association, San Francisco.

Schaubroeck, J., Ganster, D. C., & Jones, J. J. (1998). Organization and occupation influences in the attraction-selection-attrition process. *Journal of Applied Psychology, 83*, 869-891.

Schlenker, B. R., & Leary, M. R. (1982). Social anxiety and self-presentation: A conceptualization and model. *Psychological Bulletin, 92*, 641-669.

Schmidt, F. L., & Hunter, J. E. (1998). The validity and utility of selection methods in personnel psychology: Practical and theoretical implications of 85 years of research findings. *Psychological Bulletin, 124,* 262-274.

Schmidt, F. L., Hunter, J. E., & Outerbridge, A. N. (1986). Impact of job experience and ability on job knowledge, work sample performance, and supervisory ratings of job performance. *Journal of Applied Psychology, 71,* 432-439.

Schmit, M. J., & Ryan, A. M. (1993). The Big Five in personnel selection: Factor structure in applicant and nonapplicant populations. *Journal of Applied Psychology, 78,* 966-974.

Schmit, M. J., Ryan, A. M., Stierwalt, S. L., & Powell, A. B. (1995). Frame-of-reference effects on personality scale scores and criterion-related validity. *Journal of Applied Psychology, 82,* 434-443.

Schmitt, N., Gooding, R. Z., Noe, R. A., & Kirsch, M. (1984). Meta-analyses of validity studies published between 1964 and 1982 and the investigation of study characteristics. *Personnel Psychology, 37,* 407-422.

Schneider, B. (1987). The people make the place. *Personnel Psychology, 40,* 437-453.

Schneider, B. (1996). When individual differences aren't. In K. R. Murphy (Ed.), *Individual differences and behavior in organizations* (pp. 548-571). San Francisco: Jossey-Bass.

Schneider, B., Goldstein, H. W., & Smith, D. B. (1995). The ASA framework: An update. *Personnel Psychology, 48,* 747-773.

Schneider, B., Smith, D. B., & Goldstein, H. W. (2000). Attraction-Selection-Attrition: Toward a person-environment psychology of organizations. In W. B. Walsh, K. H. Craik, & R. H. Price (Eds.), *Person-environment psychology: New directions and perspectives* (2nd ed., pp. 61-85). Mahwah, NJ: Lawrence Erlbaum.

Schneider, B., Smith, D. B., Taylor, S., & Fleenor, J. (1998). Personality and organizations: A test of the homogeneity of personality hypothesis. *Journal of Applied Psychology, 83,* 462-470.

Schneider, D. J. (1991). Social cognition. *Annual Review of Psychology, 42,* 527-561.

Schneider, J. R., & Schmitt, N. (1992). An exercise design approach to understanding assessment center dimension and exercise constructs. *Journal of Applied Psychology, 77,* 32-41.

Schneider, R. J., & Hough, L. M. (1995). Personality and industrial/organizational psychology. In C. L. Cooper & I. T. Robertson (Eds.), *International review of industrial and organizational psychology* (pp. 75-129). Chichester, England: John Wiley.

Schwarz, N. (1999). Self-reports: How the questions shape the answers. *American Psychologist, 54,* 93-105.

Shepperd, J. A. (1993). Productivity loss in performance groups: A motivation analysis. *Psychological Bulletin, 113,* 67-81.

Sherwood, G. G. (1981). Self-serving biases in person perception: A reexamination of projection as a mechanism of defense. *Psychological Bulletin, 90,* 445-459.

Shore, T. H., Shore, L. M., & Thornton, G. C. (1992). Construct validity of self- and peer evaluations of performance dimensions in an assessment center. *Journal of Applied Psychology, 77,* 42-54.

Shrauger, J. S., & Osberg, T. M. (1981). The relative accuracy of self-prediction and judgments by others in psychological assessment. *Psychological Bulletin, 105,* 131-142

Silver, W. S., Mitchell, T. R., & Gist, M. E. (1995). Responses to successful and unsuccessful performance: The moderating effect of self-efficacy on the relationship between performance and attributions. *Organizational Behavior and Human Decision Processes, 62,* 286-299.

Silzer, R. F. (1986, April). *Predictions or prophecies: By data or by divinity?* Paper presented at the annual meeting of the Society for Industrial and Organizational Psychology, Chicago.

Skowronski, J. J., & Carlston, D. E. (1989). Negativity and extremity biases in impression formation: A review of explanations. *Psychological Bulletin, 105,* 131-142.

Smith, G. M. (1967). Usefulness of peer ratings of personality in educational research. *Educational and Psychological Measurement, 27,* 967-984.

Smith, P. C., Kendall, L. M., & Hulin, C. L. (1969). *The measurement of satisfaction in work and retirement.* Chicago: Rand McNally.

Smither, R., & Hogan, R. (1993). The Hogan Personality Inventory: Linking evolution, personality and psychometrics. In S. R. Briggs & J. M. Cheek (Eds.), *Personality measures: Development and evaluation.* Greenwich, CT: JAI.

Snell, A. F., & McDaniel, M. A. (1998). *Faking: Getting data to answer the right questions.* Paper presented at the annual meeting of the Society for Industrial and Organizational Psychology, Dallas, TX.

Sorrentino, R. M., & Short, J.-A. C. (1986). Uncertainty orientation, motivation, and cognition. In R. M. Sorrentino & E. T. Higgins (Eds.), *Handbook of motivation and cognition: Foundations of social behavior* (pp. 379-403). New York: Guilford.

Spence, J. T., & Helmreich, R. L. (1983). Achievement-related motives and behaviors. In J. T. Spence (Ed.), *Achievement and motives* (pp. 7-74). San Francisco: W. H. Freeman.

Springob, H. K., & Streuning, E. L. (1964). A factor analysis of the California Psychological Inventory on a high school population. *Journal of Consulting Psychology, 11,* 173-179.

Stagner, R. (1977). On the reality and relevance of traits. *Journal of General Psychology, 96,* 185-207.

Staw, B. M. (1976). Knee-deep in the big muddy: A study of escalating commitment to a chosen course of action. *Organizational Behavior and Human Performance, 16,* 27-44.

Staw, B. M. (1991). Dressing up like an organization: When psychological theories can explain organizational action. *Journal of Management, 17,* 805-819.

Staw, B. M., Bell, N. E., & Clausen, J. A. (1986). The dispositional approach to job attitudes: A lifetime longitudinal test. *Administrative Science Quarterly, 31,* 56-77.

Staw, B. M., & Ross, J. (1985). Stability in the midst of change: A dispositional approach to job attitudes. *Journal of Applied Psychology, 70,* 469-480.

Staw, B. M., & Ross, J. (1987). Behavior in escalation situations: Antecedents, prototypes, and solutions. In L. L. Cummings & B. M. Staw (Eds.), *Research in organizational behavior* (Vol. 9, pp. 39-78). Greenwich, CT: JAI.

Steel, R. P., & Rentsch, J. R. (1997). The dispositional model of job attitudes revisited: Findings of a 10-year study. *Journal of Applied Psychology, 82,* 873-879.

Sternberg, R. J. (1982). Reasoning, problem solving, and intelligence. In R. J. Sternberg (Ed.), *Handbook of human intelligence* (pp. 227-295). Cambridge: Cambridge University Press.

Stolzenberg, R. M. (1980). The measurement and decomposition of causal effects in nonlinear and nonadditive models. In K. F. Schuessler (Ed.), *Sociological methodology* (pp. 459-488). San Francisco: Jossey-Bass.

Strickland, B. R. (1977). Approval motivation. In T. Blass (Ed.), *Personality variables in social behavior* (pp. 315-356). Hillsdale, NJ: Lawrence Erlbaum.

Taylor, S. E. (1991). Asymmetrical effects of positive and negative events: The mobilization minimization hypothesis. *Psychological Bulletin, 110,* 67-85.

Taylor, S. E., & Brown, J. D. (1988). Illusion and well-being: A social psychological perspective on mental health. *Psychological Bulletin, 103,* 193-210.

Taylor, S. E., & Lobel, M. (1989). Social comparison activity under threat: Downward evaluation and upward contacts. *Psychological Review, 96,* 569-575.

Taylor, S. E., Pham, L. B., Rivkin, I. D., & Armor, D. A. (1998). Harnessing the imagination. *American Psychologist, 53,* 429-439.

Tedeschi, J. T., & Nesler, M. S. (1993). Grievances: Development and reactions. In R. B. Felson & J. T. Tedeschi (Eds.), *Aggression and violence: Social interactionist perspectives* (pp. 13-46). Washington, DC: American Psychological Association.

Tellegen, A. (1982). *Brief manual for the Differential Personality Questionnaire.* Unpublished manuscript, University of Minnesota.

Tellegen, A. (1985). Structures of mood and personality and their relevance to assessing anxiety, with an emphasis on self-report. In A. H. Tuma & J. D. Maser (Eds.), *Anxiety and the anxiety disorders* (pp. 681-706). Hillsdale, NJ: Lawrence Erlbaum.

Tellegen, A. (1993). Folk concepts and psychological concepts of personality and personality disorder. *Psychological Inquiry, 4,* 122-130.

Tett, R. P., Jackson, D. N., & Rothstein, M. (1991). Personality measures as predictors of job performance: A meta-analytic review. *Personnel Psychology, 44,* 703-742.

Thomas, K. M., & Mathieu, J. E. (1994). Role of causal attributions in dynamic self-regulation and goal processes. *Journal of Applied Psychology, 79,* 812-818.

Thompson, L., & Loewenstein, G. (1992). Egocentric interpretations of fairness and interpersonal conflict. *Organizational Behavior and Human Decision Processes, 51,* 176-197.

Thompson, S. C., Armstrong, W., & Thomas, C. (1998). Illusions of control, underestimations, and accuracy: A control heuristic explanation. *Psychological Bulletin, 123,* 143-162.

Toch, H. (1993). Good violence and bad violence: Self-presentations of aggressors through accounts and war stories. In R. B. Felson & J. T. Tedeschi (Eds.), *Aggression and violence: Social interactionist perspectives* (pp. 193-206). Washington, DC: American Psychological Association.

Tomkins, S. S. (1947). *The Thematic Apperception Test.* New York: Grune & Stratton.

Trope, Y. (1986). Self-enhancement and self-assessment in achievement behavior. In R. M. Sorrentino & E. T. Higgins (Eds.), *Handbook of motivation and cognition* (pp. 350-378). New York: Guilford.

Tupes, E. C. (1957). *Personality traits related to effectiveness of junior and senior Air Force officers* (USAF Personnel Training Reserve Center Technical Note No. 57-125). Lackland Air Force Base, TX: U.S. Air Force.

Tupes, E. C., & Christal, R. E. (1961). *Recurrent personality factors based on trait ratings* (USAF ASD Technical Report No. 61-97). Lackland Air Force Base, TX: U.S. Air Force.

Turban, D. B., & Keon, T. L. (1993). Organizational attractiveness: An interactionist perspective. *Journal of Applied Psychology, 78,* 184-193.

Turner, J. H. (1970). Entrepreneurial environments and the emergence of achievement motivation in adolescent males. *Sociometry, 33,* 147-165.

Tversky, A., & Kahneman, D. (1973). Availability: A heuristic for judging frequency and probability. *Cognitive Psychology, 5,* 207-232.

Tversky, A., & Kahneman, D. (1974). Judgment under uncertainty: Heuristics and biases. *Science, 185,* 1124-1131.

Tversky, A., & Kahneman, D. (1981). The framing of decisions and the psychology of choice. *Science, 211,* 453-458.

Tversky, A., & Kahneman, D. (1983). Extensional versus intuitive reasoning: The conjunction fallacy in probability judgment. *Psychological Review, 90,* 293-315.

Vanden Bos, G. R., & Bulatao, E. Q. (Eds.). (1996). *Violence on the job: Identifying risks and developing solutions.* Washington, DC: American Psychological Association.

Vane, J. R. (1981). The Thematic Apperception Test: A review. *Clinical Psychology Review, 1,* 319-336.

Veldman, D., & Pierce-Jones, J. (1964). Sex differences in factor structure for the California Psychological Inventory. *Journal of Consulting Psychology, 28,* 93.

Walsh, W. B., & Betz, N. E. (1995). *Tests and measurement* (3rd ed.). Englewood Cliffs, NJ: Prentice Hall.

Watson, D., Clark, L. A., & Tellegen, A. (1988). Development and validation of brief measures of positive and negative affect: The PANAS scales. *Journal of Personality and Social Psychology, 54,* 1064-1070.

Wegner, D. M., & Vallacher, R. R. (1977). *Implicit psychology: An introduction to social cognition.* New York: Oxford University Press.

Weiner, B. (1979). A theory of motivation of some classroom experiences. *Journal of Educational Psychology, 71,* 3-25.

Weiner, B. (1990). Attribution in personality psychology. In L. A. Pervin (Ed.), *Handbook of personality: Theory and research* (pp. 465-485). New York: Guilford.

Weiner, B. (1991). Metaphors in motivation and attribution. *American Psychologist, 46,* 921-930.

Westen, D. (1990). Psychoanalytic approaches to personality. In L. A. Pervin (Ed.), *Handbook of personality: Theory and research* (pp. 21-65). New York: Guilford.

Westen, D. (1991). Social cognition and object relations. *Psychological Bulletin, 109,* 429-455.

Widiger, T. A. (1992). Review of the NEO Personality Inventory. In J. J. Kramer & J. C. Conoley (Eds.), *The eleventh mental measurements yearbook* (pp. 605-606). Lincoln, NE: Buros Institute of Mental Measurements.

Williams, L. J., & Anderson, S. E. (1991). Job satisfaction and organizational commitment as predictors of organizational citizenship and in-role behaviors. *Journal of Management, 17,* 601-617.

Williams, L. J., Gavin, M. B., & Williams, M. L. (1996). Investigating measurement and nonmeasurement processes with method effect variables: An example with negative affectivity and employee attitudes. *Journal of Applied Psychology, 81,* 88-101.

Winter, D. G. (1987). Leader appeal, leader performance, and the motive profiles of leaders and followers: A study of American presidents and elections. *Journal of Personality and Social Psychology, 52,* 196-202.

Winter, D. G., John, O. P., Stewart, A. J., Klohnen, E. C., & Duncan, L. E. (1998). Traits and motives: Toward an integration of two traditions in personality research. *Psychological Review, 105,* 230-250.

Wood, J. V. (1989). Theory and research concerning social comparisons of personal attributes. *Psychological Bulletin, 106,* 231-248.

Wright, J. C., & Mischel, W. (1987). A conditional approach to dispositional constructs: The local predictability of social behavior. *Journal of Personality and Social Psychology, 53,* 1159-1177.

Index

About the Authors

Lawrence R. James holds the Pilot Oil Chair of Excellence in Management and Industrial/Organizational Psychology at the University of Tennessee. He is the author of numerous articles and papers and coauthor of a book on causal analysis. He is or has been a member of the editorial boards of the *Journal of Applied Psychology, Organizational Behavior and Human Decision Processes, Human Performance, Human Resources Management, Journal of Management,* and *Research Methods and Analysis.* He also serves as a consultant to a number of businesses and government agencies. He has been Chair of Division 19 of the Academy of Management and is currently a fellow of Divisions 5 and 14 of the American Psychological Association and a Fellow of the American Psychological Society. He earned his Ph.D. at the University of Utah in 1970, soon after which he was awarded a National Research Council postdoctorate. Following the postdoctorate, he joined the faculty at the Institute of Behavior Research, Texas Christian University, where he attained the rank of Professor and headed the Organizational-Industrial Research Group. In 1980, he moved to the Georgia Institute of Technology, where he was Professor of Psychology and Coordinator of the Industrial/Organizational Psychology Program. He moved to the University of Tennessee in 1988. As a leading researcher in industrial-organizational psychology, he has been active in building new measurement systems for personality and in studying the effects of organizational environments on individual adaptation, motivation, and productivity. His statistical contributions have been designed to make possible tests of new models in areas such as organizational climate, leadership, and personnel selection.

Michelle D. Mazerolle is the Director of Management and Organization Development at Philips Consumer Electronics North America. She received her B.A. in psychology from the College of the Holy Cross and an M.A. in industrial and organizational psychology from the University of New Haven. She is currently a doctoral student in industrial and organizational psychology at the University of Tennessee. She is a member of a number of professional organizations, including the American Psychological Association, the Society for Industrial and Organizational Psychology, the American Psychological Society, and the Society for Human Resource Management. Her current research interests include personality measurement, assessment centers, work attitudes and behavior, leadership effectiveness, and organizational climate.